File Management and
Information Retrieval Systems

File Management and Information Retrieval Systems

A Manual for Managers and Technicians

Third Edition

Suzanne L. Gill

1993
LIBRARIES UNLIMITED, INC.
Englewood, Colorado

LIBRARIES UNLIMITED, INC.
P.O. Box 6633
Englewood, CO 80155-6633

Library of Congress Cataloging-in-Publication Data

Gill, Suzanne L.
  File Management and information retrieval systems : a manual for managers and technicians / Suzanne L. Gill. -- 3rd ed.
    xvi, 267 p. 17x25 cm.
    Includes bibliographical references and index.
    ISBN 1-56308-050-8
    1. Filing systems. 2. Electronic filing systems. 3. Business records--Management--Data processing. 4. Management information systems. I. Title.
  HF5736.G56   1993
  651.5'3--dc20   92-30638
                                                                    CIP

To My Family

CONTENTS

The Paperless Files

ILLUSTRATIONS

Figures

Figures

Tables

PREFACE

During the preparation of the first edition of this work (1981), I touted the coming of the "paperless society" and lightly spoke on "other media besides paper for records," that is, microforms and computers. Since that time I have come to believe there will never be a "paperless" society. Paper's general use is currently growing 4 percent a year. In 1990 the total demand for paper was almost 43 million tons. Seventy-nine billion letters are being written a year. Five hundred seventy billion documents currently reside in storage. Today, 20 years after the "paperless office" was promulgated, 95 percent of business information is still recorded on paper. In addition, microforms, computers, CD-ROMs, and laser disks are all accepted "other mediums" of information. In fact, by the year 2001, it is predicted that 95 percent of all jobs will require workers familiar with computers.

Originally this text was created to bridge knowledge from library science to records management because of help-wanted ads such as the following:

****

LIBRARY ASSISTANT

The XXX Department Stores Company, one of the nation's largest retailing organizations, is in search of a Library Assistant to join our Corporate Legal Department. This position demands a self-starter who is detail oriented and possesses a desire to work in a Law Library. Library Technical Assistant or Records Management Assistant certification or completion of a two-year training program in either area or two years relevant experience as a Library Assistant or Records Management Assistant would be considered a plus. This is an excellent opportunity for a qualified individual to join a dynamic organization and enjoy a competitive compensation and benefits package.

Send your resume to:

XXXXXX XXX

EOE M/F/H/V

****

Requests for workshops, letters, and telephone calls make me realize that there is a large "office employee" component and their supervisors who are seeking information in this text, so this edition is intended for all those employed, or seeking employment, in an environment requiring an efficient file management system, particularly the 85 percent of companies that employ less than 200 people.

The emphasis in this text is still on creating a procedures manual, because I believe it is the essence of a file system. The area of "new technologies" has been enlarged to encompass specific software which can be used in records management. Managing recorded information is as cost-effective and beneficial as managing any other business asset. One letter-size file cabinet takes six square feet of floor space at an average cost of $900 in one firm to $2,500 in another firm.

Any executive will certainly agree that an organization, large or small, succeeds to the extent that it is able to properly manage and utilize its assets: employees, reputation, products, services—and its recorded information, its "corporate memory." Truly successful organizations appreciate the need for and contribute resources to managing such information.

An established records and information management program that provides for routine, well-documented maintenance and disposal of information affords many advantages, including

- elimination of countless hours of staff time spent in searching useless volumes of data in attempts to locate needed documentation,

- expeditiously identifying and providing information supporting the organization's decision making process,

- insuring the security of vital, sensitive and confidential information,

- enhancing and improving overall operating efficiency,

- controlling proliferation of expensive, space-consuming filing cabinets,

- saving money on the purchase of filing supplies and records storage equipment,

- freeing valuable and costly floor space,

- minimizing office clutter, and

- putting an organization on much firmer legal ground if challenged by litigation as laws requiring records and information management programs become more and more common.

The similarities of libraries and record centers are noteworthy. They both have an emphasis on service. Also, both catalog, classify information, maintain indexes, create filing systems, provide information in various media, circulate materials, survey and train users, write policies and procedures, keep statistics, maintain archives, and use the same shelving equipment and computers. Other activities are similar but have different jargon-imposed names. The former weeds a collection according to certain criteria; the latter disposes according to a retention schedule.

Many of the skills being taught in library science programs are transferable to the areas of record and information management. In addition, many library programs are expanding their program options into these areas. The Special Libraries Association now includes records management workshops in its national conference. There are also programs for record technicians on the associate, bachelor's, and master's degree levels in the United States and Canada, which incorporate library technology theory in the program. Thousands are employed in positions in which record-keeping skills are part of their implied or written job descriptions, and the employment picture for record management skills is growing. The correlative field of information management, which incorporates the job skills needed in a library, record center, archives, computer center, or information production department, is developing quickly. These new job positions are being filled by persons called information managers, information specialists, and information technicians. Even though their jobs call for multidisciplinary skills, as well as continuous training, they still need a foundation in basic organizational skills.

The emphasis in this text is on organizing material in a practical rather than theoretical fashion. *File Management and Information Retrieval Systems* is intended to be a manual that explains the basics of file management. Once those basics are understood in the traditional sense, they can be used as the foundation for creating manageable files with any of the media formats, for all technologies, no matter how sophisticated, are still basically file organizers.

The purpose of this text is to develop the skills necessary to create a procedures manual while learning file organization theory. Every record or file manual mentions the importance of a procedures manual, but none tells one how to develop one. Each filing manual will state a set of filing rules; ten such manuals will indicate how numerous are the sets of filing rules. In addition, every organization and institution has its own individual interpretation of those sets of rules. This is not bad. Each organization is unique, and it should use only those filing methods that are practical and efficient for its own records. Yet it is important for every organization to be consistent. People come and go; the company continues. Which rules and procedures are being practiced is not as important as that there be one set for that organization. Thus the procedures manual is essential; it is the document that establishes the rules practiced in that company.

Today all organizations are under tremendous pressure to process, evaluate, and report faster than before. In an era of internationalization of business, mergers, downsizing, and complying with regulations, businesses need and want "instant" information. Thus, there is a need for systematic, accurate availability of information.

Given in this textbook are various file methods, all of which are currently being practiced to organize material. As the user works through the manual he or she will be introduced to each of these filing methods for organization as well as to other steps necessary for an efficient file system. In addition, the user will be establishing a procedures manual for his or her own files. This manual will be redone on the job, perhaps in a totally new fashion, but the experience of having developed one using the theory presented here will make it easier to develop a manual for the job. Someone, already employed, will be able to use concrete rather than theoretical examples and will reap immediate benefits of a more efficient operation and quicker understanding of the why and how of filing and records management. In addition to filing rules, the text describes processing materials, retention of records, circulation procedures, and equipment and supplies, and offers some case studies.

The following vendors have kindly provided illustrations for this text: Bankers Box (1789 Norwood Ave., Itasca, IL 60143), Kardex/Sperry Rand (P.O. Box 171, Marietta, OH 45750), Lanier Business Products, Inc. (1700 Chantilly Dr., Atlanta, GA 30324), NB Jackets (Bell & Howell, P.O. Box 5430, New York, NY 10163), Oblique Files (Gaylord Brothers, Box 4901, Syracuse, NY 13221-4901), Penco Products (Brower Ave., Oaks, PA 19456), Pioneer Communications of America, Inc. (600 East Crescent Ave., Upper Saddle River, NJ 07458), Spacesaver Corporation (1450 Janesville Ave., Fort Atkinson, WI 53538-2798), Suplee Envelope Company (P.O. Box 449, Upper Darby, PA 19082).

BACKGROUND

1

RECORDS AND INFORMATION _____*MANAGEMENT*_____

We are now in what is known as an "Information Economy" and businesses are being fundamentally changed. Today's businesses are not what they were 15 years ago, before the advent of the personal computer. In 15 more years today's businesses will not resemble what they presently are—if they have survived. Information is the core of today's economy and to survive all businesses must deal with it efficiently and effectively. Information has become the main avenue to revitalizing mature businesses and transforming them into new ones.

The interest in and discovery of the need for records management and information management in industry is relatively recent, as is recognition of the need to *coordinate* records and information. Just as the student writing a term paper on "ships" discovers he or she is also investigating "transportation," "commerce," and "politics," the office worker seeking data on the production costs of a widget discovers not just separate pieces of paper but rather units of information requiring coordination. Firms with the best information systems have the competitive edge in their market. The more successful companies base their management decisions on current information not only about their own product but also about their competitors, their customers, and the economic climate. Intuition is not a very sound basis for decision making. Nor is a fragmented approach based on "bits and pieces" of information the one to take. Information based on documentation is needed. *Information* is a multi-media concept or fact that can be collected, stored, retrieved, disseminated, and used to create another concept or fact. It is vital that data, once used to solve a problem, be available again. A *record* is tangible and constitutes documentation. Figure 1.1, page 4, represents the *information cycle* that acquires and processes record documentation until it becomes a new piece of information. Companies manage two levels of records and information management: tactical and strategic. The tactical deals with short-range information needed to perform the routine tasks of daily operation. The strategic level concerns long-range information needed to make correct decisions affecting the future. It is the forest, not the trees.

A *record cycle* moves in logical steps from the creation of a record through its use, storage, and retention in active files, to its transfer to inactive files, storage, and finally disposal (see figure 1.2 below). Record management

Fig. 1.1. Information cycle.

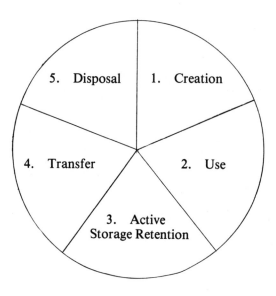

Fig. 1.2. Record cycle.

is the control of a tangible format of documentation from its birth to its death. A file is kept on each piece of paper in each step of this cycle. Even when the document has been disposed of, a record is kept establishing that step of the cycle.

What are records? Records are any media means of documenting communication in an enduring format that preserves the communication and can be recalled. Records can be written, verbal, photographic, or computer-captured. Records are information that flows from outside the company to inside, or from inside out. This flow of information can be via telephone wires, satellite, graphics, or the mail. From outside the company comes the daily mail consisting of correspondence, proposals, invoices, project reports, and answers to information problems from a database. Telecopiers, telex machines, and video cassettes also provide an on-the-job look at a particular product or project. The company also sends out correspondence and information about itself, or work completed, to other companies. Within the company circulate interoffice memos, procedures and policies, salary checks, requisition slips, and reports from each department. Information also flows from head offices to branch offices to field sales personnel or engineers. Telephone calls can be automatically taped and kept with a particular project.

Any information moving within this communication network is a record, regardless of its format. Information comes in text, data, sound, and images. Included are correspondence, memos, checks, invoices, orders, warranties, contracts, reports, pamphlets, catalogs, names and addresses, personnel records, inventory information, payroll records, sales records, requisitions, specifications, proposals, abstracts, budgets, forecasts, clippings, blueprints, computer disks, optical disks, photographs, maps, magazines, and books. The control of this information requires filing systems designed for effective retrieval, disposition, and retention. It is not funny to ask "shall I file it, or will you ever want it again?" Unfortunately, it is too often a meaningful question. The proof of how well records are managed, how good the filing system is, is how easily the material can be retrieved.

Record making and record keeping are probably the costliest part of office practices in terms of space, salaries, and equipment, yet office managers have to be sold on the value of a records system. They have to be shown cost-savings benefits before they will eliminate haphazard practices and institute effective procedures. Records are valuable assets. They are facts: facts to support decisions made and facts upon which to base future decisions; facts to communicate to employees, to customers, to potential customers, to the government, and to stockholders; facts to document the history of a company. These facts, if stored properly, improve employee morale. There is nothing more frustrating than the inability to find a record. If it takes too long to find a record, the operating costs of a company rise. The increased productivity and efficiency the implementation of a quality records management program can bring to a business can be measured in dollars and cents.

Instituting an effective records control system requires gathering concrete facts (more records!) on current time delays involved in finding information and on expenditures for duplicating records and purchasing filing equipment. One must also document clerical efficiencies that would be affected, determine legal requirements, and do a lot of public relations work. A company should be open to change, but many times implementing change needs to be handled delicately because one change can affect other components of the organization.

Unfortunately, although filing is the heart of records retrieval, few office managers place any importance on the work. Just as many people think that all a librarian does is check in and check out books, and that anyone can do that, many office managers think that anyone can file or set up a filing system. On the contrary, it takes a special person who can think very logically, someone who can create a viable classification system that places similar things together. A great deal of thought, and knowledge of a company's purpose and operation, is necessary before a logical, comprehensive, tailor-made plan can be drafted. Then the plan has to be plainly written so that anyone can follow it. When the records procedure and system of classification have been drafted well, there will be fewer records (and those will be found quickly when needed); fewer misfiles; effective discharge and return of records (which will be kept as long as necessary and no longer); fewer personnel; better utilization of floor space; and relocation of old records to less costly space.

New technologies to aid record keeping are appearing in the form of more sophisticated equipment for collecting, storing, and disseminating records. But people must judge the usefulness of the information, coordinate the flow of records, and make the decisions based on the data the records provide.

Most smaller companies do not store their information in a central resource center; rather, information is scattered in the departments with the appropriate "need to know." Whether centralized or departmentalized, information still has to be organized effectively.

In those larger companies utilizing the new technologies, there is a trend toward a multipurpose, integrated center, or a true records/library/systems/ information center. Frequently, a vice-president of information is in charge of coordinating the individual aspects of the center. There will be individual managers of the computer, records, library, and telecommunications sections, as well as technicians and clerks for each group. The department manager's goal is cooperation, not competition. A good manager is a delegator. This involves clear communication, clear definitions of what subordinates are expected to do. While providing supervision, a good manager gives subordinates the freedom to carry out their tasks. "Two-minute" management techniques will provide positive feedback to subordinates, praise for what they do well, corrective criticism on tasks done poorly, and encouragement. The use of such techniques will also provide feedback from subordinates and critical evaluation of their suggestions. The technician's role is the daily supervision of the work flow of people and machinery to keep them operating at optimum efficiency and effectiveness. Figure 1.3 is an organizational chart for such a company.

In companies with centralized files there might be a vice-president of operations who is in charge of all internal operations of the company, such as personnel, engineering, purchasing, and print production. An office manager or vice-president of personnel would be in charge of personnel, secretarial, reception and mail services, printing, and records. Again, there would be department heads, technicians, and clerks for each department. An organizational chart for this type of company could be similar to the one in figure 1.4.

The Association of Records Managers and Administrators (ARMA) is now offering certification via a six-part examination for the title of Certified Records Manager. The candidate must have three years' experience in records management and a bachelor's degree. Experience may be substituted for education on the basis of two years of experience for one year of education.

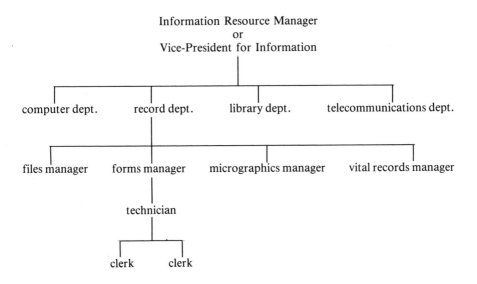

Fig. 1.3. Organizational chart.

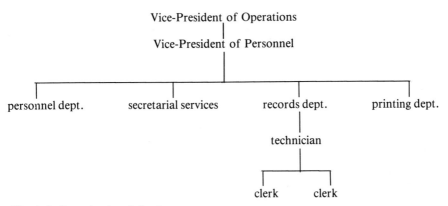

Fig. 1.4. Organizational chart.

Large organizations require a full-time records/information manager to design, implement, and direct programs to manage their information. In a small office, or in companies with departmentalized files, the secretary is frequently in charge of records as part of the job description. If there is more than one secretary for the department and each is filing into the files, it is imperative that there be a set of rules and a procedures manual, just as it is imperative in larger organizations.

Whether it is a large or small file operation, there should also be an efficient layout of the work flow. A *flowchart* is a pictorial representation of a sequence of events that shows through symbols the steps in an operation. To prepare a flowchart, analyze a routine to determine whether it is accomplishing the purpose for which it is intended with a minimum of effort and time. Diagram each step of the routine, breaking it down into details. Study each detail of the task, and if there is duplication or wasted effort, streamline the task to the essentials and draw a flowchart describing the correct method. This method can also be used for creating an efficient office layout for equipment. A flowchart for one step in the filing process, the decision whether to add or discard a record, might look like figure 1.5.

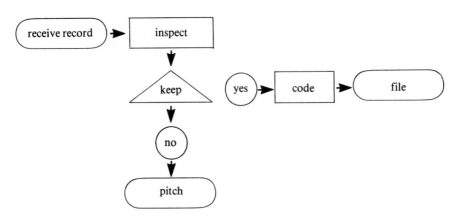

Fig. 1.5. Flowchart.

In this flowchart an oval represents both the starting and ending steps of the routines (receive record, file, and pitch). Processing steps (to inspect and to code) are represented by a rectangle. Connector symbols are small circles (yes, no). The decision step (keep) is represented by a diamond.

This book is designed to explain the basics of hand manipulation of paper or other media and files and includes guidelines for the procedures manual necessary for that hand manipulation. The next chapter will cover the history of business records. It will be followed by a section that will first provide an outline of a procedures manual and then discuss methods of arranging material for retrieval (filing classifications and codes) covering each section of the procedures manual. This section will also discuss the mechanics of filing;

retention schedules, inactive storage, and disposal; circulation procedures; equipment and supplies; and centralization versus decentralization of files. The final section discusses microfilming, computer files, and optical disks and provides case studies.

FOR FURTHER STUDY

1. For one week make a list of the types of communication media you encounter each day.

2. For one week make a list of the types of paper information you encounter.

3. From the lists you have made decide which communication is important for you to save for retrieval and give a reason why.

4. Define the "records management" problems you are going to encounter to save this material.

2

HISTORY OF
_____*BUSINESS RECORDS*_____

The management of records traces itself back to the invention of writing, and the history of keeping business records and the history of libraries parallel each other. Libraries are a repository for man's general and specific knowledge and as such are open to the public. Anyone, in theory, can use a library. A business is the repository of knowledge that concerns only that particular business and is not open to the public. Sometimes one department's information in a company is not even open, or available, to another department.

Library records and business records both have long histories. Business records form a part of our cultural heritage. The first libraries were collections of business records because it is business records that were first recorded. Literature was orally transmitted for centuries before being written, but businessmen were more concerned over misinterpretation, or loss, than were poets. Scribes, therefore, kept careful records for businesses on such matters as how many bushels of grain were collected for taxes, by whom and when, or how many oxen were sold by an individual to another.

Three thousand years before the birth of Christ, the Mesopotamian businessman had accumulated considerable technique and experience. He was seasoned in trading and knew the importance of drawing up contracts. He even protected his contracts from tampering. The scribes would imprint the particulars of a business transaction onto blocks of soft clay with a wedge-shaped stylus. Identical information was placed on two sets of square slabs or tablets. Then, a plain piece of soft clay was placed over this to create a sealed envelope. If the seal was not broken on the envelope, no one could change the contents of the tablet inside. If the outer envelope was not intact, the internal contents could be subject to litigation. If the inner tablet was changed and a new envelope placed around it, the difference in drying and shrinking between the two tablets and envelopes could be noticed. If a contract dispute arose, the two sets of tablet/envelopes would be brought before an arbitrator and judged. In Egypt, business records and correspondence were kept on palm leaves or papyrus as well as on stone. These cuneiforms and papyruses were kept in a central repository in an orderly manner. Filing systems were developed. The clay tablets were placed on racks with identifying tags visible. In Egypt, hollow skins of crocodiles were used as file cabinets for the papyrus.

Items were arranged either numerically or, after the alphabet arrived, alphabetically.

Surprisingly, a large number of business records from the ancient world have been discovered, because the ancient peoples had disposal problems too. Archaeologists have discovered they were dumped in excavations resembling landfills. At first these areas were thought to be archives because so many items were found, but later it was realized that the records that had to be retained were relocated by officials to public record offices at the provincial capitals. There were even archival depositories at the national level.

Correspondence between businessmen reveals that the traders, or salesmen, were as worried about promised and delivered shipments then as they are today. They also discussed military escorts for shipments and food supplies for the men and animals delivering the shipments of goods ordered. Governments kept census logs, property registers, land records, and laws. Diaries of events were kept by leaders. Two hundred years of found cuneiforms reveal many of the same economic and legal problems as exist today.

The Phoenicians, who lived in what is now Lebanon, developed the beginnings of the alphabet as we know it today, not to transcribe the noble thoughts of poets or philosophers, but rather to make it easier for businessmen from different parts of the world to communicate. The alphabet was an early attempt at a universal language. The Greeks expanded upon the twenty-two-letter consonant alphabet of the Phoenicians by adding vowels, by developing lower case letters, and by writing from left to right. The Greeks also added leaves, barks of trees, wax tablets, and a sharp quill to the writing equipment available to the ancient world. The Greeks also gave us the term "archives" – the place for keeping public records.

Plato's *Republic* compares the agrarian way of life with the merchant's and concludes that the power of the businessman has to be controlled. It is only the property-owning person who should be allowed to rise to a position of leadership in the government. This viewpoint of a business-dominated community differs from Aristotle's description of Carthage. Carthage was the grandest of the ancient societies ruled over by the merchant. Aristotle thought that the reason the populace of over 700,000 was so content was that the economy was based on a rich commercial system. But Carthage had no army and would not fight when Rome came looking for expansion of its empire.

Rome's rule, in principle, was also based on rule by the landowner and, while officially frowning upon the capitalistic theory, Rome laid the groundwork for the international merchant ruler of the Middle Ages. Rome was also concerned with the safekeeping of its own record of achievements. About A.D. 100 a Roman official responsible for the safekeeping of records wrote a higher official complaining that the property records office was unfit for the preservation of government records and that the higher official should authorize money to build a suitable building. Rome gave us the word *file* from the Latin *filum* meaning *thread*. Business records were strung on a thread for safekeeping. The fifteenth century provided an advancement to the thread filing, the spindle. Some firms still use the spindle, a piece of metal or wood with a sharp point upon which the records to be kept are impaled. Some merchants kept two spindles, one for unpaid bills and one for paid. When the "paid" spindle became too full, some of the older paid bills were thrown away, or a string was strung through the holes in the papers, and the papers were tied together in a bundle and stored elsewhere. Records were also kept rolled up and placed in *cubicles*, or *pigeonhole* files (see figure 2.1) with little tags hanging from them describing their contents. These two methods of storing records were used for centuries and adaptions of them are still found.

Fig. 2.1. Pigeonhole file.

During the Middle Ages (the eighth through the twelfth centuries) the Catholic church held the power of economic theory. The cities of the ancient world had fallen, giving way to small villages. The economic way of life was chiefly agricultural. Trade was considered dangerous for the soul: one person's gain was another's loss. The church fathers' philosophy called for a just price for goods bought and sold as distinct from a market price determined by the number of sellers versus the number of buyers. The producer sold directly to the consumer without a middleman. Pope Innocent III, in the year 1200, introduced the case file to hold and regulate church records. Between 700 and

1200 paper had found its way from China through the Middle East to Europe, and by the end of the twelfth century the city states in Italy were enacting statutes regulating the retention and disposal of paper files.

In the twelfth century the power of the church was broken and the development of the modern state began. Towns grew in power over the rural areas. Trade between towns became important and eventually grew powerful enough to aid in the development of the nationalist state. For a state to be strong and independent, it had to be rich and prosper economically. Thus, by the seventeenth century colonization and mercantilism had become the chief economic factors. In mercantilism the colony existed for the good of the mother country. All of this economic activity created more and more records. Documents and correspondence were collected in book form, and use of the registry system for keeping track of the documents was begun.

It has been stated that America was founded for God, Glory, and Gold. America did grow into a strong nation during that mercantilistic period. The American Constitution made possible the adoption of governmental policies that were of fundamental importance to business. The Constitution established the right of free trade both at home and abroad, the protection of private property, the inviolability of contracts, and the freedom of private enterprise.

Extant records of early American businessmen have enabled the reconstruction of business history and the history of libraries in this country. One of America's first businessmen, Robert Keayne (1596-1656) was an early advocate of setting prices by supply and demand. He left money in his will to establish the first local public library in America, continuing the tradition of libraries and businesses being interconnected. Benjamin Franklin, another businessman, was one of the founders of the subscription library, and Andrew Carnegie provided library buildings.

In the nineteenth century, businesses changed in organizational format and marketing techniques. Companies wanted to gain control over all phases of the manufacture and distribution of their products. The small, specialized owner-managed firms were transformed into large firms with stockholders and distributed goods on a national rather than regional basis. As the prime developer for the mass distribution of goods, the railroad became the first example of big business in America. At the same time, the telegraph, telephone, and typewriter revolutionized the flow of communications.

With big business came increased record-keeping problems. Prior to this time record keeping was basically descriptive. Recording by clerks of the firm's daily transactions facilitated calculations of profit and loss and helped determine the status of accounts at given points in time. With big business came capital borrowing and stockholder accountability. Additional costs in specific areas had to be recorded to serve as analytical tools for determining success or failure of a business. This introduced problems of record storage and retrieval. Several filing mechanisms appeared as attempts to organize the records of the day; each is still being used today.

The *bellows file* appeared about 1860. It is a large envelope creased like accordion bellows. Each compartment holds a separate set of information. The bellows file is convenient but limited in storage capacity. Many business people today use a bellows file as a briefcase, and offices sometimes use them as temporary sorters until documents are filed.

The *flat file*, appearing in the 1860s, was an attempt to file documents in a cabinet equipped with drawers. Papers were filed one on top of the other, and this arrangement led to its name. At first each drawer was limited to a single letter, but usage soon showed that some drawers were overfilled and others empty. Today maps, sheet music, blueprints, and art prints can be found filed in flat files (see figure 2.2).

Fig. 2.2. Flat file.

During 1875 a *file box*, shaped like a book that opened from the side, was invented. Each box contained a set of guide sheets with extension labels bearing the letters of the alphabet. This file box, or *hinge box*, is still popular for home usage, although its shape has changed considerably. (See figure 2.3.)

Fig. 2.3. File box.

The *Shannon file,* named after its inventor, appeared in the 1880s in response to a greater need for security of papers. Papers to be filed were perforated and placed on metal prongs which were secured flat. Three-ring binders and clipboards are an adaptation of the still-popular Shannon file.

The *filing cabinet* or *vertical file* is a rather recent invention, introduced in the 1890s. It was very controversial when it appeared, and many business people were quite certain the principle of filing papers vertically, or on edge, would never work. Several models, in wood, were exhibited at the Chicago World's Fair in 1892. By 1900 their success was guaranteed and steel models began to appear. An adaptation of the vertical file is the *lateral file,* which appeared in the mid-twentieth century. In the lateral file the drawer moves out from the side rather than from the front. *Hanging files* and mechanized *rotary files* are recent space savers that have enhanced filing efficiency.

The nineteenth century was also the beginning of the paper explosion problem discussed so frequently today. The advancement of technology had produced more records, not fewer. The typewriter was the first invention to spur the production of more documents, and that boon to the work force, the computer, has been another.

The Taft Commission in 1910 tried to regulate correspondence, files, and all record management functions.

In 1914 Irene Warren, librarian at the University of Chicago, brought together a group of people interested in records handling and began the Warren Filing Association. This was a by-product of the Warren School of Filing she had founded. This school was recognized then as the best for the training of file clerks and supervisors, today's technician level.

In the 1920s the Bureau of Efficiency was created by the federal government, and it survived until the 1930s when it was absorbed by the Bureau of the Budget.

In 1927 the Warren Filing Association changed its name to the Chicago Filing Association and later to the Records Management Association of Chicago.

The first large-scale application of microfilm to correspondence files occurred in the mid 1930s as a Work Projects Administration (WPA) project.

World War II created a paper avalanche. Both government and industry needed a controlled means to reduce paper files to a manageable level. During World War II the President of the United States appointed a special commission to study problems of efficiency, organization, and paperwork. Headed by former President Herbert Hoover, the commission made recommendations which became stepping stones in the field of records management. These recommendations served as the basis for the Federal Records Management Act of 1949. This initiative by the government was the first of its kind ever undertaken to bring information down to a manageable size. For the first time on a large scale people began to think about managing records. In 1950 this law was reinforced when the administrator of the General Services Administration (GSA) was given the responsibility of promoting a program to improve government record keeping. Specifically, it made him responsible for analyzing, developing, promoting, and coordinating records management within the government.

By 1954 the Records Management Association of Chicago had been hosting Midwest Annual Filing Conferences for several years. The decision was made that year to form a national association, the American Records Management Association (ARMA).

The second Hoover Commission (1955) made recommendations that called further attention to the mounting paperwork problem everywhere. It established the practice of placing responsibility for control of the problem at the high management rather than clerical level.

As a result of new records management programs, federal agencies destroyed several million cubic feet of records—the equivalent of more than a million file drawers. These savings were widely publicized and naturally caught the attention of business managers throughout the country. The job occupation and profession of records management was born. At first records management programs concentrated primarily on cleaning out accumulations of old records and on setting up retention schedules. As records managers gained recognition and experience they studied cause-effect relationships in record keeping and broadened the scope of their programs. In addition to retention schedules for all types of records, they wrote filing and records manuals. They standardized filing equipment, supplies, systems, and procedures. They became involved in studies of how information flows from department to department and how the design of forms used complements or impedes the flow. They revamped file room layouts and wrote procedures manuals for personnel. Graduates of library science programs were moving into this occupation along with many office administrators.

In 1974 ARMA began to administer the Certified Records Management (CRM) program, examinations to certify individuals who meet the qualifications for certification.

In the late 1970s junior colleges began offering technical level courses, and universities and colleges offered courses on a professional level.

Microforms are storage-saving formats that have come into wide use. For most companies it is no longer a question of whether to use microforms as it is which form. Just as time is expensive so is space, and microforms, which are photographic images of paper reduced to a small size, are a space saver.

Word processing, or text manipulation, produces both paper and electronic records. A "word processor" (see figure 2.4) can be a stand-alone unit or it can be a software program used as a computer. The most "primitive" word processor is the electric typewriter that can store and repeat a limited number of phrases. These appeared on the scene in the 1930s. Companies that use typewriters primarily for one-time typing for editing purposes still use stand-alone word processors. As companies began to place microcomputers in every workstation, word processors were replaced with software programs that run on the multifunction microcomputer. With a hard-disk drive and "window" software, a user can move from text editing to spreadsheets to document production and storage.

Fig. 2.4. Word processor/personal computer workstation. Photo courtesy of Exxon Office Systems, Hartford, CT.

The desktop computer appeared on the scene in 1980. Within 10 years, it revolutionized record production and storage. The microcomputer of today has more computing power than the early mainframes of 1950; by the year 2000, these microcomputers will run faster still and hold more information at prices comparable to the ones of 1990.

Computers have not replaced people but they have made the workplace more productive and efficient. Computers control payrolls, personnel records, accounting, production, inventory, sales records, patient records in hospitals, charge accounts, bank transactions, utility use, telecommunications, automobile speed, and room temperature. They create graphics, print newspapers, help medical science find cures, and retrieve data, literature citations, or entire documents. Computers come in all sizes from micro to mini to maxi. Maxi-computer systems are large units costing more than half a million dollars. They can perform several jobs simultaneously. The minicomputer does less work at a slower rate of speed and at less cost. Some are preprogrammed and operated by clerical personnel. A microcomputer can sit on a desk and can cost under a thousand dollars. One has to remind oneself that the microcomputer only appeared on the scene in the early 1980s because their impact has been so dramatic and they are now used everywhere.

Just as the computer married the function of the calculator and the typewriter, coming now are machines that combine the imaging capabilities of the copier, the facsimile, the printer, and the scanner into one compact unit that, when interfaced with a computer, provides the capability to input, store, retrieve, manipulate, print, copy, and transmit documents from a single keyboard. Instead of taking a picture, a multifunction machine such as a copier/printer "reads" an image like a fax machine and translates the image into a digital sequence, which is then transferred to plain paper via a laser printer. This is done with an optical character reader (OCR) scanner. This technology appeared as early as 1950, but its principal product, the compact disk (CD) did not appear until the late 1980s.

With electronic mail, or "e-mail," correspondence changes hands instantly. Words and images are electronically transmitted from place to place rather than physically transported. With electronic mail, "phone tag" is eliminated. An engineer in Boston can send an electronic query via a computer equipped with a modem to another engineer in France in the morning and have a response, with documentation, later that day. Laptop computers equipped with modems allow communication anywhere—it does not even have to take place in an office. In addition, international communication through e-mail can be cheaper than telephone or overnight mail delivery, although privacy and security may be imperiled.

Optical character scanners, CD-ROMs, video disks and multimedia presentation of text, graphics, and animation, both audio and video, viewed on a computer or television, are making rapid inroads to add "image management" to the term *record manager*. These technologies will impact business record keeping as much as the microcomputer did. A major issue that must now be addressed is the appropriate mix of media (paper, micrographics, computers). Even with all the technological advancements, 95 percent of information is still available in paper form.

Nevertheless, no matter how many technological advances occur, the information user and seeker need to know the basic methods of file organization.

FOR FURTHER STUDY

1. Research a library from the ancient world, the Middle East (1000-1400 A.D.), the Middle Ages, or Colonial America and describe the contents that would be important to a business person.

2. Do a report on the history and use of one of the following:

   a) pigeonhole file

   b) spindle file

   c) bellows file

   d) flat file

   e) Shannon file

   f) filing cabinet

   g) lateral filing cabinet

   h) hanging file

   i) the computer as a storage unit

   j) the word processor as a storage unit

   k) microphotography as a storage medium

   l) optical character readers (OCRs) or optical disks as a storage medium

THE PROCEDURES
MANUAL

3

PART I: GENERAL _____*INFORMATION*_____

The operations of every company or department are similar to, yet different from, those of every other company or department. One of the worst mistakes students can make is to leave the classroom believing they learned the "only correct way" to do something. In the classroom, students learn general principles that can be adapted to the unique requirements of every company or job situation.

This is one reason a records management procedures manual is so essential. A well-written handbook strengthens the leadership of an organization and adds dollar-and-cents benefits to the bottom line. A procedures manual is a mission statement to which an organization is committed. This manual comprises the company rules, spelling out not only general principles but also all the idiosyncracies of a particular organization. A good manual must present procedures as clearly and as fully as possible. A procedures manual enables the records manager to make good management decisions that are fair and lawful and allows the department to function at its optimum. No two organizations are alike. What is successful in one place may fail in another. Each person who uses this text should create an individualized manual, not a clone of someone else's.

A procedures manual should include the following:

Part I.   General Information
      1. Identifying name
      2. Policy statement
      3. Scope of coverage

Part II.   Methods of Classification
      1. Alphabetical
      2. Geographical
      3. Phonetic
      4. Numerical
         a. consecutive
         b. terminal digit
         c. middle digit
         d. chronological

          5.   Color-coded
          6.   Subject
          7.   Combination of methods

Part III.   Processing Materials
          1.   Location of storage files
          2.   Procedures for receiving materials into files
          3.   Instructions for assigning classification and retention codes
          4.   Procedures for filing into storage files
          5.   Instructions for updating master index file and cross-references
          6.   Recycling rules and procedures
          7.   Job descriptions for employees in the department

Part IV.   Retention of Records
          1.   Definition and list of what constitutes vital, essential, useful, and nonessential records
          2.   Retention schedule
          3.   Disaster planning

Part V.   Circulation Procedures

Part VI.   Equipment and Supplies

Part VII.   Centralization Vs. Decentralization

A sample procedures manual, like the one we will build in this text, might include some of the following information:

Part I.   General Information

Section 1.   Identifying name. Procedures manual for XYZ Company.

Section 2.   Policy statement. A policy statement is a definition establishing perimeters. For example:

> Each department of XYZ Company is responsible for developing a records program to ensure the protection of vital records; compliance with federal, state, and local laws; and the retention and preservation of the corporation's historical documents. The manager of each department is responsible for developing a records program, assigning a records manager to execute it, providing training for its implementation, and periodically auditing the program for compliance.

This definition should state whether the procedures manual applies to a company, a division, a branch, a department, or a single salesperson.

Section 3. Scope of coverage. This section specifies whether materials such as correspondence, forms, reports, samples, floppy disks, blueprints, invoices, names and addresses of clients, prospects, CD-ROM databases, videos, and vendors are covered. For example, scope of coverage of the procedures manual for the XYZ Company might read:

> The following formats of material are covered: master index file, correspondence, pamphlets, floppy disks, CD-ROM disks, professional development material, and committee reports. The following are not covered: Internal Revenue reports, supplies, books, and financial ledger.

Part II. Methods of Classification. Classification can be alphabetical, geographical, phonetic, numerical, color-coded, subject, or a combination of all or several of these indexing methods. One section of the files may be numerical and alphabetically arranged according to subject. For example, someone's personnel files may be arranged:

2	Affirmative Action
2-1	Compliance Requirements
3	Benefits
3-1	Insurance
3-1-1	Accident
3-1-2	Annuities
3-1-3	Disability
3-1-4	Hospitalization
3-1-4-1	Blue Cross
3-1-4-2	Blue Shield
6	Employee Leave
6-1	Personal
6-2	Sick
6-3	Vacation

The sales group file might be divided:

South-East
    Florida
        Carlson, Bill
    Georgia
        Henre, James
    North Carolina
        Baker, Susan
    South Carolina
        Baker, Susan
        Henre, James
South-Central
    Alabama
        Egleston, Bob
    Louisiana
        Carlson, Bill
        Egleston, Bob
South-West

Codes must be identified such as 23-61-01-10.

```
r   s   s   s
o   e   h   p
w   c   e   a
    t   l   c
    i   f   e
    o
    n
```

Part III.   Processing Materials

Section 1. Location of storage materials. You know where the storage files are, but would your successor know in your absence? Be specific in stating their location. For example:

The active storage files are located against the northeast wall of the central administrative department on the fourth floor of the office building, file range 1-15, top two drawers of each cabinet.

Inactive storage files are located against the northeast wall of the central administrative department on the fourth floor of the office building, file range 1-15, bottom two drawers of each cabinet.

Permanent storage is located at Meyer Brothers Warehouse, 10 North Broadway, third floor, file range 1-8.

Section 2.   Procedures for receiving material into storage areas. For example:

For active storage check that material has been released for filing. Releaser's initials and date of release should be on the inside cover, upper left-hand corner of all internally produced reports.

For inactive storage check that the material is dated eighteen months and coded "6" or "4." Those coded "4" are to be destroyed. Prepare the forms for destruction. Those coded "6" are to be transferred to inactive files. Material in the inactive file is to be evaluated for destruction or for transfer to permanent storage at this time.

Section 3.   Instructions for assigning classification and retention codes. For example, the procedures manual for a housing authority company states that its classification code has been based on the indexing scheme developed by the New York Municipal Library's City Planning classification code. This scheme, with its unique adaptations, has been inserted into their procedures manual. Below is a section of the scheme:

Classification is selected from the following authority file of approved numbers and subjects:

B   Planning
C   Area Planning
D   Land Use and Controls
      D 20   Land use/urban
      D 30   Commercial areas
      D 60   Zoning ordinances

The retention code is selected from the following:

1.   six months for non-policy-making memos
2.   one year for correspondence to and from the head office
3.   until superseded

The procedures for assigning classification and retention codes for this housing authority company are that the appropriate letter and number (if necessary to complete the code) are placed in the upper right-hand corner of the document in red ink. Immediately below the retention code number is written in red ink. Thus, a zoning code ordinance would be labeled:

$$\begin{bmatrix} D60 \\ 6 \end{bmatrix}$$

Section 4.   Procedures for filing into storage files. For example:

For filing into active storage remove paper clips, staple materials if required, mend torn pages, sort like material together, assign codes, and make cross-reference notations to the master authority index and in the file if necessary.

Include the procedures for transferring information from active to inactive files. List the kinds of material that are to be transferred and/or disposed of. Include forms used. Include also the procedures for receiving materials into the inactive files or at the permanent storage center and the regulations regarding disposal. Include the forms necessary for transferring, receiving, and disposing of materials.

Section 5.   Instructions for updating master index file and cross-references. For example:

For changes of address you can use the old master card to make a cross-reference card, if still in good condition, or make a new cross-reference card. Use a 3x5-inch card and begin on the second line, two spaces in from the left edge of the card, typing surname first, then forename. On the next line, in block format, give the old address using two lines. Skip a line, then six spaces in from the left side of the card write "see" and repeat the name— surname first, then forename. On the next line, four spaces in from the left side of the card, give the new address using two lines. Make a new card for the master index file with the new address beginning on the second line two spaces in from the left side of the card. Destroy the old master card or convert to a cross-reference card by adding the new information.

Index files are easy to use because of their consistency. It matters not what beginning line or indentation space is chosen, but the eye will see quicker and the mind will register that information if everything is alike.

Master Index File	Cross-Reference File
Vermeersch, Noreen	Vermeersch, Noreen
1904 Coach-N-Four	1495 Devondale
Chicago, Illinois	Detroit, Michigan

see Vermeersch, Noreen

1904 Coach-N-Four
Chicago, Illinois

For disposed records enter onto the master index card the date disposed, methods of disposition, signature of person authorizing disposition, and initials of person doing the disposing. Include copies of the forms.

Section 6. Recycling rules and procedures. Environmental issues have made recycling important. The procedures manual must not only state the philosophy of why recycling is being practiced, but also give specific instructions on what is to be recycled and how. Can paper types be mixed? Is paper to be shredded? Are cans crushed? If specific locations, pickups, or equipment are used, they should all be listed.

Section 7. Job descriptions for employees in the department. Some companies' personnel policies make all employees begin their tour of employment in either the mail room or filing department in order to "learn" the company. This has advantages in that anyone hired has "mobility" out of what may appear to be a dead-end position. But it also means that as good filers are promoted, the department supervisor must train new people, some of whom are inept in the intricacies of filing. All employees like a clear-cut description of what their job duties and responsibilities are. Most employers have employees who not only know how to perform their own jobs but who can assume some of the duties of the persons right above and below them on the organizational chart. Such overlap keeps the work flow moving in the event of an absent employee. Basically, though, each level of employment includes certain duties that the other levels do not, and spelling out these duties in the procedures manual eliminates the friction that occurs when someone feels overworked and underrecognized. These positions might be spelled out as follows:

Records Clerk. Sorts, indexes, files, and retrieves records; enters data on records; classifies materials and records; transfers records according to retention schedule.

Forms Analyst. Investigates and analyzes forms requirements; designs, drafts, and prepares finished art work masters; analyzes, revises, and consolidates existing forms; maintains records required to document and control all company forms.

Records Center Supervisor. Operates and maintains a corporate record center; selects and supervises record's center clerks; is responsible for vital records protection, storage, and disposal, recycling rules and procedures, disaster planning, and office ergonomics.

Educational and work experience requirements are frequently included with the job descriptions. Also as part of the job description, sections from the company-wide employees' handbook might be included, covering such areas as hiring criteria based upon job functions; expected employee job attitudes and conduct; military, jury, pregnancy, and paternity leave policies; grooming standards; smoking policy; break periods; personal telephone calls and/or e-mail restrictions; punctuality and inclement weather policies; and resignations, layoffs, and dismissals. Job benefits are usually enumerated, such as health, life, dental, disability, and worker's compensation insurance; continuing education reimbursement; professional dues; conference attendance; employee assistance programs; wellness programs; pension and 401K plans; flexible scheduling; collective bargaining, if applicable; sick leave, vacation, holidays, personal leave, and unpaid leaves of absence; the regular work week and overtime; credit union availability; day care provisions. Handbook sections may also re-affirm Equal Employment Opportunity commitment; explain affirmative action programs; state compliance with the Americans with Disabilities Act, not only for hiring but also in eliminating environmental barriers and in commitment with OSHA's standards for a physically safe environment; state adherence to the Immigration Reform and Control Act; and set forth employee grievance procedures, sexual, age, and sexual preference harassment policies, and complaint procedures. Many manuals include photocopies of appropriate sections from federal, state, or local laws in the procedures manual.

Include evaluation forms for job reviews. Performance measures should be specific and clear, not vague or idealistic. Unfortunately some companies/ departments are frequently managed by one of three theories: "Protestant work ethic," "top-down management," or "civil service," with rules impersonally administered and extensive records for verification. Behavioral scientists advocate a revision toward more attention to attitudes, morale, group relationship, and shaping jobs to people rather than people to jobs. There should be well-defined criteria explaining how personal growth through on- and off-the-job continuing education, contributions to the department through a service mentality, and on-the-job performance will be recognized and rewarded. If there is ongoing training to prepare for promotion, this should be spelled out.

Include an organizational chart. It is the supervisor who analyzes the job to be accomplished, trains the employees to do it, sets the job performance standards, and measures the work of the employees against those standards. In addition, supervisors as line managers have an obligation to let employees know what level of performance is expected of them and to provide frequent feedback on how they are measuring up to these expectations. Putting all of this in the department's procedure manual reminds both the supervisor and employee of the obligation.

Part IV.   Retention of Records

Section 1.   Definition and list of what constitutes vital, essential, useful, and nonessential records. For example:

Vital records are those necessary to reconstruct the company in the event of a disaster. These include, for the XYZ Company, the charter, contracts, legal documents, and patents. Essential papers are minutes of stockholders meetings and accounting ledgers.

Section 2. Retention schedule. This spells out the provisions for the eventual disposition of all records except vital records. It includes a timetable and disaster plans.

Section 3. Disaster planning. This should include location of personnel titles involved and their duties, and detailed instructions on immediate actions, as well as reconstruction plans. Sentences and paragraphs should be short. Disaster planning addresses worst-case scenarios. Less critical situations can be handled by using only the needed portions of the plan.

Part V. Circulation Procedures. This not only gives a statement of the circulation policy and procedures but also outlines screening procedures ("right to know") whenever appropriate.

Part VI. Equipment and Supplies. Included here is a description of equipment used in the storage process. Brand names can be stated, but there is less revision if only the specifications are listed. For example:

In active storage areas use lateral files, four drawers with doors and locks for all administrative and personnel files. In permanent storage areas use self-locking, steel-braced, corrugated boxes.

Include also a description of any equipment maintenance requirements. Include a list of procedures, including forms, for requisitioning supplies and equipment. If the forms for each section of the procedures manual have not been included with the steps, then include all the necessary forms now. Ergonomic considerations should be given as well as generalized facility management concerns.

Part VII. Centralization Vs. Decentralization. This decision needs to be made by each company. The increased efficiencies and control that are possible with centralization may mean a "time lag" of retrieval for workers accustomed to reaching into their own files. The results of this decision should be outlined in this section.

The procedures manual is not a static, dead tool; it is alive and always changing. For this reason, it is a good idea to have each point of coverage, or section, on its own sheet of paper. In that way only the sections being changed or adapted will have to be retyped or changed on the word processing disk, which is a backup of the procedures manual.

FOR FURTHER STUDY

1. Interview someone in a records management department and review the departmental procedures manual.

2. Begin a procedures manual. Begin with Part I, General Information. Section 1. Identifying Name; Section 2. Policy Statement; and Section 3. Scope of Coverage. This manual will be added to as additional chapters cover appropriate topics. The manual can be developed for a particular company, an organization to which you belong, or even for home use.

4

PART II: METHODS OF _____ *CLASSIFICATION* _____

Filing is a process of records control; it is arranging anything in a methodical manner. It is not easy. Filing is impossible unless one applies a set of definite criteria and carefully follows a sequence of steps. Yet, the best-known guidelines for filing—the American Library Association's rules for filing, the Library of Congress's rules for filing, and the Association of Record Managers and Administrators' rules—are based on tradition rather than scientific analysis. Many rules are imprecise, quite a few rules contradict other rules, and there are countless exceptions to rules. Computers have been forcing an objective analysis of rules and procedures and are producing yet another set of rules.

It cannot be emphasized enough that every library, records center, and information center has its own filing system. In practice, one finds countless methods for filing the same material; it is not as important what methods are followed as it is that there be a written set of rules for those methods. Unfortunately, this is not the case in many offices, and as a result many offices do not have an effective records control system. One person sets up the system, knows where everything is, moves on to another position, and tells the successor "it's alphabetical." That person begins to interfile. It may still work, but redundancies and different interpretations begin to creep in. By the time the third person begins to file, nothing can be found. A few hours spent filing from a procedures manual will save countless retrieval hours and will prevent having to begin anew.

Choosing a filing method requires a knowledge and analysis of a company's policies, objectives, organizational structure, and relationships. It also requires a knowledge of what types of information are created and received and how the information is used. What is the format? Are there blueprints, correspondence, legal-sized or standard-sized sheets, checks, invoices, microfiche, cards, computer disks, optical disks to be dealt with? What is the volume? Is the organization a hospital, an insurance company, or an engineering office?

A good filing method meets the needs of the company; it is efficient, economical, and simple, and should require the minimum in equipment, space, and personnel effort.

The basic methods of filing are: alphabetical, geographical, phonetic, numerical, color-coded, and subject. Frequently a combination of filing methods is used. One must examine each record to choose an appropriate filing method for it and to determine its life cycle.

ALPHABETICAL FILING

Let's examine some filing methods. We will begin with alphabetical filing. In the following sections you will be given various ways of filing material and problems to file according to each method. Rather than advocating that only one method is correct, I have called each a "policy."

Letter-by-Letter

Within the alphabetical system there is a policy of filing letter-by-letter. In this method all spaces are disregarded, and the material is filed as if it were one long entry.

Bloomfield Hills, Michigan is filed as if it were Bloomfieldhillsmichigan before Cleveland, Ohio, which is filed as Clevelandohio.

Take the following list and file it alphabetically letter by letter.

Chicago
Clifton
Caldwell
Cliffside Park
Carteret
Chicago Heights
Carpentersville
Calumet City

Your list should read:

Caldwell	Caldwell
Calumet City	Calumetcity
Carpentersville	Carpentersville
Carteret	Carteret
Chicago	Chicago
Chicago Heights	Chicagoheights
Cliffside Park	Cliffsidepark
Clifton	Clifton

With letter-by-letter filing it does not matter how long or short the words are, or how many words there are, the filing is handled as if it were one long string.

Word-by-Word

Official filing rules frown on letter-by-letter filing. The American Library Association's rules for filing, the Library of Congress's rules for filing, and the Association for Record Managers and Administrators' rules all say to file word-by-word.

DISREGARD ARTICLES

According to library rules this means, except for initial articles (the, a, an), filing is done alphabetically, literally word by word. However, business filing disregards nonessential words, which principally include, besides articles, conjunctions and sometimes prepositions. For instance, consider this list:

> Coiffure Lynette
> A Cut Above
> Clip Joint, Ltd.
> Colette the Beauty Spa
> Coiffures by Mira
> Coiffures by Eric's International
> Colette and Thomas
> Clip-N-Curl
> Coiffure International Beauty College

According to the policy of filing word by word, ignoring initial articles, these names would be filed as follows:

> Clip Joint, Ltd.
> Clip-N-Curl
> Coiffure International Beauty College
> Coiffure Lynette
> Coiffures by Eric's International
> Coiffures by Mira
> Colette and Thomas
> Colette the Beauty Spa
> A Cut Above

Because many businesses want to be listed first in the telephone book and other directories, they consider "A" not an article but rather as either a word or as a "nothing" letter that comes before words. Following this principle, the following list:

> A All Appliance Inc.
> A Cut Above
> A to Z Hardware
> A Rose Is a Rose
> A Fishy Deal

A Clean Sweep
A Moving and Storage
A Little Chocolate
A Able Key & Service Co.

becomes:

A Able Key & Service Co.
A All Appliance Inc.
A Clean Sweep
A Cut Above
A Fishy Deal
A Little Chocolate
A Moving and Storage
A Rose Is a Rose
A to Z Hardware

DISREGARD NONESSENTIAL WORDS

According to the filing practices of many businesses to disregard not only initial articles but also all nonessential words, the first list would be:

Clip (N) Curl	Clip Curl
Clip Joint (Ltd)	Clip Joint
Coiffure International Beauty College	Coiffure International Beauty College
Coiffure Lynette	Coiffure Lynette
Coiffures (by) Eric's International	Coiffures Eric's International
Coiffures (by) Mira	Coiffures Mira
Colette (the) Beauty Spa	Colette Beauty Spa
Colette (and) Thomas	Colette Thomas
(A) Cut Above	Cut Above

Even though they are disregarded in filing, nonessential words are included in the filing line, but traditionally they are placed in parentheses.

Take the following list and file by the policy of counting all words except initial article:

Bag Lunch
Angelo's Little Place
Angelo's in the Park
Angelo's and Marty's
Angelo's on the Hill
Bag of Chicken

Your list should be:

> Angelo's and Marty's
> Angelo's in the Park
> Angelo's Little Place
> Angelo's on the Hill
> Bag Lunch
> Bag of Chicken

Now, take the same list and file disregarding all articles, prepositions, and conjunctions. Your answers should be:

Angelo's (on the) Hill	Angelo's Hill
Angelo's Little Place	Angelo's Little Place
Angelo's (and) Marty's	Angelo's Marty's
Angelo's (in the) Park	Angelo's Park
Bag (of) Chicken	Bag Chicken
Bag Lunch	Bag Lunch

Notice how placement changes.

NAMES

Policy. If there is a forename and a surname (Suzanne Gill), file the surname first followed by the forename (Gill, Suzanne) and any middle names or initials.

Name as Written	File as
Adam R. Perez	Perez, Adam R.
David E. Perkins	Perkins, David E.
Flavius Pernoud	Pernoud, Flavius
Flavius George Pernoud	Pernoud, Flavius George
Joan Pernoud	Pernoud, Joan

PREFIXED SURNAMES

Policy. For American names of individuals with prefixed surnames, such as *A, De, Des, Du, Fitz, La, Les, Mac, Mc, O, San, Van,* and *Von,* file as one unit regardless of whether the surname is written as one word, two, or more. That is, the names are being filed letter by letter.

Name as Written	File as
Mary De La Roche	De La Roche, Mary
John Del Carmen	Del Carmen, John
Emily Deleon	Deleon, Emily
Fred Del Pizzo	Del Pizzo, Fred
Rosa De Luca	De Luca, Rosa
Bill Del Valle	Del Valle, Bill

Arrange the following names as they should appear in a file according to the policy for American names of individuals with prefixed surnames:

Leo Le Blanc
Peter Lee
John Leahy
Jerome L'Ecuyer
Stephen Le Frank
Daniel Leary

Your list should read:

Leahy, John
Leary, Daniel
Le Blanc, Leo
L'Ecuyer, Jerome
Lee, Peter
Le Frank, Stephen

Policy. Some file policies consider the prefixes *M'* and *Mc* to equal the letters *Mac* and interfile as if all were spelled *Mac*.

Name as Written	Name Inverted	File as
C. Alan McAlfee	McAlfee, C. Alan	MacAlfee
Robert R. MacDonald	MacDonald, Robert R.	MacDonald
Bernice Macdoninick	Macdoninick, Bernice	MacDoninick
Audrey M'Donnell	M'Donnell, Audrey	MacDonnell
Francis McDonnell	McDonnell, Francis	MacDonnell
Barbara MacDonough	MacDonough, Barbara	MacDonough
Dennis McDonough	McDonough, Dennis	MacDonough
Alice Macleod	Macleod, Alice	MacLeod
James Macnish	Macnish, James	MacNish

Policy. The telephone book has always placed *Mc* after all the *Ma*'s.

Name as Written	File as
Robert R. MacDonald	MacDonald, Robert R.
Bernice Macdoninick	Macdoninick, Bernice
Barbara MacDonough	MacDonough, Barbara
Alice Macleod	Macleod, Alice
James Macnish	Macnish, James
C. Alan McAlfee	McAlfee, C. Alan
Francis McDonnell	McDonnell, Francis
Dennis McDonough	McDonough, Dennis
Audrey M'Donnell	M'Donnell, Audrey

Take the following list and alphabetize it as if the prefixes *M'* and *Mc* equaled the letters *Mac*.

Rose MacNamee
Guy M'Guiness
William G. Mac Collom
Alan W. McCowan
James MacFadden
Michael MacNalley
Colin McCormick
William McGinnis
Molly McNamara
Jane M'Connell

Your answers should be:

Mac Collom, William G.
M'Connell, Jane
McCormick, Colin
McCowan, Alan W.
MacFadden, James
McGinnis, William
M'Guiness, Guy
MacNalley, Michael
McNamara, Molly
MacNamee, Rose

Take the same list and alphabetize *Mc* after all the *Ma*'s. The apostrophe should be disregarded in filing. Your list should read:

Mac Collom, William G.
MacFadden, James
MacNamee, Rose
McCormick, Colin
McCowan, Alan W.
McGinnis, William
McNamara, Molly
M'Connell, Jane
M'Guiness, Guy

HYPHENATED SURNAMES

Policy. Hyphenated surnames and compound surnames are filed as one word.

Name as Written	File as
James Carr-Kehlar	Carr-Kehlar, James
Larry Carter-Jones	Carter-Jones, Larry
Thomas FitzGerald	FitzGerald, Thomas
Kemper FitzGibbon	FitzGibbon, Kemper
Mary Peterson-Sloan	Peterson-Sloan, Mary
Harold Sloan-Peterson	Sloan-Peterson, Harold

Some computer software programs have problems with rules such as this one and *Mc* being filed as *Mac*. The names have to be keyed in as you want them printed out. Thus, *Mc* has to be keyed in as *Mac*. Hyphenated names may have to be keyed in without the hyphen, or with what is called a *hard* hyphen, or as one word: Mary Petersonsloan. Check the software's manual.

If a married couple is inserting the other's surname in front of his or her own surname, a cross-reference must be made to this fact. For example:

Mary Peterson-Sloan (Mrs.)
   see also Harold Sloan-Peterson

Harold Sloan-Peterson
   see also Mary Peterson-Sloan (Mrs.)

Remember that sometimes computers have problems with hyphens. When these words are keyed into the computer, it ignores the hyphen and the names become Mary Peterson Sloan and Harold Sloan Peterson, with the first surname treated as a middle name.

In fact, any time there is the possibility of another logical way to file something, a cross-reference must be made from the method not used to the one being used. It is better to spend the time making the cross-reference than searching for "lost" material.

MARRIED WOMEN'S SURNAMES

Policy. The legal name of a woman is her forename, her maiden name or initial, and her husband's surname. She is filed by her legal name, surname first. If her husband's name is known, make a cross-reference to it.

Name as Written	File as
Alice Marie P. Briggs	Briggs, Alice Marie P. (Mrs.)

Cross-reference
Briggs, Raymond (Mrs.)
   see Briggs, Alice Marie P.

Policy. A married woman's name is filed by preference. This may be Mary Reiffer (her maiden name, which is used professionally); her husband's name, Mrs. Thomas Fitzgerald; or Mary Fitzgerald. For safety's sake, cross-references should be made to and from all possible forms of the known names.

NICKNAMES

Policy. If a nickname is used for a forename, it is a good idea to make a cross-reference to the fuller name, but one policy is to file by nickname.

Name as Written	File as
Kiki Mitchell	Mitchell, Kiki

(List continues on page 40.)

Cross-reference
Mitchell, Kathleen
    see Mitchell, Kiki

Policy. If a nickname, or coined name, or titled name does not have a surname, file as written.

Name as Written	File as
Big Bird	Big Bird
Captain Kangaroo	Captain Kangaroo
Cookie Monster	Cookie Monster
Duke of Kent	Duke of Kent
Highland Bill	Highland Bill
Pope John Paul II	Pope John Paul II
Queen Elizabeth	Queen Elizabeth
Scotch-Lass Mary	Scotch-Lass Mary

TITLES, DEGREES

Policy. Titles and degrees are disregarded unless they are necessary to distinguish between two otherwise identical names. The title or degree is then placed at the end of the filing words and filed alphabetically. For example:

Name as Written	File as
John James Smith	Smith, John James
Col. John James Smith	Smith, John James (Col.)
John James Smith, Jr.	Smith, John James (Jr.)
Dr. John James Smith, Jr.	Smith, John James (Jr., DDS)
John James Smith III	Smith, John James (III, CPA)
Dr. John James Smith III	Smith, John James (III, MD)
Dr. John James Smith III	Smith, John James (III, PHD)
Miss Marian Teasdale	Teasdale, Marian (Miss)
Mr. Marian Teasdale	Teasdale, Marian (Mr.)
Mrs. Marian Teasdale	Teasdale, Marian (Mrs.)
Ms. Marian Teasdale	Teasdale, Marian (Ms.)

Take the following list of names and alphabetize them word by word. After each filing unit write the rule you are following.

Marie Cissoni-DeLeon
Donnie & Marie's Emporium
Sally Clarke Closson
Mary FitzPatrick
Daredevil Harry
John DeGuire
Clyde Van De Meter, Jr.
Michael and the Time Machine Disco
Father Donald Xavier
Clyde Van De Meter

Your answers should be:

Cissoni-DeLeon, Marie	Hyphenated surnames and compound surnames are filed as one word.
Closson, Sally Clarke	Names are filed surname first, followed by forename and maiden name.
Daredevil Harry	If a nickname, or coined name, does not have a surname, file as written.
DeGuire, John	For American names of individuals with prefixed surnames, file as one unit regardless of whether the surname is written as one word, two, or more.
Donnie (&) Marie's Emporium	In business filing disregard conjunctions, articles, and prepositions.
or	
Donnie and Marie's Emporium	In library filing, file word by word, disregarding only initial articles.
Father Donald Xavier	If a titled name does not have a surname, file as written.
FitzPatrick, Mary	For American names of individuals with prefixed surnames, file as one unit regardless of whether the surname is written as one name, two, or more; compound surnames are filed as one name.
Michael (and the) Time Machine Disco	In business filing disregard conjunctions, articles, and prepositions.
or	
Michael and the Time Machine Disco	In library filing, file word by word, disregarding only initial articles.
Van De Meter, Clyde	For American names of individuals with prefixed surnames, file as one unit regardless of whether the surname is written as one word, two, or more.
Van De Meter, Clyde (Jr.)	Titles and degrees are disregarded unless they are needed to distinguish between two otherwise identical names.

CORPORATE NAMES

Policy. Names of firms, corporations, and institutions are filed as written unless they contain the full name or initials of an individual.

Name as Written	File as
Bretano's	Bretano's
Casa Dia Montessori Inc.	Casa Dia Montessori Inc.
Chateau De Decors	Chateau De Decors
The Children's House	Children's House (The)
Chippewa Glass & Mirrors	Chippewa Glass & Mirrors

CORPORATE NAMES WITH AN INDIVIDUAL'S NAME

Policy. A firm or organization containing an individual's name is filed surname first followed by forename or initial(s) and any other company information.

Name as Written	File as
Jack Crowley & Assoc.	Crowley, Jack (&) Assoc.
J. E. Hanick & Assoc. Inc.	Hanick, J. E. (&) Assoc. Inc.
Esther Meyer Electrolysis	Meyer, Esther Electrolysis
Betty Phalen Temporaries	Phalen, Betty Temporaries

Take the following list and alphabetize according to the policy of first names being filed as written unless they contain the full name or initials of an individual, in which case they are filed surname first followed by forenames and additional information.

> R. G. Strassner Tennis Court Builders
> Larry Schiller Associates
> Southard Construction Company
> Seal Master
> Mel T. Stricker Auto Repair
> James Smreker Paving
> Smarko's Fish Market
> Steve's Sport Shop

Your list should read:

> Schiller, Larry Associates
> Seal Master
> Smarko's Fish Market
> Smreker, James Paving
> Southard Construction Company
> Steve's Sport Shop
> Strassner, R. G. Tennis Court Builders
> Stricker, Mel T. Auto Repair

CORPORATE NAMES WITH TWO OR MORE INDIVIDUALS' NAMES

Policy. Firm names that contain two or more full personal names are indexed under the first name with cross-references from the other names.

Name as Written	File as
William Smith & James Hawk, Attorneys	Smith, William Attorneys

Cross-Reference

Hawk, James Attorneys
   see Smith, William Attorneys

File these firm names with full personal name under the first name and make a cross-reference(s) to the other name(s).

Carl Powers and Patricia Miller, Attorneys
William H. McNamara & Richard G. Mitchell Accounting Services
Steve Gund and Elizabeth Andress Insurance

Your answers should be:

Gund, Steve Insurance

Cross-reference

Andress, Elizabeth Insurance
   see Gund, Steve Insurance

McNamara, William H. Accounting Services

Cross-reference

Mitchell, Richard G. Accounting Services
   see McNamara, William H. Accounting Services

Powers, Carl Attorneys

Cross-reference

Miller, Patricia Attorneys
   see Powers, Carl Attorneys

CORPORATE NAMES ESTABLISHED AS WRITTEN

Policy. If a personal business name has become established as written, file as written with a cross-reference.

Name as Written	File as
Colonel Sanders Fried Chicken	Colonel Sanders Fried Chicken

(List continues on page 44.)

Cross-reference
Sanders, Colonel Fried Chicken
    see Colonel Sanders Fried Chicken

Name as Written	File as
Fanny Farmer Candy	Fanny Farmer Candy

Cross-reference
Farmer, Fanny Candy
    see Fanny Farmer Candy

Name as Written	File as
John Hancock Mutual Life Insurance Company	John Hancock Mutual Life Insurance Company

Cross-reference
Hancock, John Mutual Life Insurance Company
    see John Hancock Mutual Life Insurance Company

Name as Written	File as
Kay Williams Personnel	Kay Williams Personnel

Cross-reference
Williams, Kay Personnel
    see Kay Williams Personnel

This policy is an exception to the general policy of filing surnames first, and not all companies follow this policy. My feeling is that the fewer exceptions to rules that appear in your procedures manual, the better.

CORPORATE NAMES AS WRITTEN

This policy and the one that follows are contradictory, but each is used in some offices.

Policy. File business names as written.

Name as Written	File as
Captain Brown Shoes	Captain Brown Shoes
Madame Rosa's Dress Shoppe	Madame Rosa's Dress Shoppe
Doctor Scholl Foot Comfort Shop	Doctor Scholl Foot Comfort Shop

CORPORATE NAMES WITH TITLES

Policy. Firm or corporate names that have titles as their first word are indexed by name. Titles are disregarded, but cross-references are made.

Name as Written

Captain Brown Shoes

Cross-reference

Captain Brown Shoes
 see Brown Shoes (Captain)

File as

Brown Shoes (Captain)

Name as Written

Madame Rosa's Dress Shoppe

Cross-reference

Madame Rosa's Dress Shoppe
 see Rosa's Dress Shoppe (Madame)

File as

Rosa's Dress Shoppe (Madame)

Name as Written

Doctor Scholl Foot Comfort
 Shop

Cross-reference

Doctor Scholl Foot Comfort Shop
 see Scholl Foot Comfort Shop (Doctor)

File as

Scholl Foot Comfort Shop
 (Doctor)

Take the following list and alphabetize it by the policy of surname first, followed by forename or title.

Montgomery Ward Company
Grandpa Pigeon's Emporium
Mr. Pip's Tips
Castaway Bob Jones Boat Rack
Grandma Smith's Apple Pies Inc.

Your answers should be:

Jones, Bob Castaway Boat Rack
Pigeon's Emporium (Grandpa)
Pip's Tips (Mr.)
Smith's Apple Pies Inc. (Grandma)
Ward, Montgomery Company

Take the same list and alphabetize it by the policy that corporate or firm names are filed as written. Your answers should be:

Castaway Bob Jones Boat Rack
Grandma Smith's Apple Pies Inc.
Grandpa Pigeon's Emporium
Mister Pip's Tips
Montgomery Ward Company

Here are two more contradictory policies.

HYPHENATED CORPORATE NAMES

Policy. Hyphenated firm names are indexed as separate words:

Name as Written	File as
A-1 Auto Company	A One Auto Company
Am-Vets Thrift Center	Am Vets Thrift Center
Anglo-American Car Rental	Anglo American Car Rental
Brod-Dugan Paint Company	Brod Dugan Paint Company

Policy. Hypenated firm names are indexed as a single word.

Name as Written	File as
A-1 Auto Company	Aone Auto Company
Am-Vets Thrift Center	Amvets Thrift Center
Anglo-American Car Rental	Angloamerican Car Rental
Brod-Dugan Paint Company	Broddugan Paint Company

In many filing systems, the practicalities are that these words will fall into the same place no matter which policy is followed. But in very large or very specialized filing centers, which policy is practiced makes a difference in how the filing develops. Another policy that is correlative to these is that any word that can be written as one word or two can be filed as one word or two. Thus, it is possible to find each of these three policies in force in companies.

TWO WORDS WRITTEN AS ONE WORD

Policy. Any word written as two words which can be written as one word is filed as one word.

Name as Written	File as
Inter State Trucking	Interstate Trucking
Mid West Library Service	Midwest Library Service
North Eastern Coal Company	Northeastern Coal Company

Policy. Any word written as two words which can be written as one word is filed as two words.

Name as Written	File as
Inter State Trucking	Inter State Trucking
Mid West Library Service	Mid West Library Service
North Eastern Coal Company	North Eastern Coal Company

GEOGRAPHIC TERMS

Policy. Each word in compound geographical terms is a separate filing unit, including prefixes, and is filed as written.

Name as Written	File as
Des Moines Hatchery	Des Moines Hatchery
Los Angeles Freeway, Inc.	Los Angeles Freeway Inc.
San Diego Ship Company	San Diego Ship Company

Policy. Two-word geographical names are considered one word.

Name as Written	File as
Des Moines Hatchery	Desmoines Hatchery
Los Angeles Freeway, Inc.	Losangeles Freeway, Inc.
San Diego Ship Company	Sandiego Ship Company

Take the following list and arrange it by the policy that hyphenated compound geographical words, and words that can be compounds but are not, are filed as separate words.

Lake Side Dock & Barge Company
Play-Rite Courts
Des Peres, Missouri
Los Gatos, California
Pan-American Truck Lines
La Grandee, Oregon
Dos Palos, California

Your answers should be:

Des Peres, Missouri	Des Peres Missouri
Dos Palos, California	Dos Palos California
La Grandee, Oregon	La Grandee Oregon
Lake Side Dock & Barge Company	Lake Side Dock & Barge Company
Los Gatos, California	Los Gatos California
Pan-American Truck Lines	Pan American Truck Lines
Play-Rite Courts	Play Rite Courts

Take the same list and arrange it by the policy that hyphenated, compound geographical words and words that can be compounded are filed as one word. Your answers would be the same as the first list.

Des Peres, Missouri	Desperes Missouri
Dos Palos, California	Dospalos California
La Grandee, Oregon	Lagrandee Oregon
Lake Side Dock & Barge Company	Lakeside Dock & Barge Company
Los Gatos, California	Losgatos California
Pan-American Truck Lines	Panamerican Truck Lines
Play-Rite Courts	Playrite Courts

In practice, more and more you will find that words thought of as a unit are filed as a unit. More and more, filers are trying to think in terms of retrieval and not merely the mastering of myriad rules. Also, as more "coined words" appear, they are thought of as a complete unit.

COINED WORDS

Policy. Coined words, consisting of phonetic spellings, trade words, syllable prefixes or suffixes, or combined forms that require the combination to be complete, are filed as one unit.

Name as Written	File as
Bona-Fide Bond Company	Bonafide Bond Company
Glo-Art Embroidery	Gloart Embroidery
Take-hom-a-sak	Takehomasak

Take the following list and alphabetize it by the policy that coined words, trade words consisting of phonetic spellings, prefixes and suffixes, and words that can be combined are filed as one unit.

Tel-Rep Cable TV
Policy-Quip Cable TV
Remco TV Rental
Arch Way TV Service
Photo-Scan Video Systems
Bi-Rite TV Sales Company
Panasonic Closed Circuit TV
Polyester Fabrics
Telephone Communi Tronics
Tele-Foto Cameras

Your answers should be:

Arch Way TV Service	Archway TV Service
Bi-Rite TV Sales Company	Birite TV Sales Company
Panasonic Closed Circuit TV	Panasonic Closed Circuit TV
Photo-Scan Video Systems	Photoscan Video Systems
Polyester Fabrics	Polyester Fabrics
Poly-Quip Cable TV	Polyquip Cable TV
Remco TV Rental	Remco TV Rental
Tele-Foto Cameras	Telefoto Cameras
Telephone Communi Tronics	Telephone Communitronics
Tel-Rep Cable TV	Telrep Cable TV

INITIALS

The following policies reflect other means of dealing with initials and abbreviations.

Policy. Initials and single letters file before words beginning with the same letters.

Name as Written	File as
NAACP	N A A C P
NAB Exhibit Office	N A B Exhibit Office
NAC Finance Corp.	N A C Finance Corporation
NAMPA Administration	N A M P A Administration
NAPA Distribution Center	N A P A Distribution Center
NMC Research	N M C Research
N & V Television Sales	N V Television Sales
Naam, Nashaat	Naam, Nashaat
Naar, Sheldon	Naar, Sheldon
Naas, Lee	Naas, Lee

The problem occurs when the initials or single letters really stand as abbreviations and the filer does not know this.

Policy. Whenever initials are an abbreviation, make a cross-reference notation on the card that will stand in the file as letters.

NAACP
>   see National Association for the Advancement of Colored People

M.A.A.P.
>   see Middle American Awareness Plan

MDRT
>   see Million Dollar Round Table

TABS
>   see Total Abstinence and Benevolent Society

List the following as they would appear in a file:

MARC
>   see Machine-Readable Cataloging

MGM Hotel
M Brand Popcorn Company
MGC Inc.
Maack, Albert
M Transportation Co.
MAA Inc.
MGM
>   see Metro Goldwyn Mayer

M-A Jobbing and Equipment Co.
Maack Auto Parts
MAB Paint Store
MFA Insurance Co.

Your list should read:

M Brand Popcorn Company
M Transportation Co.
M-A Jobbing and Equipment Co.
MAA Inc.
MAB Paint Store
MARC
    see Machine Readable Cataloging
MFA Insurance Co.
MGC Inc.
MGM
    see Metro Goldwyn Mayer
MGM Hotel
Maack, Albert
Maack Auto Parts

ACRONYMS

Another problem occurs with acronyms, that is, initials that spell a word. Is NATO an abbreviation, letters by themselves, or an acronym? Depending upon circumstances, it can be all three. Whenever possible the filer should find out. If it is determined that it is an acronym or an abbreviation, make a cross-reference from the letters. Unfortunately, sometimes a filer cannot find out what AAA means. It could be Agricultural Adjustment Association, American Automobile Association, or American Air Aviation. WARP could be a word or stand for Women Against Rotten Politics.

File the following list of acronyms as words:

UNESCO
CAB
ERA
SEATO
NASA
ANSI
COMPAID
SWAT
OSHA
UNCLE

Your answers should be:

American National Standards Institute
Civil Aeronautics Board
Compute Order Material Planning and Instrumentation Drawings
Equal Rights Amendment
National Aeronautics and Space Administration
Occupational Safety and Health Administration
Southeast Asia Treaty Organization

Special Weapons and Tactics
United Nations Crime Law Enforcement
United Nations Educational, Scientific, and Cultural Organization

File the same list with the acronyms filed as letters or initials with a "see" cross-reference interwoven with the acronyms spelled out. Your answers should be:

ANSI   see American National Standards Institute
American National Standards Institute
CAB   see Civil Aeronautics Board
COMPAID   see Compute Order Material Planning and Instrumentation Drawings
Civil Aeronautics Board
Compute Order Material Planning and Instrumentation Drawings
ERA   see Equal Rights Amendment
Equal Rights Amendment
NASA   see National Aeronautics and Space Administration
National Aeronautics and Space Administration
OSHA   see Occupational Safety and Health Administration
Occupational Safety and Health Administration
SEATO   see Southeast Asia Treaty Organization
SWAT   see Special Weapons and Tactics
Southeast Asia Treaty Organization
Special Weapons and Tactics
UNCLE   see United Nations Crime and Law Enforcement
UNESCO   see United Nations Educational, Scientific, and Cultural Organization
United Nations Crime and Law Enforcement
United Nations Educational, Scientific, and Cultural Organization

Judgmental decisions, such as whether something is a word whose letters stand for something or simply a set of letters, make filing difficult. If you do not know, then it is best to file these as letters. This is often referred to as the "nothing before something rule," nothing meaning it does not stand for anything. Symbols (-,*,#,') are each an example of something that stands for nothing. Letters that do not form an acronym or a word are also considered "nothing." According to this principle, radio and TV call letters are filed before words. For example:

KMOX
KSDK
KSD-TV
KSS
Kay, Sheila

PARENT COMPANY

Policy. Names of subsidiaries, divisions, and affiliates are filed by parent company with cross-references from the subsidiary.

Name as Known	File as
Stromberg Carlson, a division of General Dynamics	General Dynamics

Cross-reference

Stromberg Carlson
   see General Dynamics

Policy. Names of subsidiaries, divisions, and affiliates are filed according to the name on their letterhead with cross-references to the parent company.

Name on Letterhead	File as
Remington Rand, division of Sperry Rand	Remington Rand
Library Bureau, division of Sperry Rand	Library Bureau

Cross Reference

Sperry Rand
   see also Library Bureau
        Remington Rand

Take the following list of subsidiaries and file by parent company with a cross-reference from the subsidiary:

Tinius Olsen Testing Machines Division of Labquip Corporation
Zeuschel Equipment Company Dealers for Bacharach Instruments
West Point Division of Pepperell Inc.
Martex Division of Pepperell Inc.
Zeis Tinplate Division of Bakewell Corporation

Your answers should be:

Bacharach Instruments
Bakewell Corporation
Labquip Corporation
Martex
   see Pepperell Inc.
Pepperell Inc.

Tinius Olsen Testing Machines
    see Labquip Corporation
West Point
    see Pepperell Inc.
Zeis Tinplate
    see Bakewell Corporation
Zeuschel Equipment Company
    see Bacharach Instruments

Take the same list and index by letterhead name with a cross-reference from the parent company. Your answers should be:

Bacharach Instruments
    see Zeuschel Equipment Company
Bakewell Corporation
    see Zeis Tinplate
Labquip Corporation
    see Tinius Olsen Testing Machines
Martex
Pepperell Inc.
    see Martex
        West Point
Tinius Olsen Testing Machines
West Point
Zeis Tinplate
Zeuschel Equipment Company

ABBREVIATIONS

Policy. File abbreviations as spelled in full.

Abbreviation	File as
AAA	American Automobile Association
Dr.	doctor
Dr.	drive
FBI	Federal Bureau of Investigation

Policy. File *Mrs.* and *Ms.* as *Mrs.* and *Ms.*

Name as Written	File as
Mr. Chips	Mister Chips
Mrs. Miniver	Mrs. Miniver
Ms. Magazine	Ms. Magazine

Some more conflicting policies follow.

APOSTROPHE

Policy. Disregard the apostrophe in elisions and possessives, and file as written.

Name as Written	File as
Alice Boy	Boy, Alice
Boy Scouts of America	Boy Scouts of America
T. R. Boy Manufacturing Co.	Boy, T. R. Manufacturing Co.
Doreen Boye	Boye, Doreen
Boy's Candy Company	Boy's Candy Company
Charles Boys	Boys, Charles
Boys' Clubs of America	Boys' Clubs of America
Ralph Boys	Boys, Ralph
Boy's Wearing Apparel	Boy's Wearing Apparel
I'll Go-N-Stop	I'll Go-N-Stop
Ill Pill Shop	Ill Pill Shop

Policy. Apostrophe-s ('s) indicating possessive case is not considered in indexing and filing, but s-apostrophe (s') is. Thus, the previous list would be filed as:

Boy, Alice
Boy Scouts of America
Boy, T. R. Manufacturing Co.
Boy('s) Candy Company
Boy('s) Wearing Apparel
Boye, Doreen
Boys, Charles
Boys' Clubs of America
Boys, Ralph
I'll Go-N-Stop
Ill Pill Shop

Notice that *Boye, Doreen*, *Boy's Wearing Apparel*, and *Boys, Charles* have all moved from their previous positions. One letter does make a difference in filing. This is why the rules an organization follows must be documented in a procedures manual.

Take the following list and alphabetize disregarding the apostrophe-s ('s) but counting the s-apostrophe (s'):

Flora Browns
Mark E. Brown
Brown's Food Shop
Browns' Meat Market
Brown's Sons of Fenton
Browns' Brothers Shoes

Your list should read:

Brown('s) Food Shop
Brown, Mark E.
Brown('s) Sons of Fenton
Browns' Brothers Shoes
Browns, Flora
Browns' Meat Market

Take the same list and disregard all apostrophe marks. Your list should read:

Brown, Mark E.
Browns' Brothers Shoes
Browns, Flora
Brown's Food Shop
Browns' Meat Market
Brown's Sons of Fenton

GUARDIANS, RECEIVERS, TRUSTEES

Policy. Guardians, receivers, and trustees are indexed under the names of the individuals or organizations for whom they act, with a cross-reference made for the name of guardian, receiver, or trustee.

Name as Written	File as
Jack Lutz, administrator Estate of Brian Gill	Gill, Brian, estate of

Cross-reference
Lutz, Jack, administrator
see Gill, Brian, estate of

Name as Written	File as
Commerce Bank, trustee Estate of James Gill	Gill, James, estate of

Cross-reference
Commerce Bank, trustee
see Gill, James, estate of

Take the following list of guardians, receivers, and trustees and index under the name of the individuals or organizations for whom they act, with a cross-reference made for the name of guardian, receiver, or trustee.

Doris Shreve, guardian of Daniel Boenkleman
Shreveport Bank, trustee of Philo Beckman's estate
Pamela Stoll Law Firm, receivers of Baucair's Bistro bankruptcy
Linda Beckmann, 1901-1969, Bruce Sheraton trustee

Your answers should be:

Baucair's Bistro, bankruptcy
Beckman, Philo, estate of
Beckmann, Linda, 1901-1969, estate of
Boenkleman, Daniel
Sheraton, Bruce, trustee
    see Beckmann, Linda, 1901-1969, estate of
Shreve, Doris, guardian
    see Boenkleman, Daniel
Shreveport Bank, trustee
    see Beckman, Philo, estate of
Stoll, Pamela Law Firm, receivers
    see Baucair's Bistro, bankruptcy

COMMON NAMES

Policy. Associations, banks, churches, clubs, colleges, hospitals, hotels, libraries, motels, newspapers, periodicals, schools, unions, and universities are filed under their distinctive names. If necessary, the location is placed after the distinctive name and secondary filing is made by location. (In geographical filing, location would go first and primary filing would be by location, then distinctive name.)

This is a practical policy because, depending upon the company or organization, there could simply be too many filing units beginning with the same word. Libraries follow this same policy when they choose not to file under "history of" or "story of" simply because of the number of entries involved.

Name as Written	File as
Third District Missouri Nurses Association	Nurses Association, Missouri Third District
Wellston Chamber of Commerce	Chamber of Commerce, Wellston
District Number 2 Marine Engineer Beneficial Association	Marine Engineer Beneficial Association, District Number 2
National Association of Housing (&) Redevelopment Officials	Housing (&) Redevelopment Officials, National Association
Bank of Crestwood	Crestwood Bank
Bank of Ellisville	Ellisville Bank
Citizen's Bank of Pacific	Citizen's Bank of Pacific
First National Bank of Arnold	First National Bank of Arnold
First National Bank of Clayton	First National Bank of Clayton
St. Paul's Church	St. Paul's Church (Catholic)
St. Paul's Church	St. Paul's Church (Episcopal)

St. Paul's Church	St. Paul's Church (Lutheran)
Hiram Sumner High School	Sumner, Hiram High School
University of Denver	Denver University (of)
Fermin Desloge Hospital	Desloge, Fermin Hospital
Hotel Mayo	Mayo Hotel
Hotel Windsor	Windsor Hotel
St. Louis Post-Dispatch	Post-Dispatch, St. Louis

Listing entries under distinctive titles presents a problem whenever something is known locally by a "popular" name. For example, does one file under the name as known: Memorial Hospital; or under the official name: St. Mary of the Sepulcher Memorial Hospital; or under place: Illinois. Cahokia. St. Mary of the Sepulcher Memorial Hospital? All three methods could be considered "correct." More and more, filing is done by popular name with cross-references from the official name.

Policy. File by distinctive, popular name. Make a cross-reference from the official name.

File as	Cross-reference
Elks Club	Benevolent and Protective Order
	of Elks
	see Elks Club

Filing under official name with a cross-reference from the popular name is also done.

Policy. File by official name. Make a cross-reference from the distinctive popular name.

File as	Cross-reference
Benevolent and Protective	Elks Club
Order of Elks	see Benevolent and Protec-
	tive Order of Elks

File the following by distinctive, popular name with a cross-reference from the official name.

Pioneer District's Camp Zoa, Boy Scouts of America, known as Camp Zoa

Kirkwood's Free and Accepted Masonic Lodge, known as Masonic Lodge

Carondelet Lodge Loyal Order of Moose, known as Moose Lodge

Your answers should be:

Boy Scouts of America. Pioneer District
   see Camp Zoa
Camp Zoa. Boy Scouts of America. Pioneer District

(List continues on page 58.)

Free and Accepted Masons. Kirkwood Lodge
    see Masonic Lodge. Kirkwood
Loyal Order of Moose. Carondelet Lodge
    see Moose Lodge. Carondelet
Masonic Lodge. Kirkwood
Moose Lodge. Carondelet

File the same list under official names with cross-references from the popular names. Your list should read:

Boy Scouts of America. Pioneer District. Camp Zoa
Camp Zoa
    see Boy Scouts of America. Pioneer District. Camp Zoa
Free and Accepted Masons. Kirkwood Lodge
Loyal Order of Moose. Carondelet Lodge
Masonic Lodge. Kirkwood.
    see Free and Accepted Masons. Kirkwood Lodge
Moose Lodge. Carondelet
    see Loyal Order of Moose. Carondelet Lodge

GOVERNMENT DEPARTMENTS

Government departments pose the same problem of whether to file under popular or official name. And with most federal, state, and local government departments there is frequently a hierarchy of bodies which must also be taken into account. Should material on the "Gateway Arch," its popular name, be filed under "National Park Service," its sponsoring agency, "Jefferson National Expansion Memorial," its official name, or "United States Department of the Interior," its highest sponsoring body?

FEDERAL GOVERNMENT DEPARTMENTS

Policy. Federal departments are indexed and filed under "United States Government" and are subdivided by name of department in a hierarchical arrangement showing the sequential order of authority and reporting lines. For example:

United States Government. Department of the Interior. National Park
    Service. Jefferson National Expansion Memorial.

Cross-reference

Gateway Arch
    see United States Government. Department of the Interior.
    National Park Service. Jefferson National Expansion
    Memorial.

To keep abreast of all the federal changes of departments, the latest edition of the *United States Government Manual* (Washington, DC: Superintendent of Documents) is invaluable. It is also useful for many United Nations departments. *Statesman's Yearbook* (New York: St. Martin's Press) is useful for foreign governments and United Nations departments.

As with names, though, the trend is to file directly by popular name and cross-reference from the fuller hierarchy.

File the following by United States government hierarchy of departments.

Urban renewal with HUD
FHA mortgages
Federal Register's Code of Federal Regulations
Civil Defense bomb shelters
Affirmative Action guidelines

Your answers should be:

United States Government. Department of Housing and Urban Development. Urban renewal.
United States Government. Federal Housing Administration.
United States Government. Federal Register Division. Code of Federal Regulations.
United States Government. Department of Defense. Office of Civil Defense.
United States Government. Department of Labor. Office of Economic Opportunity.

Alphabetically these agencies would fall:

United States Government. Department of Defense. Office of Civil Defense.
United States Government. Department of Housing and Urban Development. Urban renewal.
United States Government. Department of Labor. Office of Economic Opportunity.
United States Government. Federal Housing Administration.
United States Government. Federal Register Division. Code of Federal Regulations.

Filing directly, the same list would produce:

Civil Defense Office
Code of Federal Regulations
Equal Opportunity Employment
Federal Housing Administration
Housing and Urban Development

STATE AND LOCAL GOVERNMENT
DEPARTMENTS

Policy. State and local governmental units are filed first by state or governmental name and then by department. The words, "state," "city," or "county" may have to be added for clarity but are assumed within an individual state, city, or county.

New York (City) Board of Aldermen
New York (State) Department of Education
St. Louis (City) Department of Planning
Chesterfield. Department of Public Safety

File the following by name of state or local government and department:

Commission for the Blind, Commonwealth of Pennsylvania
Cook County Department of Welfare
City of Boston. Tourism Board
Clayton Parks and Recreation Department

Your answers should be:

Boston. Board of Tourism.
Clayton. Department of Parks and Recreation.
Cook County. Department of Welfare.
Pennsylvania. Commission for the Blind.

Just as distinctive names are being used for filing schools, hospitals, and associations, one finds distinctive names increasingly being used for governmental bodies. Place is important, but filing is going directly to the unique department, rather than relying upon the complete hierarchical history. Even common words such as "department," "bureau," and "commission" are being ignored.

Boston. Tourism (Board)
Clayton. Parks and Recreation (Department)
Cook County. Welfare (Department of)
Kirkwood. Public Safety (Department)
New York (City) Aldermen (Board)
New York (State) Education (Department of)
Pennsylvania. Blind (Commission for)
St. Louis (City) Planning (Department of)
United States Government. Census (Bureau).
     not: United States Government. Department of Labor. Bureau
       of Census.

Policy. File governmental units by place and then distinctive name. Take the following list and arrange by place and distinctive governmental name:

Regional Planning Board of Princeton, New Jersey
Center for Urban Policy Research, Princeton, New Jersey
Ohio census for 1800-1850
United Nations Department of Economic and Social Affairs

Your answers should be:

New Jersey. Princeton. Regional Planning (Board)
New Jersey. Princeton. Urban Policy Research (Center for)
United Nations. Economic and Social Affairs (Department of)
United States Government. Census (Bureau) Ohio. 1800-1850

In the state of New Jersey, the state could have been eliminated and filing done by city:

Princeton. Regional Planning (Board)
Princeton. Urban Policy Research (Center for)

Whenever you are dealing with a governmental unit, it is an excellent idea to write the full filing unit onto each document to be filed. Do not leave it to chance that the filer will automatically think "United States Government" before "census (Bureau)," or "Alabama" before "National Guard."

FOREIGN WORDS

Foreign words, names, and governments also present several filing options. The first decision to be made is whether to Americanize the words or to follow the rules and spellings of the country.

As an American citizen "Kurt von Gotard's" last name is "Von Gotard, Kurt," but as a German citizen his last name is "Gotard, Kurt von."

If you have a very small file of foreign names, it is easiest to interfile them with your regular list of names with a cross-reference from the form not used to the one used. But if you have a large proportion of foreign (not American citizens') names or corporations, then a separate file is easier. Even with a separate file you must determine whether to attempt again to "Americanize" the procedure or to carefully follow the rules for each country. Let's examine some policies from which one could select procedures for individual filing systems.

FOREIGN INDIVIDUALS' NAMES

Policy. If it is possible to determine a given, middle, and last name, file surname first, followed by given and middle names as if they were American names.

Name	File as
Eva St. John	St. John, Eva
Maria Lo Piccolo	Lo Piccolo, Maria

Policy. Names are filed alphabetically according to the customs of the country.

Spanish: The father's surname is followed by the mother's surname.
Julio Parra y Rodriquez is filed as Parra y Rodriquez, Julio.

Portuguese: The mother's surname precedes the father's surname.
Julio Rodriques y Parra is filed as Parra, Julio Rodriques y.

French: With names containing a preposition and an article (not a contraction of the two), the article precedes and the preposition follows the name.
Jean de La Fontaine is filed as La Fontaine, Jean de.

Chinese: Chinese names frequently occur in the order of surname first followed by given names. They are to be filed surname first.
Wong, Ha Yi is filed Wong, Ha Yi.

Policy. If it is not possible to determine an individual's surname and given names, index and file as written.

Kang Kiang is filed as Kang Kiang.
Ari Ibn Sahav is filed as Ari Ibn Sahav.

Policy. Foreign place names should be translated into English.

Bruxelles is filed as Brussels.
Habana is filed as Havana.

Policy. Foreign place names are filed as written.

Bruxelles is filed as Bruxelles.
Habana is filed as Habana.

FOREIGN CORPORATE NAMES AND GOVERNMENTAL DEPARTMENTS

Policy. Foreign company names and governmental bodies are translated into English and filed.

La Banque Provinciale du Canada is filed as Provincial Bank of Canada.
Conseil d'Etat is filed as France. Municipal Court.

Policy. Foreign company names and governmental bodies are filed as written, placing country or city in front if it is a governmental unit.

La Banque Provinciale du Canada is filed as La Banque Provinciale du Canada.
Conseil d'Etat is filed as France. Conseil d'Etat.

Translate the following geographical terms into English:

Bastenaken
Cracow
Firenze
Helsingfors
Kjobenhaven
Lisboa
Milano
Moskva
München

Your answers should be:

Bastogne
Krakow
Florence
Helsinki
Copenhagen
Lisbon
Milan
Moscow
Munich

Policy. Foreign company names are filed first alphabetically by place and then by company.

England. Abbey Life Insurance Company, Ltd.
England. Affiliated Factors Limited
Italy. Alfa Romeo

Policy. Foreign company names are interfiled into one alphabet with foreign individual names regardless of country.

Abbey Life Insurance Company Ltd.
Affiliated Factors Limited
Alfa Romeo
Ari Ibn Sahan

Take the following list and alphabetize it into one alphabetic sequence disregarding place:

Abeille. Milan, Italy
All Parts Auto Supply Company. Toronto, Canada
Agricultural and General Insurance Ltd. Kent, England
N. B. Amev. Utrecht, The Netherlands
Allianz Lebensversicherungs. Husum, West Germany
Allparts Ltd. London, England
Agrippina Ruckeversicherung. Husum, West Germany
Ajax Engineering Products. Kent, England

Alleanza Assicuragioni. Milan, Italy
Albingia Versicherungs. Aschaffenburg, West Germany
Alexander and Aris Ltd. London, England
Alcan Aluminum Corporation. Montreal. Canada

Your answers should be:

Abeille
Agricultural and General Insurance Ltd.
Agrippina Ruckeversicherung
Ajax Engineering Products
Albingia Versicherungs
Alcan Aluminum Corporation
Alexander and Aris Ltd.
All Parts Auto Supply Company
Alleanza Assicuragioni
Allianz Lebensversicherungs
Allparts Ltd.
Amev, N. B.

Take the same list and alphabetize first by place, then by company or name. Your answers should be:

Canada. Montreal. Alcan Aluminum Corporation
Canada. Toronto. All Parts Auto Supply Company
England. Kent. Agricultural and General Insurance Ltd.
England. Kent. Ajax Engineering Products
England. London. Alexander and Aris Ltd.
England. London. All Parts Ltd.
Italy. Milan. Abeille
Italy. Milan. Alleanza Assicuragioni
Netherlands. Utrecht. Amev, N. B.
West Germany. Aschaffenburg. Albingia Versicherungs
West Germany. Husum. Agrippina Ruckeversicherung
West Germany. Husum. Allianz Lebensversicherungs

Obviously, no matter which policies are adopted by an individual records department, a lot of cross-references will still have to be made from logical headings to the one(s) actually being used, and all policies will need to be fully documented in the procedures manual.

CONSECUTIVE SEQUENCE AND NUMBERS SPELLED OUT

Policy. Filing units starting with numerals of any number of digits are arranged in strict numeric sequence, are not spelled out, and are filed preceding the entire alphabetic file. Numbers already spelled out (not numerals) are filed alphabetically.

3-Hour Dry Cleaners
23rd Avenue Drug Store
905 International Inc.
Adam, Samuel
Forty-Four Club

Policy. Numerals appearing in other than the first position are filed immediately preceding the first similar name without a numeral.

Edie's 600 Club
Edie's Furniture
Tony's 9th Pit Stop
Tony's 10th Pit Stop
Tony's Bar and Grill

NUMBERS AS SPOKEN

Policy. Numbers are filed as though spelled out and as spoken. The numeric designation is filed alphabetically as one word. Thus, the number "1989" can be filed as:

one thousand nine hundred eighty nine, if it is a consecutive number

one-nine-eight-nine, if it is a house number and

nineteen eighty nine if it is a year.

The following list shows filing numbers, as spoken, in alphabetical order:

15th Street Auto Parts
5th Avenue Fashion Shops
5th Baptist Church
1st Army Battalion
1st Avenue Irregulars
First Productions Inc.

SYMBOLS

Policy. If symbols can be spoken, they are filed alphabetically as spoken, otherwise they precede the alphabet according to the number of symbols and the words that follow.

**Disco
???Magic Shoppe
Able, Thomas
Baker, Charles
$5 Daily Rentals (Five Dollar Daily Rentals)
#1 Food Shop (Number One Food Shop)
Olliver, Bradford J.

File the following using the policy that all numbers are filed consecutively before the letters of the alphabet, and that numbers within filing units precede similar filing units without a numeral.

Tony's 23rd Avenue Repair Shop
401 Garden Center
Top of the 230
Tony's 5th Pizza Parlor
Tony's Television Service
Fourth Pen and Pencil Inc.
4th Avenue Irregulars
Top of the 9th
1400 West 51st Street Apartments
Top of the Avenue
Tony's Pizza Parlor

Your answers should be:

4th Avenue Irregulars
401 Garden Center
1400 West 51st Street Apartments
Fourth Pen and Pencil Inc.
Tony's 5th Pizza Parlor
Tony's Pizza Parlor
Tony's 23rd Avenue Repair Shop
Tony's Television Service
Top of the 9th
Top of the 230
Top of the Avenue

Take the same list and file the numerals as spoken no matter where they fall within the filing unit. Your answers should be:

401 Garden Center (Four-O-One)
4th Avenue Irregulars
1400 West 51st Street Apartments (Fourteen Hundred)
Fourth Pen and Pencil Inc.
Tony's 5th Pizza Parlor
Tony's Pizza Parlor
Tony's Television Service
Tony's 23rd Avenue Repair Shop
Top of the Avenue
Top of the 9th
Top of the 230 (Two-thirty)

It is obvious that filing will fall into different places depending upon which policies one is following.

Policy. Inclusive numbers are sequenced by the lowest numeral of the sequence.

89-92 West Hampton Apartments is filed under 89 West

Policy. When identical filing units are distinguished only by numbers, they are arranged in numerical consecutive sequence.

Vitamin B-1
Vitamin B-12

Take the following and arrange by the policy of sequence by the lowest number and consecutive sequence for identical units except for number:

Highway 312
1411-1415 Manchester Road
1402-1410 Manchester Road
Highway 101
1407 Manchester Road
1412-1414 Manchester Road
Highway 206
Highway 201

Your answers should be:

1402 (-1410) Manchester Road
1407 Manchester Road
1411 (-1415) Manchester Road
1412 (-1414) Manchester Road
Highway 101
Highway 201
Highway 206
Highway 312

ADDRESSES

What do you do if there are two medical doctors named Robert John Bruner, or two companies named Presto Incorporated? You will have to use address location to distinguish them. As their addresses change, their positions in the files may have to change.

Policy. When the same name appears with different addresses, the arrangement is:

1) alphabetical by name
2) alphabetical by city
3) alphabetical by state
4) alphabetical by street name
5) alphabetical by direction: east, north, northeast, south, etc.
6) streets without direction designation are filed ahead of streets with direction designation
7) numerical by house or building numbers
8) when a building name and street name are included in the address, disregard the building name in favor of the street name.

For example, the following are in correct order according to this policy:

Smith, John Joseph
  Denver, Colorado
  8202 Church Road

Smith, John Joseph
  Denver, Iowa
  5421 East Devonshire

Smith, John Joseph
  Des Peres, Missouri
  1102 Kendon Drive

Smith, John Joseph
  Des Peres, Missouri
  1102 Kendon Lane

Smith, John Joseph
  Des Peres, Missouri
  1114 Kendon Lane

Arrange the following list by address location:

Enterprise Insurance
  Evanston, Louisiana
  4135 North Central

Enterprise Insurance
  St. Charles, Illinois
  4135 West Central

Enterprise Insurance
  Evanston, Illinois
  4135 North Central

Enterprise Insurance
  St. Charles, Missouri
  4135 Central

Enterprise Insurance
  Evanston, Louisiana
  4135 South Central

Enterprise Insurance
  St. Charles, Illinois
  4135 Western Ave.

Enterprise Insurance
  St. Charles, Missouri
  4135 East Central

Enterprise Insurance
  Evanston, Illinois
  4139 North Central

Your answers should be:

> Enterprise Insurance
> Evanston, Illinois
> 4135 North Central
>
> Enterprise Insurance
> Evanston, Illinois
> 4139 North Central
>
> Enterprise Insurance
> Evanston, Louisiana
> 4135 North Central
>
> Enterprise Insurance
> Evanston, Louisiana
> 4135 South Central
>
> Enterprise Insurance
> St. Charles, Illinois
> 4135 West Central
>
> Enterprise Insurance
> St. Charles, Illinois
> 4135 Western Ave.
>
> Enterprise Insurance
> St. Charles, Missouri
> 4135 Central
>
> Enterprise Insurance
> St. Charles, Missouri
> 4135 East Central

INDIVIDUALS' NAMES WITH PHRASES

Now the question arises as to how to interfile individuals' names and phrases. As usual, there is more than one method.

Policy. Words are interfiled in strict alphabetical order disregarding punctuation and phrases.

Name as Written	File as
Charles	Charles
A. Charles	Charles, A.
Albert Charles	Charles, Albert
Charles the Baker	Charles (the) Baker
Charles Baker Corporation	Baker, Charles Corporation
A. Charles Plumbing	Charles, A. Plumbing
Al Charles Travel Company	Charles, Al Travel Company
Charles' and Ray's Cleaning	Charles' and Ray's Cleaning
Charles-Wright Inc.	Charles-Wright Inc.

To file this list in strict word-by-word alphabetical order disregarding punctuation, the list would read:

Baker, Charles Corporation
Charles
Charles, A.
Charles, A. Plumbing
Charles, Al Travel
Charles, Albert
Charles (the) Baker
Charles' (and) Ray's Cleaning
Charles-Wright Inc.

Policy. Individuals' names standing alone precede phrases, even if the phrase contains an individual's name. The preceding list now becomes:

Baker, Charles Corporation
Charles
Charles, A.
Charles, Albert
Charles, A. Plumbing
Charles, Al Travel
Charles (the) Baker
Charles' (and) Ray's Cleaning
Charles-Wright Inc.

File the following list by the policy of strict alphabetical order disregarding punctuation:

John Del Mar
Delmar Street Car Line
Delmar Civic Association
Jack Delmar Grocery Store
Del Mar-Johnson Corporation

Your list should read:

Delmar Civic Association
Delmar, Jack Grocery Store
Del Mar, John
Del Mar-Johnson Corporation
Delmar Street Car Line

Take the same list filing by the policy of individuals' names preceding phrases, including those containing an individual's name. Your list should read:

Del Mar, John
Delmar Civic Association

Delmar, Jack Grocery Store
Del Mar-Johnson Corporation
Delmar Street Car Line

CROSS-REFERENCES

Although the term, *cross-reference*, has been used several times, and examples have been included, further discussion is needed. A cross-reference leads from a term not being used to one that is being used. For example:

Automation
    see Data Processing

This means the term, "Automation," is not being used in the file. Anything that might go into such a category is being placed, instead, in a file labeled "Data Processing."

Another form of cross-reference is a "see also" reference. This is used when the term you are seeking is being used, but more information may be found under another. For instance, Mary Ebeling Jones is the wife of Robert Charles Jones. In the file for Robert Charles Jones there is a "see also" reference to the file of Mary Ebeling Jones. A simple cross-reference leads from a term not being used to one that is being used; "see also" cross-reference leads to all possible terms being used.

Cross-reference notations can take many formats. They can be on cards, computer tape, or sheets of paper. At this point we have been discussing name files that frequently appear on 3x5-inch cards. A file is efficient to use because like things always appear in the same place. The eye expects to see certain things in certain places because the file has been programmed in that way.

One format for creating a name cross-reference on a 3x5-inch card is to begin the name not being used one space from the left side of the card and one carriage roll from the top of the card. Skip a line and indent four spaces and type "see" or "see also" followed by the term(s) to be investigated (see figure 4.1, page 72).

On six 3x5-inch cards make the following cross-references using the illustrated format:

Wright-Charles Inc.
    see Charles-Wright Inc.

Barbara Kadlec McDonough
    see also Dennis B. McDonough

Dennis B. McDonough
    see also Barbara Kadlec McDonough

Automation
    see also Computers, Data Processing

Computers
    see also Automation, Data Processing

Data Processing
    see also Automation, Computers

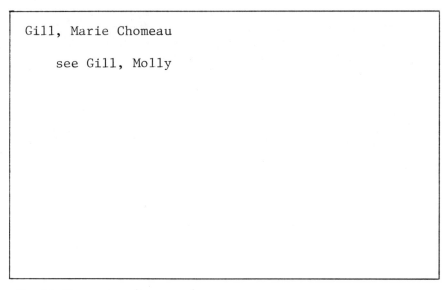

Fig. 4.1. Name cross-reference card.

For Further Study

1. Photocopy the list of names and addresses given (unless you need typing practice!). Cut each filing group apart and transfer it to its own 3x5-inch card. These cards will become a file to manipulate in several ways.

   a) Arrange the file alphabetically, word by word, disregarding punctuation, conjunctions, and apostrophe-s ('s). Hyphenated words are filed as two words. Acronyms and initials are filed as "nothing before something" rule. File surnames, first names. Interfile names and phrases. Answers are given on pages 251-52.

   b) Go through your file and write on a sheet of paper all the policies you used to create your file.

   c) Take the file and rearrange alphabetically word by word with individuals' names coming before phrases. File hyphenated words as one word. Acronyms and initials should be filed as words. File ampersands and conjunctions as words. Do not disregard them. Answers are given on pages 252-53.

   d) Check your file for any additional policies you might have used to create your filing list.

2. Obtain a list of 100 names and addresses. If you work for an organization as either an employee or a volunteer, use the list of names available to you there. If not, use a telephone book. You are now going to add to your procedures manual Part II, "Methods of Classification. Section 1. Alphabetical." You must decide which policies you will follow to create your file. Every rule you use must go into your procedures manual. Use your list of names as examples to clarify each rule you have written.

LIST FOR USE WITH "FOR FURTHER STUDY"

A-Abasco Fire Extinguishers Co.
  Inc.
Oakdale, Pennsylvania 15071
378-221-994

A-Admiral Rentals & Sales Co.
Oak Ridge, New Jersey 07438
378-438-088

A-1 Auto Drive School
Oakdale, Louisiana 71463
378-382-364

APA & Associates
Oak Ridge, Tennessee 37830
378-425-541

A-1-AA Book Shop
Oakridge, Oregon 97463
478-490-286

AA Addressing and Office Machines
Oakdale, California 95361
478-681-198

A-A Award Studio
Oakdale, Iowa 52319
478-210-243

A & A Graphics Inc.
St. Louis, Missouri 73101
478-727-180

AAA Ace Photographers of Canada
Montreal (Quebec) Canada
388-682-782

A-Able Information Service
Oak Ridge, Louisiana 71264
488-787-649

A-1 Auto Parts Locating Service
Oakdale, Wisconsin 54649
488-691-774

A-1 Auto Parts and Supply Co.
Oak Ridge, North Carolina 27310
488-926-449

A-Z Auto Parts Inc.
Oakdale, Nebraska 68761
398-435-638

A to Z Insurance Programs Inc.
Denver, Iowa 50622
398-921-682

AA see Alcoholic Anonymous

AA Importing Co. Inc.
Oak Ridge, Louisiana 71264
398-430-646

A & A Meat Sales
Oakdale, Wisconsin 54649
498-327-544

AAA Auto Parts Inc.
Oakridge, Oregon 97463
498-390-969

(List continues on page 74.)

AAA Auto Air Conditioning
Oakdale, Pennsylvania 15071
388-923-255

AAA Automobile Club
Oak Ridge, New Jersey 07438
388-374-569

A-AAA Amusement Co.
Oakdale, Nebraska 68761
488-676-109

AAA see Automobile Club of
  America

A. E. Miller Lock & Key Co.
Oak Ridge, North Carolina 27310
448-921-608

A. E. Schmidt Co.
Oakdale, Wisconsin 54649
448-688-756

A & S Auto Service
Kirkwood (St. Louis), Missouri
448-928-185

A & S Automotive Inc.
Oakdale, California 95361
358-317-897

AAA Auto Parts Co.
Oak Ridge, Mississippi 39180
498-436-066

AAA Auto Salvage
Oakdale, Louisiana 71463
498-431-191

A. B. Lester Booksellers Limited
Oak Ridge, Mississippi 39180
348-954-125

A & E Brake Engineers
Oak Ridge, Louisiana 71264
348-675-016

A & E Company Printers
Oak Ridge, New Jersey 07438
448-432-721

AFIA Worldwide Insurance
Oakdale, Nebraska 68761
458-433-090

A & E Electronics Corp.
Oak Ridge, New Jersey 07438
368-727-332

A & E Guttering Co.
Oakdale, Louisiana 71463
368-316-617

A & E Square Deal Auto Salvage
Oakdale, Pennsylvania 15071
368-921-884

A & H Auto Parts
Oakridge, Oregon 97463
368-322-149

AAA Insurance Agency
Oak Ridge, Tennessee 37830
408-374-569

AABC National Insurance Agency
Oakdale, California 95361
408-462-552

A-AAA Amusement & Vending Co.
Oakdale, Iowa 52319
438-437-363

ABC Battery & Auto Parts Warehouse Inc.
Oakdale, California 95361
438-684-419

ABC Insurers
Oak Ridge, Tennessee 37830
348-317-086

A. B. Dick Products Co. of St.
  Louis
St. John (St. Louis), Missouri
348-697-098

A Builders
Denver, Iowa 50622
358-462-932

A-Okay Apartments
Hibbing (St. Louis), Minnesota
358-433-034

AABCO National Insurance Agency
Denver, Iowa 50622
358-655-091

A Bee C Television Service Co. Inc.
Oakdale, Iowa 52319
468-314-722

A Better System Dog Training
Oak Ridge, Louisiana 71264
468-928-771

A-O-K Home for the Elderly
Oakdale, Louisiana 71463
468-376-364

A-Te-Anna Coiffures
Oak Ridge, Tennessee 37830
468-431-141

Assurances Générales de France
Vaucresson, France
Rue de Gaulle
128-210-245

Associated Engineering Limited
Warwickshire, England
60 Kenilworth Road
128-210-244

Avions Marcel Dassault-Breguet
Vaucresson, France
33 Rue de Professor
218-430-647

BMW see Bayerische Motoren
   Werke Aktiengesellschaft
München, West Germany
40 Haus
128-410-969

AAFP Group Disability Plans Inc.
Kirkwood (St. Louis), Missouri
458-433-528

ABCO Insurers
Oakdale, Iowa 52319
458-675-254

A & B Linen Service
Hibbing (St. Louis), Minnesota
458-437-794

Roy L. Aach
14120 Forestvale
228-321-431

Edward G. Asche
119 E. First Ave.
228-432-593

Edward Ash
11923 Claymont
138-692-198

Roy L. Ash
2910 Santiago
138-721-780

Roy L. Oesch Construction Co. Inc.
2929 Robert Dr.
138-467-484

Roy L. Aach
112 South Hanley Road
238-682-682

Avon Insurance Co. Ltd.
Stratford-on-Avon, England
3 Church St.
228-327-543

Aach see also Asche, Ash, Ashe,
   Oesch

Roy L. Aach
14122 Forestvale
228-691-431

Abbey Life Assurance Co. Ltd.
London, England
3 St. Paul's Churchyard
168-422-692

(List continues on page 76.)

Abeille
Milano, Italy
15 Via Leipardi
168-442-692

Affiliated Factors Limited
Kent, England
Turnpike Road
168-433-073

Albingia Versicherungs
Aürich, West Germany
28 Aurilusstrasse
168-420-646

Ajax Engineering Products
Kent, England
Haslemere Rd.
268-737-180

Roy L. Aach & Associates, Inc.
24 Brown Rd.
148-420-867

Edward Asche
119 E. First St.
148-922-355

Edward H. Ash
21 E. 31st
148-422-962

Roy L. Ashe
14 South 31st Ave.
148-223-420

Roy L. Oesch, Jr.
2929 Robert Dr.
248-467-488

Rosalind Apple, DDS
Toronto (Ontario), Canada
6124 Kendon
138-423-074

Audi NSU
München, West Germany
8070 Ingolstadt
238-727-180

Automotive Products Limited
Montreal (Quebec), Canada
33 Rue de la Place
238-430-645

Alcan Aluminum Corporation
Montreal (Quebec), Canada
10 Plaza West
268-440-646

All Parts Auto Supply Co.
Toronto (Ontario), Canada
3128 Hampton
268-672-782

Allianz Versicherungs Aktiengesell-
    schaft
München, West Germany
22 Haus
268-933-255

Allparts Ltd.
London, England
79 Station Road
178-380-969

Ansvar Insurance Co. Ltd.
East Sussex, England
St. Leonard's Road
178-423-072

Alva Booker
Denver, Iowa 50622
178-400-969

Roy L. Aach
112 North Hanley Road
248-691-198

Avon Rubber Company Limited
Wiltshire, England
Bath Road
238-682-781

Afro-American Museum
Oak Ridge, Tennessee 37830
158-200-243

Agricultural & General Insurance
Ltd.
Kent, England
219 High Street
158-220-243

Alfa Romeo
Milan, Italy
45 Via Gallanetta
158-337-544

Alexander & Aris Ltd.
London, England
Broad Street at Warwick
158-317-544

Alleanza Assicuragioni
Milan, Italy
34 Via San Gregorio
258-692-782

Allianz Lebensversicherungs
München, West Germany
7 Stuttgart
258-913-255

Jane Addams Vocational High
School
St. Louis, Missouri 63101
248-413-073

Agrippina Ruckeversicherung
München, West Germany
14 Stuttgart
248-717-180

Caen, Leach & McLean Insurance
Agency
Oakdale, Wisconsin 54649
188-787-650

Chapman-Sander Inc.
Oakridge, Oregon 97463
188-691-775

E & E Insurance Company
Oak Ridge, North Carolina 27310
288-926-490

Emcasco
Oak Ridge, Mississippi 39180
288-490-287

Joe Graves & Associates
Hibbing (St. Louis), Minnesota
288-921-684

Al's Auto Parts
Oakdale, Wisconsin 54649
198-384-099

A. Allen Guns Inc.
Oak Ridge, North Carolina 27310
198-438-087

Am Versucherungen
Aureliusstrasse
Aürich, West Germany
258-432-691

Aetna Life & Casualty
Oakdale, California 95361
178-785-770

Al's Auto Salvage
Oakdale, Pennsylvania 15071
278-782-319

All American Life Insurance
Oakdale, Louisiana 71463
278-221-993

Allendale Insurance
Oak Ridge, New Jersey 07438
278-383-363

Allstar National Agency
Oak Ridge, Mississippi 39180
278-926-448

Allstate Insurance Co.
Oak Ridge, Tennessee 37830
188-926-490

C P Service Company
Oakdale, California 95361
188-221-995

(List continues on page 78.)

Allsparts Insurance
Oakdale, Nebraska 68761
198-691-773

Automotive Agency of America
Oakdale, Iowa 52319
298-425-542

Bomar-Thomas Insurance Agency
Oak Ridge, North Carolina 27310
298-425-542

Cage, George H.
Oakdale, Louisiana 71463
298-438-089

Campbell & Konering
Oakdale, Pennsylvania 15071
298-382-365

Eighty-Eight Insurance Consultants
Inc.
Oak Ridge, New Jersey 07438
208-425-542

Ellis-Rodes-Meers & Co.
Oakdale, Nebraska 68761
208-490-285

Emes, Walter J.
Oak Ridge, Tennessee 37830
208-435-639

Airbanc of Canada
Toronto (Ontario), Canada
328-392-523

Assurances Générales Compagnie
Financière et de Réassurance du
Groupe
Brussels, Belgium
208-671-198

Aabar Express Co.
Oakdale, Wisconsin 54649
308-327-416

Aabco Welding Co. Inc.
St. Louis, Missouri 63101
308-655-133

Aaron, Carl L.
Oak Ridge, North Carolina
308-318-222

Aaron, James H. Lt.
Oak Ridge, New Jersey 07438
308-490-680

Aaron, James H. Capt.
Oakdale, California 95361
318-320-050

Aaron-Jones Service Station
Oak Ridge, Louisiana 71264
318-327-255

Aarons, Albert
Kirkwood (St. Louis), Missouri
318-377-894

Aaron-Abbott Commercial Service
Oakdale, Pennsylvania 15071
328-374-788

Aaron, Alex G.
Oak Ridge, Mississippi 39180
328-316-055

Aaron, Ferer & Sons Inc.
Oakdale, Nebraska 68761
328-214-235

Aaron, John H.
Hibbing (St. Louis), Missouri
428-431-534

Aaron, Jon
Denver, Iowa 50622
428-220-616

Aaron's Catering Service
Denver, Iowa 50622
428-729-197

Abatis Insurance Agency
St. Louis, Missouri 63101
428-223-958

ABACO Auto Transport
Oakdale, Wisconsin 54649
338-659-442

Aboussie Insurance Service
Oak Ridge, North Carolina 27310
338-327-048

Aarons' Plumbing and Sewer Clean
  ing Co.
Oakdale, Louisiana 71463
318-314-841

Abel, Emmett
Oakdale, Pennsylvania 15071
418-432-035

Alex Aboussie & Son Insurance
Oakridge, Oregon 97463
418-677-160

Ackrit Automotive Inc.
Oakdale, Nebraska 68761
418-375-376

N. B. Amev
Utrecht, The Netherlands
10 Archamedeslaan
258-432-693

Elizabeth Elias
Oakdale, Iowa 52311
288-921-683

Abramson, Mettzer Insurance
  Agency
Oak Ridge, New Jersey 07438
338-392-043

Adams & Associates Agency
Oak Ridge, Tennessee 37830
338-654-117

C. Stanley Adkinson Dr.
Oakdale, Iowa 52319
438-677-454

Ad-Mac & Associates, Inc.
Oak Ridge, Mississippi 39180
418-375-168

All Risk Agency Inc.
Oakridge, Oregon
198-787-648

GEOGRAPHICAL FILING

If location is more important than name, then geographical filing should be used. If a company has widespread geographical outlets, geographical filing might be the answer for keeping track of personnel. For utilities, government files, address plates, publishers, and meteorological, geological, and aeronautical files, geographical arrangement is logical.

Just as there is more than one way to alphabetize, there is more than one way to arrange geographical subdivisions. Arrangement can be by:

1. Continent. Country. City. Firm or individual name.
   Europe. Belgium. Brussels. L'Aluminium Belge Société Anonyme.

2. Country. City. Firm or individual name.
   Belgium. Brussels. L'Aluminium Belge Société Anonyme.

3. State. County. Town. Firm or individual name.
   Missouri. St. Louis. Creve Coeur. Monsanto Company.

4. State. Town. Firm or individual name.
   Ohio. Dayton. National Cash Register.

5. Town. State. Firm or individual name.
   Clayton. Missouri. Edwards, A. G.
   (This method is not used as frequently because of the similarity of so many town names.)

6. Territory or area. Firm or individual name.
   Europe. L'Aluminium Belge Société Anonyme.
   Southwest. Parra, Alfred.

7. Street filing.
   Compton Heights. Block 1. 325-355.

8. Sales routes. Town or Territory. Name.
   101-110. Des Moines. McNamara, Frank.

9. Addresses. Addresses can be in an alphabetical arrangement without being in a geographical arrangement. Either way, the order for identical names but different addresses is:

   a) Alphabetical by city.
      Chicago. Acme Travel.
      Chicago. Bridge & Iron Works.

   b) Alphabetical by state.
      Maine. Portland. Union Bank.
      Oregon. Portland. Union Bank.

   c) Alphabetical by street name.
      Hargrove
      Kendon

   d) Numerical street names before or after alphabetical.
      Sixth Street
      Tenth Street

   e) Alphabetical by street designation.
      Hargrove Drive
      Hargrove Lane
      Hargrove Street

   f) Numerical by house number.
      1021 Kendon
      1023 Kendon
      1025 Kendon

Arrange the following list by the policy of "Continent. Country. City. Firm or individual name."

University Press at Oxford, England
Maria von Schuschnigg, Salzburg, Austria
L'Etol, Paris, France
Great Assurance Ltd. in London, England

Diamonds Unlimited, Cape Town, South Africa
John Quigley, London, England

Your answers should be:

Africa. South Africa. Cape Town. Diamonds Unlimited.
British Isles. England. London. Great Assurance Ltd.
British Isles. England. London. Quigley, John
British Isles. England. Oxford. University Press.
Europe. Austria. Salzburg. Schuschnigg, Maria von.
Europe. France. Paris. L'Etol.

Arrange the same list by "Country. City. Firm or individual name." Your
list should be:

Austria. Salzburg. Schuschnigg, Maria von.
England. London. Great Assurance Ltd.
England. London. Quigley, John.
England, Oxford. University Press.
France. Paris. L'Etol.
South Africa. Cape Town. Diamonds Unlimited.

Arrange the following list by the policy of "State. County. Town. Firm or
individual name."

Walt's Tires and Batteries, Troy, Missouri, Lincoln County
Sterling Engineering at Birmingham, Alabama, Jefferson County
Rock & Quarry Mining Inc., St. Louis County, Hibbing, Minnesota
Phoenix's First National Bank, Maricopa County, Arizona
St. Louis Community College at Florissant Valley, Missouri
Walt's Tires & Batteries, Pike County, Troy, Alabama
Maricopa County's Commerce Bank, Phoenix, Arizona

Your answers should be:

Alabama. Jefferson. Birmingham. Sterling Engineering.
Alabama. Pike. Troy. Walt's Tires & Batteries.
Arizona. Maricopa. Phoenix. Commerce Bank.
Arizona. Maricopa. Phoenix. First National Bank.
Minnesota. St. Louis. Hibbing. Rock & Quarry Mining Inc.
Missouri. Lincoln. Troy. Walt's Tires and Batteries.
Missouri. St. Louis. Florissant. St. Louis Community College.

Arrange the same list by the policy of "State. Town. Firm or individual
name." Your answers should be:

Alabama. Birmingham. Sterling Engineering.
Alabama. Troy. Walt's Tires & Batteries.
Arizona. Phoenix. Commerce Bank.
Arizona. Phoenix. First National Bank.

(List continues on page 82.)

Minnesota. Hibbing. Rock & Quarry Mining Inc.
Missouri. Florissant. St. Louis Community College.
Missouri. Troy. Walt's Tires and Batteries.

Arrange the same list by the policy of "Town. State. Firm or individual name." Your answers should be:

Birmingham. Alabama. Sterling Engineering.
Florissant. Missouri. St. Louis Community College.
Hibbing. Minnesota. Rock & Quarry Mining Inc.
Phoenix. Arizona. Commerce Bank.
Phoenix. Arizona. First National Bank.
Troy. Alabama. Walt's Tires & Batteries.
Troy. Missouri. Walt's Tires and Batteries.

File the following list by the policy of "Territory or area. Firm or individual name."

Southeast. Sterling Engineering.
North Central. Rock & Quarry Mining Inc.
Midwest. St. Louis Community College.
Southeast. Walt's Tires & Batteries.
Midwest. Walt's Tires and Batteries.
Southwest. Commerce Bank.
Southwest. First National Bank.

Your answers should be:

Midwest. St. Louis Community College.
Midwest. Walt's Tires and Batteries.
North Central. Rock & Quarry Mining Inc.
Southeast. Sterling Engineering.
Southeast. Walt's Tires & Batteries.
Southwest. Commerce Bank.
Southwest. First National Bank.

Speed of reference to specific geographical areas is the main advantage of a geographical file. Also, all the advantages of alphabetical filing are inherent in this method since it is basically an alphabetical arrangement.

The volume or records within any given geographical area can be seen by glancing at the files. An analysis of the information contained in a geographical file section could be used in sales work to note areas with the most complaints, to note aggressive selling efforts or the lack thereof, to note areas where additional work seems needed, or to assist in allocating territories. If one is using territories for filing, they can be combined, enlarged, or subdivided readily. Each location is a unit or a group, and the shifting of groups is relatively easy. Many geographical systems use color as a safeguard to give the file technician another check against misfiling. All the records of one geographical section would be one color.

A disadvantage of geographical filing may be the complexity of the guide cards and folders. The very nature of the geographical method calls for variety. A geographical file is not as easy to set up as a straight alphabetical name file. Similarity between names may cause confusion. There are a lot of cities named Columbus and Springfield across the United States. Many geographical files are actually numerical files arranged by zip code. In addition, frequent cross-referencing and refiling of names are necessary as people and businesses move. One file has to be kept, at least for a period, referring from the old location to the new. Finally, a separate alphabetical index by firm or individual name is needed as a key to the filing unit. An example of this would be:

Anderson, Andrew T. and Company
   Des Moines, Iowa 50301
   4269 Springfield Avenue

   filed under Midwest. Anderson, Andrew T. and Company.

For Further Study

1. From the file of 3x5-inch cards that you established in the Alphabetical Filing section, pull all cards having non-United States addresses. From the United States file, pull all cards labeled "Oakdale, California; Oakdale, Iowa; Oakdale, Louisiana; Oakdale, Nebraska; Oakdale, Pennsylvania; and Oakdale, Wisconsin; and all Aach, Asche, Ash, Ashe, and Oesch cards.

    a) Arrange the foreign cards following the policies of filing by "Continent. Country. City. Firm or individual name," and alphabetizing word by word, disregarding punctuation. Type your answers on a sheet of paper.

    b) File the same cards by "Continent. Country. City. Firm or individual name," with individual names coming before phrase names. Type those answers that differ from arrangement (a) on a sheet of paper.

    c) Arrange the same cards by the policy of "Country. City. Firm or individual name," alphabetizing word by word. Type those answers that differ from arrangement (a) on a sheet of paper.

    d) Arrange the "Oakdale" cards by the policy of "State. Town. Firm or individual name," alphabetizing word by word. Disregard conjunctions. File hyphenated words as two words. Type the answers on a sheet of paper.

    e) Arrange the "Oakdale" cards by the policy of "State. Town. Firm or individual name," alphabetizing individual names before phrase names. File hyphenated words as one word. Consider conjunctions. Do not ignore them. Type those filing sections that differ from (d) on a sheet of paper.

    f)   Arrange all the 3x5-inch cards by the policy of "Town. State. Firm or individual name," alphabetizing word by word, disregarding punctuation.

    g)   Disregard the names of Aach, Asche, Ash, Ashe, and Oesch and file by the policy of addresses.

2.   Take your own list of names and if they can be filed by "State. Town. Firm or individual name," make such an arrangement and document the policy and finished examples in your procedures manual under Part II, "Methods of Classification. Section 2. Geographical."

3.   If your list of names is not conducive to "State. Town" arrangement (or, even if it is, after completing that arrangement), arrange by address policy, disregarding individual or firm names and filing instead alphabetically by street name, incorporating the policies of street designation, direction, or number if need be. Document all the policies you followed in your procedures manual using your cards as examples for the rules.

PHONETIC FILING

In large files with names that sound alike, a phonetic method of filing might be considered. The phonetic method is also an invaluable tool when many names are given over the telephone or one has to decipher handwriting or a mistyped version of a name.

The phonetic system is for all words that sound alike, or could be misinterpreted as another name by similar spelling. An example would be the names "Janson, Jahnsen, Jansen, Janssen, Jantzen, and Jensen." These words would all be filed alphabetically after the first possible spelling of the name with cross-references to the correct filing word wherever it would fall in the file.

    Jahnsen
    Jansen
    Janson
    Janssen
    Jantzen
    Jensen

The cross-reference cards would number five and would read:

    Card 1:
    Jansen
      This name is filed phonetically and alphabetically after "Jahnsen."

    Card 2:
    Janson
      This name is filed phonetically and alphabetically after "Jahnsen."

Card 3:

Janssen

This name is filed phonetically and alphabetically after "Jahnsen."

Card 4:

Jantzen

This name is filed phonetically and alphabetically after "Jahnsen."

Card 5:

Jensen

This name is filed phonetically and alphabetically after "Jahnsen."

In a small office rather than filing by sound alphabetically, the first filing words, regardless of spelling, could be interfiled and the second words in the names filed alphabetically.

Thus, we can formulate two policies.

Policy. File together words that sound alike or could be misinterpreted by spelling; arrange alphabetically.

Policy. File together words that sound alike or could be misinterpreted by spelling; interfile the first word and arrange alphabetically by the second word.

Arrange the following list by the policy of phonetic filing, interfiling the first filing unit and arranging alphabetically by the second filing unit.

No-Mor File Company
Nomar Shall Enterprises
Gamble, Beatrice
Gamble for Bucks
Nomore, Larry
Nomore North West Gallery
Gambill's Shoes
No More Cleaning
Gam-bill for Bucks
No-More Northwest Real Estate
Gambill & Hamilton Associates
Gamble Street Apartments

Your answers should read:

Gamble, Beatrice
Gamble (for) Bucks
Gam-bill (for) Bucks
Gambill (&) Hamilton Associates
Gambill('s) Shoes
Gamble Street Apartments
No More Cleaning
No-Mor File Company
Nomore, Larry

(List continues on page 86.)

Nomore North West Gallery
No-More Northwest Real Estate
Nomar Shall Enterprises

Arrange the same list by the policy of filing phonetically and alphabetically by the first filing unit. Your answer should be:

Gam-bill (for) Bucks
Gambill (&) Hamilton Associates
Gambill('s) Shoes
Gamble, Beatrice
Gamble (for) Bucks
Gamble Street Apartments
Nomar Shall Enterprises
No-Mor File Company
No More Cleaning
Nomore, Larry
Nomore North West Gallery
No-More Northwest Real Estate

"Nomore, Larry" could also be filed before "No More Cleaning" if it is
the office policy to file individual names before phrase names.

Remington Rand has taken phonetic spelling and numerically coded the
sounds. Their system is called "Soundex." Every name is filed by initial letter
and a numerical code of three numbers. The Soundex method does not always
work, but it works so often that it is used by many filers for similar-sounding
names.

The Soundex method does not code vowels or the letters *h, w,* or *y*. This
alone helps to solve the misinterpretation of the handwritten *a, o, u, ie, ei, v,
w, h,* and *k*. The code is:

Letters	Code Number
B, F, P, V	1
C, G, J, K, Q, S, X, Z	2
D, T	3
L	4
M, N	5
R	6

The rules that go with this code are:

1. To code a name use three digits. When no consonants or insufficient
   code consonants appear in a surname or organization name, add
   one, two, or three zeros to give a three digit code.

   For example, the name, *Conder*, is *C536*. The first letter of the word
   is not coded but is used to begin the code. The *o* is ignored since it is
   a vowel. The code for the letter *n* is *5*. The letter *d* is coded *3*. The

vowel *e* is ignored. The code for the letter *r* is *6*. Thus, *Conder* equals *536*.

Gail is *G400* because the *a* and *i* are ignored. *L* is *4*. Three digits are needed, so "0" and "0" are added.

Lutz is *L320*.

Finley is *F540*.

Bratvogel is *B631*. You only go as far in the name as you need to create three digits. The remainder of the name is ignored.

2. Two letters together (double letters) are considered as one letter (single letter).

   Gill is *G400* (*ll*).

   Gill and *Gail* would be filed together because they are names which sound alike or for which the spelling could be misinterpreted.

   Dippold is *D143* (*pp*).

   Farrell is *F640* (*rr*) (*ll*).

   Bugg is *B200* (*gg*).

3. Consider any combination of two or more equivalent letters (from the same code category) as having the same number as a single letter.

   Opffer is *O160* (ff are double letters; p and f are equivalent letters).

   Herschal is *H624* (the *6* is for *r*; *s* and *c* are equivalent letters and so they count only once as *2*; *4* represents *1*).

4. When the first letter of a name is followed immediately by an equivalent letter or the same letter, the letters are considered together as one first letter and are not coded.

   Lloyd is *L300* (Ll are considered together as an initial letter *L*; the *o* and *y* are not coded; *d* is represented by *3*; and since the system calls for three numerals, two zeros are added).

   Schumann is *S550* (S and c are equivalent letters and are represented by the letter *S*; *h* and *u* are disregarded; *m* is coded *5* and the vowel *a* is ignored; *nn* are double letters and are coded as one *n*; to make three digits a zero is added).

5. The vowels and the consonant *y* are not counted in the code, but they are separators. Consonants having a code number when separated by vowels or *y* are coded individually. *H* and *w* are not separators, are not coded, and are thus considered nonexistent in the name when coding.

   Czeko is *C200* (C and Z are equivalent letters and are represented by the letter *C*; the vowel *e* acts as a separator; thus, *k* is no longer an equivalent and is coded *2*; to make three digits, two zeros are added).

Van Sickle is *V522* (V begins the code; *5* represents the *n*; *S* is represented by *2*. The vowel *i* acts as a separator; *c* and *k* are equivalents and are represented by *2*; the *l* need not be coded because there are already three digits).

Code and arrange the following names according to the Soundex system:

Quigley
Scuzzo
Hagenhoff
Schields
Hawk
Wannemacher
McNamara
Mitchell
Powers
Sweeney
Seeley
Stricker
Schiller
Monnig
Wilson
Dolan
Dolen
McCormick
Springer

Your answers should be:

Dolan	D450
Dolen	D450
Hawk	H200
Hagenhoff	H251
McNamara	M255
McCormick	M265
Mitchell	M324
Monnig	M520
Powers	P620
Quigley	Q240
Springer	S165
Scuzzo	S220
Stricker	S362
Seeley	S400
Schields	S432
Schiller	S460
Sweeney	S500
Wilson	W425
Wannemacher	W552

Notice that *Hagenhoff, McNamara, McCormick, Springer, Scuzzo, Stricker, Seeley, Schields, Sweeney*, and *Wannemacher* fall out of place alphabetically.

Foreign names can also be converted to Soundex coding by remembering a few policies.

Policy. Names with prefixes (d, da, de, Fitz, M' O, van) are considered part of the surname no matter how they are spaced and written.

Walter Von Broun is V516.
Sean O'Casey is O220.

Policy. Compound or hyphenated surnames are considered as a single name for coding purposes.

Anthony Armstrong-Jones is A652.
Alice Perez y Parra is P621.

Policy. All abbreviations are spelled in full before coding.

Eva St. John = Eva Saint John is S532.

Policy. When a surname cannot be distinguished from a forename, code only the first word of the group.

Tai Yat Sung is T000.

J. L. Campbell has written a very simple Apple computer program, using the "Applesoft II" language for Soundex. It is listed below so you can try it if you would like to.

```
1    Rem Soundex
3    Rem Written by J. L. Campbell
10   TEXT: CLEAR: POKE 216,0:A = FRE(0)
15   NR$ = "01230120022455012623010202
17   REM NUMBERS REPRESENT ALPHABET LETTERS
20   HOME: PRINT:PRINT TAB (12) "*** SOUNDEX
***":PRINT
30   INPUT "ENTER LAST NAME = ";LN$
40   GOSUB 2000
50   PRINT:PRINT "SOUNDEX CODE = ";S$
60   VTAB (20): INPUT "ANOTHER NAME? (Y/N) ";A$
70   IF LEFT$ (A$,1) = "Y" THEN 20
80   END
2000 REM SOUNDEX SUBROUTINE
2010 L$ =" "
2020 S$ = LEFT$ (LN$,1)
2030 IF LEN (LN$)<2 THEN 2200
2040 FOR I=2 TO LEN (LN$)
2050 E$ = MID$ (LN$, I, 1)
2060 E = ASC (E$)-64
```

```
2070   IF E >26 OR E <1 THEN 2160
2080   REM SELECT CODE
2100   K$ = MID$ (NR$, E, 1)
2120   IF K$ = L$ OR K$ = "O" THEN 2160
2140   S$ = S$ + K$
2150   IF LEN (S$) >3 THEN 2200
2160   L$ = K$
2170   NEXT I
2200   S$ = LEFT$ (S$ + "000",4)
2210   RETURN
```

Some advantages of the Soundex method of phonetically grouping names are:

1. Every name has a positive, unchanging number.

2. Most family names and their variants are automatically grouped regardless of spelling. For example, Maran, Mahren, Marin, Mehrin and Moran would all be together. But remember Scuzzo and Stricker fell out of their alphabetical sequence, as would Mehrin and Moran.

3. Only six numbers are used. Some numeric codes for the alphabet have, of course, 26 numbers.

4. Unlimited expansion is possible. There are 294 number combinations for each letter of the alphabet.

5. The alphabet with all its complexities is simplified to numerical sorting, filing, and finding, and numbers are easier to handle than letters of the alphabet.

6. Error checking of the file is rapid because numbers out of place are easier to spot than letters out of order.

For Further Study

1. Take the pack of 3x5-inch cards that you established in the Alphabetical Filing section, disregard all cards beginning with letters that signify nothing but letters, and code the remaining cards according to the Soundex method. Place the code in the upper right-hand corner of the card. Arrange the cards by number code.

2. Add to your procedures manual Part II, "Methods of Classification. Section 3. Phonetic." Decide whether your policy will be to file phonetically and alphabetically or according to the Soundex system. Whichever method you choose, write the necessary rules required in your procedures manual. If your own list of names does not provide twenty-five samples to place in the manual, use the telephone directory to select some appropriate examples.

NUMERICAL FILING

The Soundex phonetic system of filing discussed on pages 86-90 is also a numerical system of filing. Once a number has been assigned, filing and retrieval is done numerically rather than alphabetically. For large files with many identical names, the Soundex code can become more distinct by adding birth dates expressed in numbers. Michael Gill born July 1, 1967, would be G400-070167.

An alphanumeric system very familiar to library/media technicians is the Library of Congress Classification schedule (HF5549.2 is personnel management). A very familiar all-numerical system is, of course, the Dewey Decimal System (658.8 is personnel management).

Records that are filed numerically can be set up so that the numbers are arranged consecutively, by terminal digit, or by middle digit; or the numbers can represent dates, subjects, or letters of the alphabet. Files greater than 20,000 records are handled better numerically than alphabetically. Number arrangement is also excellent for records that are prenumbered (such as checks, invoices, purchase orders, licenses), or in situations where a number is assigned to documents (insurance policies, claims, credit applications, patient case histories, mortgages, loans, blueprints). Numerical filing is also very useful in situations where privacy is important. In fact, the United States privacy act will force an increasing number of records to be arranged numerically. There is nothing less personal than a number, and we exist in more files by our social security, driver's license, and credit card numbers than we do by our names. Yet, problems still arise regarding the confidential nature of the files and the "right to know" of the person seeking information. Records can literally affect our fates, and, with a computer's capacity to process, match, and retrieve information at high speed, file management policies can become a moral or ethical problem. How much control do individuals have over the files that concern them? Who has, or should have, access to those records? What information needs to be recorded and what does not? A file by its mere existence acquires a certain authority, a certain permanence, a facelessness that is lacking in person-to-person communication. The composite picture created by these bits of stored information may or may not resemble the real person. Who is to decide?

There are several types of numerical systems. The most commonly used are:

1. consecutive

2. terminal digit

3. middle digit

4. chronological

5. alphanumeric

6. subject

All numerical systems are indirect filing systems, which means they require double sorting, once by words and once by numbers. There must always be a word key, or cross-reference, to the meaning of the number. People do not usually request information by number, but rather by words. Usually this key is alphabetical and can serve a dual purpose. For example, it can serve as an address mailing list or contain birth dates or territories.

There must also be a key to assigning the next number. This is called an accession book, or register. When someone asks for a file by name, the first key is checked to obtain the number and also to determine if a number has been assigned to that person or item or if it is a new file acquisition. The second key has to be checked for the next available number for all new file material to be added to the collection. Next to the number is the name assigned to it. For further information you have to use the card index filed by name.

An example from a key index:

103   Dippold, Joyce
        Florissant, Missouri 63135
        2240 Wheatfield
        837-8825

An example from an accession book:

101   Gill, Molly
102   McDonnell, Anne
103   Dippold, Joyce

Consecutive numbering is serial numbering in a straight numerical sequence, beginning low and continuing: 1, 2, 3, 4, 5, etc. Numbers are assigned in order, then filed in strict sequence from the oldest to the newest numbers. This arrangement requires that space always be available at the end of the sequence for the latest incoming numbered records. When old files are pulled for storage, the folders must be back-shifted to make room for growth that always occurs at the end of the file. After papers have been destroyed, the numbers can be reused. By using "fifth cut" file folders, a missing number becomes conspicuous by the gap it leaves (see figure 4.2).

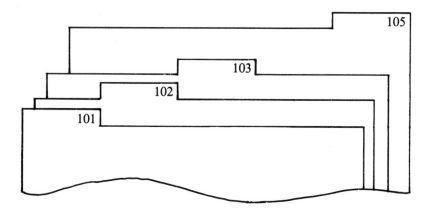

Fig. 4.2. "Fifth cut" file folders.

Numerical systems based on nonconsecutive numbering are terminal digit and middle digit filing.

Terminal digit filing spreads records evenly throughout the file. Numbers are read from right to left in groups of either two or three. For instance, the social security number 487-44-6283 can be filed terminally by dividing the number 487-44-6283, reading from right to left. The groups of digits are called: primary (283), secondary (446) and final or tertiary (487). Numbers are divided by dashes for easier, faster identification. All files ending with the same last two or three numbers come together in the same section.

4-20-54	or	4-20-54	or	487-446-283
4-21-54		11-20-54		487-447-283
4-22-54		16-20-54		487-448-283

The following is a longer example of terminal digit arrangement:

37-46	1-37-46
	2-37-46
	3-37-46
	4-37-46
	5-37-46
	6-37-46
38-46	1-38-46
	2-38-46
	3-38-46
	4-38-46
	5-38-46
	6-38-46
39-46	1-39-46
	2-39-46
	3-39-46
	4-39-46
	5-39-46

Expansion in terminal digit filing would be like:

00	37-46	1-37-46
		2-37-46
		3-37-46
		4-37-46
		5-37-46
10	37-46	10-37-46
		11-37-46
		12-37-46
		13-37-46
		14-37-46
		15-37-46

(List continues on page 94.)

20	37-46	20-37-46
		21-37-46
		22-37-46
		23-37-46
		24-37-46
		25-37-46

The numbers 00, 10, 20, 37-46, 38-46, and 39-46 are guide numbers to the file.

Arrange the following list by terminal digit filing:

391-023-409	391-432-279	381-723-569
385-732-959	361-023-558	361-732-360
361-723-717	391-132-367	385-623-140
385-732-200	391-123-271	385-732-734
391-023-100	361-532-754	385-723-570
385-032-981	361-023-523	391-832-560
381-023-981	361-632-908	361-423-687
381-332-535	385-523-927	361-432-752
361-723-994	361-132-170	381-423-357
391-032-272	381-023-847	381-432-150
361-423-449	385-332-887	361-423-303
391-132-647	385-223-456	381-432-436
385-823-143	391-732-212	391-623-161
361-832-358	381-623-634	391-632-592
381-823-182	381-632-639	391-323-579
385-132-803	361-723-554	381-432-900
385-023-471	391-632-387	

Your answers should be:

100	391-023-100
	385-623-140
	385-823-143
	381-432-150
	391-623-161
	361-132-170
	381-823-182
200	385-732-200
	391-732-212
	391-123-271
	391-032-272
	391-432-279
300	361-423-303
	381-423-357
	361-832-358
	361-732-360
	391-132-367
	391-632-387

400	391-023-409
	381-432-436
	361-423-449
	385-223-456
	385-023-471
500	361-023-523
	381-332-535
	361-723-554
	361-023-558
	391-832-560
	381-723-569
	385-723-570
	391-323-579
	391-632-592
600	381-623-634
	381-632-639
	391-132-647
	361-423-687
700	361-723-717
	385-732-734
	361-432-752
	361-532-754
800	385-132-803
	381-023-847
	385-332-887
900	381-432-900
	361-632-908
	385-523-927
	385-732-959
	381-023-981
	385-032-981
	361-723-994

Once the technician has been trained to file using terminal digits, fewer errors occur than with a system based on consecutive numbering. Because the folder numbers are divided into groups of two or three digits, the files technician is concerned with only two or three numbers at a time. Transpositions and misreading of numbers is less likely to occur. Several file technicians can be looking for consecutively numbered folders at the same time because they need not wait until someone else moves; they are working in separate drawers or file areas. Numeric filing works best in shelf files but it can be done in drawers as well.

One disadvantage of terminal digit filing arises when a large block of consecutively numbered folders must be moved to storage. The files technician must go to each of many locations in the system to pull the folders. One advantage is that shifting is never necessary as with consecutive numbers when folders are pulled.

Arrange the following list by terminal digit filing:

39-10-23	36-11-32
38-57-32	38-10-24
36-17-24	38-53-32
38-57-33	38-52-23
39-10-24	39-17-32
38-50-32	38-16-32
38-10-23	39-16-32
38-13-32	38-17-23
36-17-23	36-17-32
39-10-32	38-56-23
36-14-23	38-14-31
39-11-32	39-18-32
38-58-23	36-14-32
36-18-32	38-14-23
38-18-23	38-14-32
38-51-32	36-14-24
38-50-23	38-14-33
39-14-32	39-16-23
39-11-23	39-16-33
36-15-32	39-13-23
36-10-23	38-57-23
36-16-32	38-16-23

Your answers should be:

36-10-23	39-10-32
38-10-23	36-11-32
39-10-23	39-11-32
39-11-23	38-13-32
39-13-23	36-14-32
36-14-23	38-14-32
38-14-23	39-14-32
38-16-23	36-15-32
39-16-23	36-16-32
36-17-23	38-16-32
38-17-23	39-16-32
38-18-23	36-17-32
38-50-23	39-17-32
38-52-23	36-18-32
38-56-23	39-18-32
38-57-23	38-50-32
38-58-23	38-51-32
38-10-24	38-53-32
39-10-24	38-57-32
36-14-24	38-14-33
36-17-24	39-16-33
38-14-31	38-57-33

The second numerical system based on nonconsecutive numbering is middle digit filing. *Middle digit filing* is a modification of terminal digit filing in that middle numbers are considered for the first sorting. For the number 487-446-283, with middle digit sorting, "446" becomes the primary sorter, "487" the secondary, and "283" the final or tertiary group of digits.

All records with the middle group of digits, "446," are filed in one drawer or section of the file. Sequence within the drawer or section is determined by the digits at the left, and then by the digits to the right. Guide numbers are determined by the secondary digits to the left.

487	487-446-283	or	20	20-10-01
	487-446-284			20-10-02
	487-446-285			20-10-03
	487-446-286			20-10-04
488	488-446-001	or	21	21-10-01
	488-446-002			21-10-02
	488-446-003			21-10-04
	488-446-004			21-10-05
	488-446-005		22	22-10-01
489	489-446-001			22-10-02
	489-446-002			22-10-03
			23	23-10-01

Middle digit filing has the same advantages as terminal digit filing: even distribution of filed material behind each guide and in each section of the file, ease of sorting, elimination of shifting, convenient expansion when required, reduction of misfiles, and speed of operation. In addition, it is easier to move records filed by the middle digit system because a block of 100 consecutive numbers can be moved together. Therefore, if one is going to convert from a straight consecutive filing method to digit, middle digit is the logical choice.

Middle and terminal digit filing are very efficient for large files. Area work stations can be assigned with full assurance of equalized workload, and it is easy for the supervisor to check on the competence, accuracy, and speed of the technicians.

Take the lists for terminal digit filing and arrange by middle digit filing. Your answers for the first list should be:

361-023-523	385-332-887	391-632-387
361-023-558	361-423-303	391-632-592
381-023-847	361-423-449	361-723-554
381-023-981	361-423-687	361-723-717
385-023-471	381-423-357	361-723-994
391-023-100	361-432-752	381-723-569
391-023-409	381-432-150	385-723-570
385-032-981	381-432-436	361-732-360
391-032-272	381-432-900	385-732-200

(List continues on page 98.)

391-123-271	391-432-279	385-732-734
361-132-170	385-523-927	385-732-959
385-132-803	361-532-754	391-732-212
391-132-367	381-623-634	381-823-182
391-132-647	385-623-140	385-823-143
385-223-456	391-623-161	361-832-358
391-323-579	361-632-908	391-832-560
381-332-535	381-632-639	

Your answers for the second list should be:

36-10-23	38-16-32
38-10-23	39-16-23
38-10-24	39-16-32
39-10-23	39-16-33
39-10-24	36-17-23
39-10-32	36-17-24
36-11-32	36-17-32
39-11-23	38-17-23
39-11-32	39-17-32
38-13-32	36-18-32
39-13-23	38-18-23
36-14-23	39-18-32
36-14-24	38-50-23
36-14-32	38-50-32
38-14-23	38-51-32
38-14-31	38-52-23
38-14-32	38-53-32
38-14-33	38-56-23
39-14-32	38-57-23
36-15-32	38-57-32
36-16-32	38-57-33
38-16-23	38-58-23

Chronological filing is also numerical. It is most frequently used for "follow-up" material and is often called a *tickler file*. A set of date guides is needed, showing the months, quarters, or weeks of the year, and then the days, weeks, and/or hours. Information to be followed up on is placed behind the appropriate date guide.

April			
	1		
	2		
	3		
	4	9 a.m.	Dr. Leta Webster
		10 a.m.	Dean Betty Duvall
		11 a.m.	Prof. Harry J. Lutz
	5		
	6		
May			

Create a chronological file for the following information:

> Reconfirm on September 15 Raymond Briggs's appointment with Barbara Vandivort on September 18 at 10 a.m.
>
> Carol Madalon to contact Amy Michelle Lutz on August 3 and set up an appointment for week of September 12 at 2 p.m.
>
> Christopher Schildz to install fixtures Barret Warehouse Inc. on August 28.
>
> Raymond Briggs's appointment with Barbara Vandivort, 10 a.m., September 18.
>
> Joan Cambria to contact Jim Wehner on August 3 and set up appointment for September 12 at 9:30 a.m.
>
> Tom McDonnell to fly to Alabama for meeting with Quigley Enterprises August 30, flight 519.
>
> Call for tickets for Tom McDonnell August 10 for Alabama trip on August 30, flight 519.
>
> Reconfirm Barret Warehouse fixture job for August 28 on August 12.

Your answers should be:

August	3	Cambria, Joan contact Jim Wehner for September 12, 9:30 a.m. appointment
		Madalon, Carol contact Amy Michelle Lutz for September 12, 2 p.m. appointment
	10	Call for tickets for Tom McDonnell to Alabama on August 30, flight 519
	12	Reconfirm Christopher Schildz installing fixtures Barret Warehouse on August 28
	28	Barret Warehouse installation of fixtures by Christopher Schildz
	30	McDonnell, Tom to Alabama — flight 519
Sept.	12	9:30 a.m. Cambria, Joan appointment with Jim Wehner
		2:00 p.m. Madalon, Carol appointment with Amy Michelle Lutz
	15	Briggs, Raymond reconfirm appointment with Barbara Vandivort, September 18, 10 a.m.
	18	10:00 a.m. Briggs, Raymond appointment with Barbara Vandivort

Another form of numerical filing is *alphanumeric filing*. With alphanumeric filing the letters of the alphabet are assigned numbers to keep them in order. Thus, files are asked for by name, but refiled by number.

31-87-0	Bac
31-87-1	Bach
31-87-12	Back
31-87-13	Backa
31-87-14	Backe
31-87-5	Baf
31-87-6	Bah

Often in assigning numbers in such a system, gaps of 100 are left between the sections of the alphabet or names so that new names that fall between the original names can be accommodated. In this way the alphabetic arrangement can be maintained. Sometimes it might be necessary to add a decimal point.

100	Baa
101	Bac
101.1	Back
101.2	Backa
101.3	Backe
102	Bag
200	Beb
300	Bib
400	Bob

A good means of assigning numbers to names would be to assign numbers to the vowels only:

A is 1
E is 2
I is 3
O is 4
U is 5

Consonants which fall after the vowel can be coded with the number of the vowel that precedes them in the alphabet. Thus, "m" is "3" because it appears after "i" but before "o." The system devised by Charles Ammi Cutter employs this method. If you are familiar with this system, you know that each number assigned relies on what has been assigned before. No two numbers are exactly alike. Each is "unique." Sometimes, in order for items to remain in alphabetical order, a very contrived number occurs. Frequently, decimal numbers are used. Two departments within the same company might code the same material differently, depending upon which material was handled first.

Using the code for vowels and assigning the number of the vowel preceding the consonant, assign three-digit numbers, each unique, to the following names. Disregard the initial letter, "M."

Doris Meyer
Albert Maescher
Susan Mansfield
Marilyn Mitchell
John Miller
Keith Mauldin
Rosalie Meert
David Muckerman
John Morrison
Thomas Meyer
Paul Meiners
Diane Molner
Rita Mooney
Rita Moriarty
Louis Monnig

Your answers could be:

Maescher, Albert	124
Mansfield, Susan	134
Mauldin, Keith	153
Meert, Rosalie	224
Meiners, Paul	233
Meyer, Doris	254
Meyer, Thomas	262
Miller, John	333
Mitchell, Marilyn	341
Molner, Diane	433
Monnig, Louis	434
Mooney, Rita	443
Moriarty, Rita	444
Morrison, John	444.5
Muckerman, David	513

Some numerical filing is combined with subjects, and the subjects can be arranged alphabetically. This becomes a classification system just as the Dewey Decimal System is a numerical classification for libraries.

500	Science
510	Mathematics
521	Astronomy
522.1	Observatories
523.2	Solar System

An example of a *numeric-subject-alphabetic classification* is the Million Dollar Round Table Information Retrieval System (MDRT-IR) developed for insurance companies.

2300.00	Educational Insurance
2400.00	Employee Benefits and Executive Compensation
2410.00	Employees Stock Ownership Trusts
2500.00	Estate Planning

Notice the gaps in numbers to allow for new subjects to fall alphabetically when needed.

The MDRT-IR is also decimal in development:

3300.00	Group Insurance
3300.01	Accidental Death and Dismemberment
3300.02	Annuities
3300.04	Blue Cross/Blue Shield

Another method for allowing expansion numerically within an area would be to code with hyphens.

3	Employee Benefits
3-1	Group Insurance
3-1-1	Accidental Death and Dismemberment
3-1-2	Annuities

Develop a logical sequence and a number code using hyphens for the following subjects:

Education
  college
  elementary school
  nursery school
  primary grades
  middle grades
  high school
  junior college
  adult continuing education
  junior high school
  graduate professional school

Your sequence and code could look like this:

1	Education
1-1	nursery school
1-2	elementary school
1-2-1	primary grades
1-2-2	middle grades
1-3	junior high
1-4	high school
1-5	adult continuing education
1-5-1	junior college
1-5-2	college
1-5-3	graduate/professional school

For Further Study

1. Each of your 3x5-inch cards that you established in the Alphabetical Filing section has a nine digit number on it. File the pack first by terminal digit.

2. File the same pack by the middle digit filing method.

3. Precede the zip code numbers on your own packet of cards with zeros, and file your list of names by the last two terminal digits; then refile the pack by the middle two digits.

4. Add to your procedures manual a section in Part II, "Methods of Classification. Section 4. Numerical." Now decide whether your list of names is to be filed by terminal or middle digit filing and write the rules for following that system in your manual.

COLOR-CODED FILING

Color-coded arrangement of files is frequently combined with another system of filing to provide a dual system, or secondary, subsidiary filing to the main system. Color can be used to designate dates for follow-up, weeding, or storage; to designate types of medium; to separate letters of the alphabet or numerical sequences; to identify cross-references or subjects; as a training tool; or to indicate materials that have been checked out. In short, colors can designate whatever the records filer desires, so long as the significance of each color is documented in the procedures manual.

Color is attractive, relieves the monotony of filing and retrieval, decreases misfiling, and aids in learning and retention. The only danger is overdoing it. A few colors or color families work; too many are a disaster. The rainbow spectrum is a good starting—and stopping—point.

There are many commercial color filing systems on the market. This means you buy folders already keyed to certain breakdowns of the letters of the alphabet or numbers, as well as matching guide cards, labels, and "out" cards.

One system for alphabetic color keying might work with five colors, each color keyed to a vowel or to certain consonant letters consistently throughout the folder. For instance, one could have five colors: red for "a," yellow for "e," green for "i," blue for "o," and purple for "r." Thus all files beginning Aa, Ba, Ca, Da, and so on, would be red; all files beginning Ae, Be, Ce, De, and so on would be yellow. "Harold Bacon" would be in a folder color keyed red. "Patricia Adkinson" would also be in a folder color keyed red because "Ad" is before "Ae" which would be the next color change. Folders can still be misfiled, but if they are placed in a different color series, it is readily apparent. This substantially reduces searching for lost materials.

For the following names use the color coding of red for "a," yellow for "e," green for "i," blue for "o," and purple for "r." Arrange the names alphabetically by the initial letter of the surname and by color using the second letter of the surname.

Martha Graham	Donald Gentry	Chris Einig
Billie Gillespie	Peter Gentile	Marianne Kasper
Brian Gill	Ginny Gerwitz	Loretta McCormick
Mary Ann Graf	Andy Gieselman	Carolyn Hendry
Bob Gleason	Bernard Glazer	Dorothy Johnson
John Gorman	Bruce Glazier	Duane Hertel
Katherine Graczak	Terry Gold	J. B. Allison
Judy Gray	Louis Goetz	Mary Claire Lipic
Mary Grubb	Philo Beckmann	A. J. Koller
Judy Geoghegan	Alice Marie Briggs	Donna Krebs
Gene Gaffney	Pat D'Amico	Jennifer Lutz
Richard Gandy	Joan Diehl	Natalie Lutz
		Samuel Adams

Your answers should be:

red	Adams, Samuel	blue	Goetz, Louis
green	Allison, J. B.	blue	Gold, Terry
yellow	Beckmann, Philo	blue	Gorman, John
purple	Briggs, Alice Marie	purple	Graczak, Katherine
red	D'Amico Pat	purple	Graf, Mary Ann
green	Diehl, Joan	purple	Graham, Martha
green	Einig, Chris	purple	Gray, Judy
red	Gaffney, Gene	purple	Grubb, Mary
red	Gandy, Richard	purple	Grubb, Mary
yellow	Gentile, Peter	yellow	Hendry, Carolyn
yellow	Gentry, Donald	yellow	Hertel, Duane
yellow	Geoghegan, Judy	blue	Johnson, Dorothy
yellow	Gerwitz, Ginny	red	Kasper, Marianne
green	Gieselman, Andy	blue	Koller, A. J.
green	Gill, Brian	purple	Krebs, Donna
green	Gillespie, Billie	green	Lipic, Mary Claire
green	Glazer, Bernard	purple	Lutz, Jennifer
green	Glazier, Bruce	purple	Lutz, Natalie
green	Gleason, Bob	red	McCormick, Loretta

Colors can also be assigned to numbers. One color can be used for each digit from 0 to 9. Misfiles are apparent because the visible pattern of color is broken. Different bars of color in a folder break down longer numbers into smaller groups. Notches can be used for dating material for weeding.

Using the following key, we can build some color-arranged files:

0	red		5	gold
1	gray		6	yellow
2	blue		7	brown
3	orange		8	pink
4	purple		9	green

Although every digit could be color-coded, let's use three colors for terminal or middle digit filing.

On a file folder there will be three colors. The middle bar of color represents the first number of the terminal digit. The bottom bar represents the last number of the terminal digit, and the top bar represents the first number of the middle digits. Therefore, for the number 487-446-283 the colors would be blue for 2, the first number of the terminal digit sequence 2-8-3; orange for 3, the last number of the terminal digit sequence 2-8-3; purple for the first number of the middle digit sequence, 4 of the sequence 4-4-6. The color scheme would be arranged purple, blue, orange.

For middle digit filing, the middle color band represents the first number of the sequence of primary filing numbers, the bottom bar the last number of the primary filing sequence, and the top bar the first number of the secondary filing sequence. The color scheme for 487-446-283 would now be purple for the first 4 of the sequence 4-4-6, yellow for the last digit 6 of the sequence 4-4-6, and purple for the first number 4 of the secondary filing scheme of 4-8-7. The color sequence would now be purple, yellow, purple.

Take the following numbers using the same color key (0, red; 1, gray; etc.) and color-code their arrangement by middle digit filing.

361-532-754	385-532-754
361-723-717	361-832-569
381-723-569	381-732-716
385-223-456	361-723-454
361-223-455	381-823-182
391-832-560	385-823-182
385-732-734	391-523-454
391-223-456	

Your answers should be:

orange blue orange	361-223-455	orange brown orange	381-723-569
orange blue orange	385-223-456	orange brown blue	381-732-716
orange blue orange	391-223-456	orange brown blue	385-732-734
orange gold orange	391-523-454	orange pink orange	381-823-182
orange gold blue	361-532-754	orange pink orange	385-823-182
orange brown orange	361-723-454	orange pink blue	361-832-569
orange brown orange	361-723-717	orange pink blue	391-832-560

Color can also be used in other ways to enhance filing systems whether alphabetical, numerical, or alphanumeric. In offices that have several doctors or lawyers, colored file folders provide quick identification as to whom they belong. Having new employees place a color guide after each record filed helps with training, with the guides identifying problems. The card remains with the incorrectly filed items until the error is reviewed with the employee.

Small colored labels, which come in several sizes and shapes, can provide additional information. For example, it is easy to identify an inactive record if a red dot is placed on the folder. Should an inactive record fall into the active files by mistake, it is again recognized, thanks to the red dot.

The latest advance is the use of taupe-colored file folders. They provide a neutral background for bright color-coded labels, making each color stand out. When these folders are placed in taupe-colored open-shelf units, the visual distraction produced by manila folders is eliminated.

Color-coded file holders have also been developed for microfilm and computer formats.

Color-coded files can be used by color-blind people because of the consistency with which a color-blind person sees color and its shades. Commercial color-coded labels are bold and widely separated in the spectrum and thereby easily distinguishable.

Many manufacturers have produced trade-name systems, most of which are based on the alphabet or numbers and colors. These systems have certain devices or characteristics that are intended to speed up filing and retrieving and to provide a deterrent to misfiling. A list of some manufacturers is given in the bibliography.

For Further Study

1. Take your packet of 3x5-inch cards that you established in the Alphabetical Filing section and color-code the cards by placing the appropriate color on the right-hand side of the card in the upper right-hand corner with a felt tip pen. Then arrange alphabetically with the colors. Use the following key:

    Red is for foreign names.

    Yellow is for automobile names.

    Blue is for insurance names.

2. Take the same packet of cards, and with a felt tip pen, on the left-hand side of the card in the upper right-hand corner color-code the numbers by terminal digit; the top bar represents the first number of the middle digits.

0 red	5 gold
1 gray	6 yellow
2 blue	7 brown
3 orange	8 pink
4 purple	9 green

3. Color-code each of your name cards by middle digit, filing by the zip code numbers. Create your key and place it and the rules you are following in your procedures manual under the heading, "Methods of Classification. Section 5. Color-Coded."

SUBJECT FILING

Arranging material by subject is another method of filing. It, too, can be combined with other methods. Thus, there is alphabetical subject filing, numerical subject filing, and color-coded subject filing.

Filing by subject means arranging records according to what they are about. This is the most difficult filing arrangement to develop and administer and therefore can be very costly and time-consuming.

Only someone who has worked for a company for some time, and preferably in several departments, should develop the classification system. Such experience is necessary because it takes a thorough knowledge of an organization—its purposes, history, departments, and use of records—to formulate the filing categories that are needed. Any system developed must have an understandable logic built in, be flexible, and allow for growth.

To develop a subject classification, begin by studying the routine operations of the company or office. Put the work being done into words. Keep a diary for a week or a month of the kinds of activities taking place in the records center. How is material being requested? Obtain a good manual that covers the workings of your type of organization or industry and use it as a base for developing the thesaurus, index, or authority file. These handbooks are available at the library for most fields of employment, whether it be advertising, trucking, engineering, insurance, law, medicine, food, or appliances. Also obtain a dictionary of synonyms.

Then derive "obvious" subject phrases from a stack of documents and write each on a separate sheet of paper. Whenever the same topic has a different subject phrase possibility, add it to the sheet of paper started for that subject. When the same phrase begins to appear repeatedly, make a check mark next to the phrase each time it appears. For example, a sheet of paper could develop looking like this:

> education
> colleges
> continuing education ✔✔✔✔
> universities
> adult education ✔
> correspondence schools
> workshops
> seminars ✔
> convention conferences

Using your industry's handbook, check the index and table of contents to see if the subject phrases you have found are obtainable in the manual. Mark those headings on the other side of your list.

> ✔✔ continuing education
> ✔ seminars ✔✔

Look for additional similar phrase headings in the manual and add them to your list. Check the dictionary of synonyms for any additional words to add. Continue until you have examined all the documents once.

Now you can begin to establish your authority list of words. Select the word(s) under which all documents pertaining to that broad subject will be filed. Create a cross-reference in the authority list from all the other possible word(s) that could be used to retrieve material. For example:

Adult education
    see Continuing education

Education
    see Continuing education

Seminars
    see Continuing education

The downfall of most subject classifications is redundancy. Nearly every-thing can be expressed in more than one way. The object is to have as few subject headings as possible. Yet, all possible access points for the material need to be provided with references to the term(s) being used. The time spent in preparing the master authority file pays off in faster filing and retrieval.

Now all documents need to be examined for sub-subject headings. Every organization develops these headings according to its special needs. They should be as simple as possible yet should provide thorough coverage. For example, one set of sub-subjects could be developed for the formats of materials:

administrative policies
budget
catalog
computer tape
correspondence
interoffice memos
microfiche
requisitions
vouchers

Thus, a subject file could be developed:

Accounting
    Accounting-Computer tapes
    Accounting-Correspondence
    Accounting-Interoffice memos

Advertising
    Advertising-Administrative policies
    Advertising-Budget
    Advertising-Correspondence

Continuing education
    Continuing education-Administrative policies
    Continuing education-Budget
    Continuing education-Catalogs
    Continuing education-Requisitions

One goal is to design the subjects and their sub-categories so that anyone, in theory, can go to the authority index and files and find the exact informa-tion needed. The less technical knowledge a system requires, the quicker the user can become proficient at using it. Remember that the proof of any successful filing system is in the retrieval. Many people have a dread of libraries and files because they quite frankly do not understand the system, and too few librarians and filers are patient enough to help. Complicated filing systems do not impress; they alienate.

The words used in a subject system must be concise, definitive, and uniform. Consistency, as always, is the key. Preparation of materials for the subject files always takes longer than any other method of filing because every paper must be thoroughly and carefully read; scanning will not suffice. But subject files are ideal for administrators, since all aspects of a particular topic are grouped together. For managerial decisions individual pieces of paper become units of a whole picture.

Papers in a subject file are not filed by author. People come and go in a department, but the department remains. Thus, papers would be filed by department (accounting) or position (personnel manager). But because papers often will be asked for by author, a cross-reference from author to filing subject should be included in the authority file or master index.

Combination of Methods

A small subject file can be inserted into an alphabetical author file, but usually it is kept separate, which means you are maintaining two, or maybe more, files. It is possible for an organization to have author, geographical, subject, color-coded, and numerical files all within one department. This requires, again, an excellent cross-referencing index, which should be developed to all the files. Creating and maintaining this index is time-consuming, and thus expensive, but it does pay off in fewer lost items and quicker retrieval, even though the initial filing is slower.

Examples of alphabetical subject files:

Accounting
Advertising
Charity
Competition
Government regulations
Taxes
Unions

Examples of numerical subject files:

5	Population (General)
5.2	Population-U.S.A.
5.21	Urban planning
5.3	Population-Environment
5.31	Population-Natural resources
5.31.1	Man adapting
5.32	Population-Food

(The above example is from the Katherine Dexter McCormick classification for Planned Parenthood.)

1	Equipment
1-1	Equipment-Desks
1-1-1	Equipment-Desks-Rolltop
1-1-2	Equipment-Desks-Flattop
1-1-3	Equipment-Desks-Modular
1-2	Equipment-Chairs

Examples of color-coded subject files:

brown	graphics/art
light green	architecture-general
dark green	architecture-aspects
blue	landscape

(The above color classification is for Hellmuth, Obata & Kassabaum, Architects.)

Take the following list of topics that can be found in an insurance company, devise a subject classification system for them, and develop an index, or authority file, to your system.

mutual funds	boat
nondrinkers	suburbs
home	handicapped
sickness	airline
auto	business
franchise	motorcycle
military	family
health	hospitalization
life	key man
midcity	airplane
juvenile	motor home
taxes	recreational vehicle
tax shelters	youthful driver
collision	senior citizens
cancer	nonsmokers
flood	cancelled drivers
malpractice	sports car
corporate	fire
estate planning	burglary
livestock	commercial
transportation	worker's compensation
accident	pensions
fleet	annuities
crime	liability
inland marine	truck
property	group
casualty	mortgage
endowments	title
marine	whole life insurance

trusts
innercity
high-risk
profit sharing
disability
retirement
individual insurance
gift
associations
business
divorce
travel

Blue Cross/Blue Shield
educational insurance
employee stock ownership trust
government benefits
social security
dental
major medical
international insurance
partnerships
underwriting
wills
term insurance

Your system may differ completely, but below is a general breakdown of the system devised for the insurance industry by the Million Dollar Round Table (John P. Bell, Des Plaines, IL).

100.00 Accident & health insurance (individual)
100.01   Blue Cross/Blue Shield
100.02   Hospital-Surgical
100.03   Disability income
100.04   Major medical
200.00 Accidental death insurance
200.03   Trip insurance
300.00 Accounting
400.00 Advertising/Public relations
500.00 Agency
600.00 Agent as a businessperson
700.00 Annuities
800.00 Articles
900.00 Assignments
1000.00 Associations (civic, professional, religious, educational, etc.)
1100.00 Attribution
1200.00 Beneficiaries
1300.00 Business agreements
1400.00 Business insurance (not employee benefits)
1500.00 Cassettes (audiovisual)
1600.00 Charity
1700.00 Common law/Community property
1800.00 Communications
1900.00 Competition
2000.00 Computers
2100.00 Corporations
2200.00 Divorce
2300.00 Educational insurance
2400.00 Employee benefits & executive compensation
2400.01   Automobiles and airplanes

(List continues on page 112.)

2400.09   Education
2400.24   Vacation homes and yachts
2410.00 Employee stock ownership trusts
2500.00 Estate planning
2600.00 Fact sheet
2700.00 Financed life insurance
2800.00 Form letters
3000.00 Gifts
3200.00 Government benefits
3200.04   Social security
3300.00 Group insurance
3300.01   Accidental death and dismemberment
3300.02   Annuities
3300.04   Blue Cross/Blue Shield
3300.06   Dental
3300.08   Fire and casualty
3300.09   Franchise
3300.10   Hospital
3300.11   Life
3300.111   Ordinary
3300.112   Permanent
3300.113   Term
3300.12   Long term disability income
3300.13   Major medical
3300.18   Travel
3800.00 International insurance
3900.00 Interview techniques
4200.00 Juvenile insurance
4300.00 Key man insurance
4400.00 Life insurance
4600.00 Mass marketing
4600.01   Auto
4600.02   Fire
4600.03   Homeowners
4600.04   Liability
4600.05   Malpractice
4900.00 Mortgage insurance
5300.00 Partnerships
5400.00 Pensions
7400.00 Taxes
7400.01   Excess profit taxes
7400.02   Federal
7400.03   Local taxes
7400.05   State
7500.00 Tax shelters
7500.01   Annuities
7500.03   Cattle-citrus
7500.04   Farming-forestry
7700.00 Term insurance

8000.00 Trusts
8100.00 Underwriting
8500.00 Wills

Notice that the MDRT-IR classification schedule places more emphasis on estate planning than it does on insuring modes of transportation. Individual agents may set up their files with more emphasis on transportation by expanding the "Mass marketing" section, and not use other areas.

Three other logical methods for arranging the categories of material are:

Method 1

1.0   Life insurance
   1.1   Accident
   1.101   participating
   1.102   nonparticipating
   1.2   Annuities
   1.201   participating
   1.202   nonparticipating
   1.3   Endowments
   1.4   Family
   1.5   Group
   1.6   Juvenile
   1.7   Key man
   1.8   Mutual funds
   1.9   Military
   1.10   Nonsmokers
   1.11   Pensions
   1.12   Profit sharing
   1.13   Retirement
   1.14   Travel

2.0   Health insurance
   2.1   Accident
   2.103   individual
   2.104   group
   2.2   Cancer
   2.203   individual
   2.204   group
   2.3   Disability
   2.4   Group
   2.5   Hospitalization
   2.6   Senior citizen
   2.7   Sickness
   2.8   Worker's compensation

3.0   Professional liability
   3.1   Malpractice
           file alphabetically by profession

(Method 1 continues on page 114.)

4.0	Property - Commercial	
5.0	Business	
	5.1	Burglary
	5.2	Casualty
	5.3	Crime
	5.4	Fire
	5.5	Flood
	5.6	Mortgage
	5.7	Title
6.0	Carriers	
	6.1	Airlines
	6.2	Fleet
7.0	Franchise	
8.0	Inland marine	
9.0	Marine	
10.0	Transportation	
11.0	Property - Private	
	11.1	Real property
	11.1005	Home Area
	11.1005.1	high-risk
	11.1005.2	innercity
	11.1005.4	suburbs
	11.1105	Coverage
	11.1105.01	casualty
	11.1105.02	burglary
	11.1105.03	fire
	11.1105.04	flood
	11.1205	Mortgage
	11.1305	Title
	11.2	Tangible property
	11.2006	boat
	11.2007	livestock
12.0	Vehicle	
	12.1	Auto
	12.121	coverage
	12.1211	collision
	12.1212	liability
	12.122	exceptions
	12.1220.1	cancelled drivers
	12.1220.2	handicapped
	12.1220.3	high-risk
	12.1220.4	nonsmokers
	12.1220.5	youthful drivers
	12.2	Motorcycle
	12.3	Motor home

12.4   Recreational vehicle
12.5   Sports car
12.6   Truck

Method 2

I. Corporate
   A. Business
      1. franchise
      2. key man
      3. livestock
      4. malpractice
      5. transportation
   B. Group insurance
      1. accident
      2. casualty
         a. worker's compensation
         b. disability
         c. handicapped
      3. life insurance
   C. Profit sharing
   D. Pensions
   E. Commercial: fleet
      1. airline
      2. truck
      3. marine
      4. inland marine

II. Military

III. Family
   A. Auto
      1. collision
      2. liability
      3. rates vary according to:
         a. juvenile
         b. nondrinkers
         c. nonsmokers
         d. high-risk
            1) cancelled drivers
            2) youthful drivers
   B. Property
      1. home
         a. burglary
         b. fire
         c. flood
         d. mortgage

(Method 2 continues on page 116.)

                    e. title
                    f. by area
                        1) innercity residence
                        2) midcity residence
                        3) suburban residence
                2. recreational vehicles
                    a. airplane
                    b. boat
                    c. motorcycle
                    d. motor home
                    e. sports car
        C. Sickness
            1. cancer
            2. health
            3. hospitalization
        D. Senior citizens
            1. annuities
            2. mutual funds
            3. retirement
            4. estate planning
                a. endowments
                b. trusts

Method 3

    1. Assigned-risk insurance
            1-1   cancelled drivers
            1-2   high-risk
            1-3   senior citizens
            1-4   youthful drivers

    2. Business-Professional insurance
            2-1   airline
            2-2   business
            2-3   commercial
            2-4   corporate
            2-5   franchise
            2-6   key man
            2-7   malpractice
            2-8   profit sharing
            2-9   worker's compensation

    3. Family planning insurance
            3-1   annuities
            3-2   endowments
            3-3   estate planning
            3-4   family
            3-5   juvenile
            3-6   life
            3-7   mutual funds

      3-8   pensions
      3-9   retirement

4. Health and accident insurance
      4-1   accident
      4-2   casualty
      4-3   liability

5. Homeowners insurance
      5-1   burglary
      5-2   crime
      5-3   fire
      5-4   flood
      5-5   home/property
              5-5-1 innercity residents
              5-5-2 midcity residents
              5-5-3 suburban residents
      5-6   mortgage
      5-7   title

6. Livestock insurance

7. Marine insurance
      7-1   boat
      7-2   inland marine
      7-3   marine

8. Medical insurance
      8-1   cancer
      8-2   disability
      8-3   group
      8-4   handicapped
      8-5   hospitalization
      8-6   sickness

9. Military insurance

10. Travel insurance
      10-1   airplane
      10-2   auto
      10-3   boat

11. Vehicle insurance
      11-1   auto
      11-2   collision
      11-3   fleet
      11-4   motorcycle
      11-5   motor home
      11-6   nondrinkers
      11-7   nonsmokers
      11-8   recreational vehicle
      11-9   sports car
      11-10 truck

From these examples it is obvious that three people can work with the same list of subjects and from them make three different logical groupings, or classifications. Thus, three secretaries or three agents working at different times could set up the files for one insurance agency in three different ways. How is an agent going to be able to use the files? And, how is the next secretary going to be an immediate asset? Inconsistent filing results in the loss of valuable selling and training time.

For Further Study

1. Pull all the automobile cards from the file that you established in the Alphabetical Filing section and devise a subject method of filing the cards.

2. Save everything that comes into your office or home for a week, regardless of format, and devise a subject classification for it. Add this classification system and examples to your procedures manual Part II as "Methods of Classification. Section 6. Subject."

5

PART III: PROCESSING
MATERIALS

Filing is one phase of the records management process. Filing is also one step of the *filing* process—not the first but the sixth. The first five steps are: inspecting the document; coding the document for retrieval and weeding; preparing cross-references; preparing the index, file folders, and labels; and sorting.

INSPECTING THE DOCUMENT

The first step of the filing process is to inspect the document to be certain it has been released for filing. Someone may still be using it. There should be initials and a date somewhere on the document, always in the same location, if possible. If the document is not initialed and dated, return it for official release.

If it is material that comes directly to the records center, immediately stamp it with the company's name and the day's date. While you still have the envelope, check the document for source. It is amazing the numbers of papers, pamphlets, and computer printouts whose sources or dates of issue are not identifiable. By saving the envelope you should be able to identify the record if it is not labeled. By stamping the date of receipt onto the document, you will have a guide for weeding purposes.

CODING THE DOCUMENT

Once a record has been released for filing, it is time to identify it for disposal, storage, and weeding, that is, to code it or date it for disposal or removal to storage. Examine it again for retention or immediate disposal. Filing too many unnecessary records makes for poor records management.

If company procedure calls for all files to be moved to storage after a set period, then the material does not have to be coded individually. But if files randomly go to storage, then each document or folder must be marked for storage. The code used may be anything but it must be written into the procedures manual. For instance, the code could be a date, a color code, a symbolic number, or a letter of the alphabet that would indicate when the document should be moved or destroyed.

Each record is now assigned its classification method according to company procedure. This means you must decide whether an alphabetical, numerical, color-coded, geographical, phonetic, subject classification, or a combination of these, is to be used. If the method is alphabetical, the correct rule for alphabetizing must be applied. This is a mental process that takes just moments for an experienced filer, but a less experienced filer may have to refer to the procedures manual.

The record must now be physically coded for filing units. Many filers place circles around, or underline in colored pencil, the name, subject, or number. Refiling time is quicker if the code is always placed in the same area for each document. If the same subjects or numbers are used over and over, it is economical and faster to preprint labels or to have stamps made to code the record. A coded sheet of correspondence might look like figure 5.1.

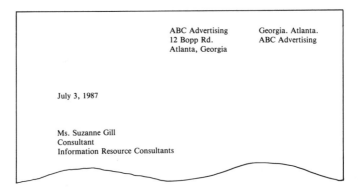

Fig. 5.1. Coded sheet of correspondence.

PREPARING CROSS-REFERENCES

Cross-references should be made now if they are necessary. Do not skimp on cross-references. They pay off in faster retrieval. There are two types of cross-references: one is document, and the other is master index.

With a *document cross-reference* the document, or item, is placed in the file under one method of classification. At the same time the filer must identify other places where the item might logically be sought. This is frequently done by placing an "X" under the filing method's classification code with the other logical places listed. In the other filing places, a full sheet of paper will be found identifying and describing the item, and giving its storage location. For example, a photograph might be coded and cross-referenced as in figures 5.2 and 5.3.

Filing Code	Format	Subject	Description	Date Acquired	Location
163141 x Dred Scott x St. Louis— history	photograph	Old Courthouse	northeast exter- ior view, 1863, lithograph; P. Bugnitz photographer	9/30/41	inactive storage Gallery wing B box 141

Fig. 5.2. Coding and cross-referencing a photograph.

```
                              Basic file number: 16314
                              Date acquired: 9/30/41
                              Subject: St. Louis—History
This material is filed in: 163141  Old Courthouse
    Format:
        correspondence          microfilm
        drawing                 microfiche
      X photograph 8x10-inches  serial
        report                  slide
    Description:
        northeast exterior view, 1863, lithograph
        Patrice Bugnitz (1820-1881) photographer
    Location: inactive storage, Gallery wing B, box 141
```

Fig. 5.3. Cross-reference sheet.

The cross-reference form for the Million Dollar Information Retrieval Index is similar (see figure 5.4, page 122).

As many cross-reference sheets as necessary are placed in the files, all telling where the actual document is filed. If there is only one cross-reference and only one or two pages to the document, the document is frequently photocopied, marked, and filed in the other file areas.

The other type of cross-reference is the *master index file*, which is usually used for:

1.   Names when documents are filed by number. For example:

Original Card
284 McDonough, Patrick (Dr.)
   Dr. Patrick McDonough
     (D.D.S.)
   1017 Haversham
   Des Plaines, Illinois 60016

Cross-reference
McDonough, Patrick (Dr.) 284
Dr. Patrick McDonough
   (D.D.S.)
1017 Haversham
Des Plaines, Illinois 60016

Basic File Number

Date

Cross-Reference Form

☐ Cross-reference to Information Retrieval File Number   ————————————————————

☐ Hard-bound book   ————————————————————

☐ Magazine or bulletin kept in binder   ————————————————————

☐ Audio-visual material   ————————————————————

Subject:

Title:

Author:

Date of publication:

Location:

Information synopsis:

MORT Information Retrieval Index

Fig. 5.4. Sample cross-reference form.

2. Foreign names. For example:

Original Card
Ahadi, Mahmood (Dr.)
Dr. Mahmood Ahadi (Ph.D.)
12134 Olive Street Blvd.
Nashville, Tennessee 37201

Cross-reference
Mahmood Ahadi (Dr.)
12134 Olive Street Blvd.
Nashville, Tennessee 37201
   see
Ahadi, Mahmood (Dr.)

3. Married names for women. For example:

Original Card
Lutz, Pamela Stoll (Mrs.)
Mrs. Pamela Stoll Lutz
6006 Geddes Circle
Denver, Colorado 80112

Cross-reference
Lutz, H. John (Mrs.)
6006 Geddes Circle
Denver, Colorado 80112
   see
Lutz, Pamela Stoll (Mrs.)

If records also exist under her maiden name, "Stoll," a "see" or "see also" cross reference should be made there as well.

Original Card
Lutz, Pamela Stoll (Mrs.)
Mrs. Pamela Stoll Lutz
6006 Geddes Circle
Denver, Colorado 80112
  see also
    Pamela Stoll

Cross-Reference
Stoll, Pamela
Mrs. Pamela Stoll Lutz
6006 Geddes Circle
Denver, Colorado 80112
   see
Lutz, Pamela Stoll

4. Compound company names. For example:

Original Card
143 Tully & Krebs & Brand
Tully & Krebs & Brand
834 Smithfield
Springfield, Virginia 22152

Cross-Reference
Krebs & Tully & Brand 143
834 Smithfield
Springfield, Virginia 22152
   see
143 Tully & Krebs & Brand
Brand & Tully & Krebs 143
834 Smithfield
Springfield, Virginia 22152
   see
143 Tully & Krebs & Brand

5.   Parent companies and divisions. For example:

Original Card   Cross-reference
Gamco Inc.   Galesbury Manufacturing Company
Gamco Inc.   see
6221 Devonshire   Gamco Inc.
Brentwood, California 94513

6.   Abbreviations and initials. For example:

Original Card   Cross-reference
American Telephone & Telegraph   AT & T
                                      see
                                      American Telephone & Telegraph

7.   Changes in name or address. For example:

Original Card   Cross-reference
Schauf, Tom   Schauf, Tom
Mr. Tom Schauf   109 Beaumont Drive
Amoseas   San Jose, California 95129
Barkley Camp   see Schauf, Tom
Avqaiq, Saudi Arabia   Amoseas-Barkley Camp
                                      Avqaiq, Saudi Arabia

8.   Foreign words translated into English. For example:

Original Card   Cross-reference
Sweden   Sverige
                                         see Sweden

Original Card   Cross-reference
Mueller   Müller
                                         see Mueller

9.   See also cross-references. For example:

Original Card   Cross-reference
General Grocers Inc.   General Grocers Inc.
General Grocers Inc.   937 Couch
937 Couch   Des Moines, Iowa 50310
Des Moines, Iowa 50310   see also
                                      Night and Day Foods
                                      Cuyahoga Falls, Ohio 44221
                                      Sav-Well Grocery
                                      Fargo, North Dakota 58102

Original Card   Cross-reference
Braun, Alice   Brown
                                         see also
                                      Braun
                                      Broun
                                      Browne

PREPARING INDEX CARDS, FOLDERS, AND LABELS

The fourth step in the filing process is to type index cards and labels for the folders. There are many ways to prepare these, but the method must be uniform for one company. Uniformity of style in the typing of cards and labels makes the filing and finding of the cards easier. Therefore, whatever style is adopted should be followed consistently.

One method is to begin two typewriter carriage rolls down from the top of the card and/or label and three spaces from the left edge. The name or heading should be typed in index form. For names, type surname first, given name or initial second, and the middle name or initial third. Use a comma to separate the surname from the other filing units in the name. A title that is not an indexing unit but might become one (Dr., Jr.) should be typed in parentheses after the last indexing unit on the top line. Words not needed for indexing purposes may be abbreviated (Co., Inc.)

The filing words at the top can be in all capital letters, all in red, or a combination of upper and lower case; or you might use all capital letters for only the units needed for filing. Whatever method you select, be consistent. A combination of upper and lower case letters are always easier to read than all upper or all lower. Do not strike over or hand correct an error. Spell out abbreviations if they are considered in filing. Type arabic numbers as numbers, but beneath the numerals spell them out as they are filed.

Triple space after the name in index form and give the name as spoken and the address in block form, as on an envelope. Some examples of these principles are shown in figure 5.5.

Buechner, Barbara

Barbara Buechner
4040 S. Indianola
Scottsdale, Arizona 88018

10-14 Delivery Service

ten fourteen
10-14 Delivery Service
3900 North Outer Drive
Ferguson, Missouri 63135

Fig. 5.5. Sample format for cards and labels.

Some companies number their labels even though they retrieve alphabetically. This is easy to do if the file has already been established. Then you can refile by numbers. Folders can be added with additional digits. For example:

McCormick, Colin	22
McCormick, Loretta	22-1
McCormick, Paula	23

Some companies date the label for weeding purposes. For example:

361-149-375   9/88

For inactive records, three-part carbonless forms can be used to make effective labels. The top part can be taped to the end of the box (do not use ordinary tape or it will yellow and fall off). One copy is returned to the originating department for its files and one is kept by the records supervisor.

A bar code is a label that speeds up the process of keeping track of material, increases productivity, improves efficiency, and generally saves money. Bar codes can be produced in-house or purchased commercially. They also come in a two-dimensional version, horizontally and vertically, so that both numbers and the alphabet can be identified.

SORTING

Material should now be sorted according to filing schemes. Commercial sorters that break the alphabet or numbers into smaller sections are available. They also help to hold material in a first breakdown before they are filed.

FILING

We have finally reached the last step of the filing process: placing the information into its proper folder. If filing is nothing more than placing the correct document in the correct folder, why are there so many errors? Because many simple procedures are ignored. Some hints for successful filing follow.

Mend torn papers before they are filed, not with ordinary transparent tape but with "invisible mend" or "Japanese tissue," a special paper.

Attach odd-size papers to standard-size sheets of paper with staples or tape, or fold to standard size.

Never use paper clips to hold papers together; use staples.

Store papers in the folder, not in the space between folders or guides.

Do not allow folders to become thicker than one inch before you make a second folder.

Eliminate unnecessary duplicates of letters or memos.

Label drawers with first and last filing divisions.

Use sufficient guide cards, about 25 per drawer.

Regularly check miscellaneous folders to see if they contain a sufficient number of related documents to warrant setting up separate folders. An arbitrary number—usually four or five items—is selected and recorded in the procedures manual to prescribe when a separate folder should be created. Miscellaneous folders are a peculiarity of business files. Generally one exists for every letter of the alphabet and is used to store isolated documents that do not fall into any existing file category. Information in the miscellaneous folder is filed alphabetically, and the folder is placed either at the front or the end of the letter of the alphabet to which it refers, but always in the same place.

File everything as soon as possible. The longer it goes unfiled, the more apt it is to become lost.

File from the side of the filing cabinet, not the front.

Pull the folder high enough to make certain the information is going into the correct folder.

For your own comfort use rubber fingertips for easier and faster handling of papers.

Use a stool to file in the bottom drawer.

Do not pull open more than one drawer at a time.

MISFILES

Three percent of documents are misfiled. Executives spend more than 150 hours annually looking for information that is misplaced, misfiled, mislabeled, or missing at a cost of $200 to recover each file.

What if you have done everything right in filing a document and you can't find it? Begin a systematic approach. Always look in the same fashion and you'll soon discover the source of continuing problems. For example:

Check the charged-out material.

Check the material to be filed in the sorter.

Check the day's filing to be sorted.

Check through the correct folder thoroughly. The document may be misfiled there.

Check the folder in front of and behind the correct folder.

Check the bottom of the file drawer.

Check for transpositions in names or numbers
(Thomas Anthony, Anthony Thomas; 6273, 6237).

Check folders with initials and names with similar spellings or sound.

Check the cross-reference folders and the miscellaneous folders.

Last (far too often the solution), ask the requester, the boss, and the boss's secretary to check their desks, files, and briefcases. Very often the document was not checked out properly to begin with or had never been released for filing.

If, after this search, the document is really gone, make a note to that effect so you do not waste time searching again. Place a description in a special "lost" file. If an entire folder has been lost, place a duplicate in the file where it would belong, but mark it "lost." The file folder used might be a different color. If a single document has been lost, make a notation in the file on a large, perhaps colored, sheet of paper that such and such a document is lost. Or, try to obtain a duplicate copy. If that is not possible, send a "lost" notification to those requesting the document.

FORMATS

Material that is frequently stored comes in many formats. Some of these formats, and methods for handling them, are:

Correspondence comprises a sizeable number of the documents appearing in any organization's file. The newer pieces of correspondence should be filed in front of earlier pieces. Correspondence of a general nature is frequently kept for two years. McDonnell Douglas Corporation has a 43-page procedures manual dealing just with "controlled correspondence," which is defined as "correspondence, both incoming and outgoing, [which] deals primarily with legal, contractual or obligatory technical and financial matters relating to company business" (MCAIR Policy Statement, p. 1, 8 June 1989).

Memoranda. Memos can be very useful to a company or person and also very sensitive. Handwriting on or anything added to a typed memo creates a second memo. Frequently exchanged by executives among themselves, memos are often considered outside the record center's province, yet by their existence they are a legal entity. In fact they can, thanks to the copier, become a very prolific legal entity. E-mail is another form of a memo.

Forms are papers or hand-held computers that have been designed for entry of information. Part of the paper or screen is preprinted with space available for updating information. One-third of all documents used in businesses are forms. Forms are intended to help a company run more efficiently and officially. They do not always do this, though. Problems arise because of using poorly designed forms; requiring duplication of effort, such as handwriting on the form and then inputting the completed form into the computer, thus doubling the opportunity for errors; storing obsolete forms that are then inadvertently used; not having the necessary forms available when needed; and finally, requiring too much time to fill in the form. With the advent of desktop publishing, many software programs have become available to produce very specific, in-house forms. Some of the programs provide templates, while others allow you to design the form's text and graphics any way you want. Various software programs must be evaluated for specific needs. If many forms are to be used, the software package should be used to create the master only, and have the copies produced by a commercial printer. Using a copying machine is cheaper than the laser printer connected to the computer, but if storage is a problem, or only a few forms are needed, then it is more efficient and cost-effective to produce them as needed from the software directly.

There are also "electronic" programs, which allow the user to see the form (template) and data together on the screen, but file the form and data separately in the computer. This allows the data to be used by other software applications or database systems, such as accounting, without the need to key in the information more than once. Field engineers or shop supervisors increasingly are using hand-held computers to store information on a software form which is later added to a larger mini- or mainframe computer database. Electronic form software is more expensive than form design software. Forms are created in endless variety and for myriad purposes. They can be filed by

department functions
title
number
job performed by form, that is, by subject.

Clippings are usually filed by subject and should always be marked with date and source. It is best not to fold clippings, but rather store them in large envelopes or binders. If valuable, they should be stored in acid-free environments.

Invoices, bills of lading, and *checks* are filed by the number printed on them, or those that refer to the same item are stapled together and filed with the correspondence relating to them.

Blueprints and *reports* are frequently filed by the job number assigned to the project. All items pertaining to that job should be cross-indexed. For example:

893724   Clarence Darrow Dam

This file consists of:
correspondence
bid proposal
specifications
soil samples
original drawings
contracts
interoffice memos
subcontractor's proposals
vendor proposals

(List continues on page 130.)

> preliminary report
> intermediary report
> blueprints
> purchasing records
> cost control and estimate records

Large items such as the original drawings for blueprints, maps, and artwork are filed flat in narrow flat file boxes or drawers of files. Working blueprints can be rolled and kept in cylinder files. Originals for engineering drawings, maps, and artwork, if they are to be kept permanently, should be prepared on linen paper, backed with cloth, or laminated between sheets of plastic.

Paper computer printouts are filed in large binders or bound between pressed board covers.

Computer tape has to be kept away from magnetic fields such as transformers and fluorescent lights. The handler should touch metal to eliminate any static electricity before handling computer tape. Tape can be kept in fibreboard containers but metal cans are more common.

Microfilm and microfiche should be in acid-free containers. These can be plastic, paper, or metal.

The *floppy disks* used with microcomputers and word processors can be filed either in cabinets or in binders.

CD-ROM disks can also be kept either in cabinets, jukeboxes, or special holders.

Serial subscription services can be anything from the daily newspaper, to magazines, to free catalogs, to very expensive updating services. They may be filed together or scattered. A time limit should be placed on storing serial information that is obtainable from a local library. If it can be obtained there, material that is not used frequently and is no longer being actively used does not have to be kept.

Updating subscription/continuation services cover every subject and range from being free to costing several thousand dollars a year for one manual. A subscription service is information that arrives periodically (daily, weekly, monthly, etc.) on one general topic and is added to a manual. As it is added it supersedes older material, which must be pulled. In an engineering office this could be vender catalog material, which covers price, products, and specifications for a company's product line.

It is a very simple procedure to update these manuals. In the updating packet is a cover page telling you to insert page 21 and pull old page 21. For example:

ABC Electronics   Los Angeles, California

   Please file the following parts lists numerically in your ABC Electronics parts lists book. Discard revised sheets bearing an earlier date.

PL-4568   January 1988   Model 130MC single station cascade
                                        controller
PL-4570   January 1988   Model 130MD console control stations

The difficulty for most companies is that this information, which arrives so frequently and in such large numbers, never seems to be on the priority list of daily filing in a small office. As a result, it piles up until it becomes a chore and a filing problem, especially if someone decides to throw a portion of it away. This means there is either a gap in the numerical sequence or in the revising dates.

It is best to file these updates regularly. It is also a good idea to initial and date in pencil what is being interfiled, as a check for errors if several people are doing the interfiling. If there is a numerical or date gap, it will eventually be caught up as newer revised material to be inserted arrives, but until that time it can be very costly in terms of lost information. Never discard unfiled portions of revised or updated pages of a subscription service even if you believe the pile to be filed is so large it has superseded itself. You cannot be positive until the material has been arranged for interfiling.

The Paperwork Reduction Act of 1980 did not lessen the creation of papers. The Paperwork Reduction Act of 1991 probably will not either. This act involves "only" the record-keeping requirements of a business for the federal government and, like the earlier act, is intended to make it easier for businesses to comply with federal regulations by making government forms easier to fill out and nonduplicative. The 1991 Act extends the agencies to which act applies. It is a good idea for all companies to review their own paper-generating and record-keeping processes to instigate their own reduction acts.

FOR FURTHER STUDY

Add to Part III of your procedures manual the following sections under "Processing Materials." Include detailed instructions.

Section 1. A. Location of active storage files.

Section 2. A. Procedures for receiving material into records center, active storage files.

Section 3. A. Instructions for assigning classification and retention codes.

Section 4. A. Procedures for filing into storage files, active storage files.

Section 5. A. Instructions for creating master index file and for making cross-references for all files.

6

PART IV: RETENTION
_____*OF RECORDS*_____

Media horror stories abound of companies that lost court cases because they still had records in their files that were not legally required to be kept — but, because the records existed, they became admissible evidence. Other stories concern retired employees with company files in their attics and memos with embarrassing handwritten wisecracks in the margins.

Valueless records cost equipment, space, staff time, and money. However, fines, penalties, or other legal consequences may be imposed if a company does not keep records long enough or destroy them properly. In the average business, less than 10 percent of records should be kept permanently; 20 percent should be retained in current files only; 35 percent should be transferred to less costly space for longer term retention; and 35 percent should be disposed.

The proliferation of multimedia information formats calls attention to the importance of good record retention. Electronic media have enlarged the scope and need for a written records retention policy. With home computers, modems, networks, copy, and facsimile machines, the possibility of a record duplicating itself to outrageous proportions is not small.

A records retention program should retain records of value and historical interest, protect vital records, destroy records that have outlived their usefulness, and maintain records in a proper, safe, and legal manner.

To establish a systematic records retention program, begin with a records *inventory*, that is, a systematic collection of information on the contents of the file by record series name. Such information will permit a proper evaluation of the records, their function, and their use. It will also tell what records actually exist in a given office, how they are used, and what that office's needs are for usage, storage, and retrieval. This process involves interviews with users, examination of existing filing systems, and compilation of lists of records or record series.

To begin an inventory, forms can be given to each department for completion by its personnel. (See figures 6.1 and 6.2, pages 133 and 134.) This has the advantage of speed and less disruption of normal duties. Also, since each department completes its own inventory, the results should be accurate, because each department should be familiar with its own files.

(Text continues on page 135.)

RECORD SERIES INVENTORY/INTERVIEW WORKSHEET

INVENTORY DATA:	Custodian Name/No.	Division/Department	Building
Record Series Name			

USE AND PURPOSE OF THE RECORD SERIES:

Is Record a package? ___ Yes ___ No If yes, list record types within the package.

Current storage in: ___ File Cabinet ___ Desk ___ Pile ___ Safe ___ Fire-resistant cabinet ___ Shelf ___ Box	Inclusive Dates	Listed on an approved Records Retention Schedule? ___ Yes ___ No

Analyst Name/Date

RETENTION REQUIREMENTS:	Disposition Authority
Retention Instructions:	

Transfer Instructions:

Office of Origin:	Office of Record:

Analyst Name/Date

INTERVIEW DATA:	Are records of this series uniquely identified? ___ Yes ___ No Is there a Controlled Index for this record series? ___ Yes ___ No Does this record series go through revisions? ___ Yes ___ No Is this record series distributed with receipt requirements? ___ Yes ___ No Is this record series on a Controlled Records List? ___ Yes ___ No

Applicable Procedure	Applicable Requirement

Number of copies typically distributed _____
Distributees/retrievers/users of this record series (orgs):

Preferred retrieval format (Prioritize): ___ Index ___ Record Image ___ Searchable Text	Level of retrieval requests (a few? many?) Specify quantities per period: ____ /Day ____ /Week ____ /Month ____ /Year

Ease in finding the right information: ___ Fast/easy ___ Somewhat slow/hard ___ Very tedious

Total number of these records _____
Number created monthly _____
Average number of pages per record _____
Is there a single, sitewide, approved form? ___ Yes ___ No
Would a standardized, electronic form facilitate creation? ___ Yes ___ No

Would status-tracking/workflow control facilitate review and approval/authentication? ___ Yes ___ No
Would view and markup/raster cleanup facilitate review? ___ Yes ___ No

Analyst Name/Date

Fig. 6.1. Record series inventory/interview worksheet. Reprinted by permission of the Association of Records Managers and Administrators, Prairie Village, KS. By Alice Gannon, *Records Management Quarterly*, April 1992.

RECORDS INVENTORY AND ANALYSIS WORKSHEET

INVENTORY DATA:	Location:		Department/Section:	Building/Floor/Room:
Record Series Name:				

DESCRIPTION OF FILES/USE AND PURPOSE:

Physical Form/Media: _____ Hardcopy, _____ Computer Printout, _____ Aperture Card, _____ Roll Film, _____ Microfiche, _____ Other_____.

Volume:	Inclusive Dates:	Present Retention:

Office of Origin:	Office of Record:

Other Offices Receiving Copies:

Analyst Name/Date

RECORD ANALYSIS AND APPRAISAL:	Legal Requirements:	
Preliminary Retention Recommendation:		Final Retention Recommendation:
Office:		Office:
Records Center:		Records Center:
Remote Site:		Remote Site:
Total:		Total:
Analyst Name/Date		

DEPARTMENT INTERVIEW:		
Operational Value:		Expires After:
Audit Requirements:		Expires After:
Potential Legal Value:		Expires After:
Historical/Archival Value:		
Other Comments/Recommendations:		
Interviewee Name/Date:	Interviewee Name/Date:	Tax Name/Date:
Interviewee Name/Date:	Accounting Name/Date:	Audit Name/Date:

Fig. 6.2. Records inventory and analysis worksheet. Reprinted by permission of the Association of Records Managers and Administrators, Prairie Village, KS. By Alice Gannon, *Records Management Quarterly*, April 1992.

Or the records manager can conduct the inventor
continuity and attention to detail. If the records
tory, a departmental person should also be invol
and security requirements. Regardless of met
personnel is essential for success.

Standard inventory procedures should be
sketch of the offices or departments or areas
included. Any indexes or records listing the act
obtained and attached to the inventory forms. Be sure to
words used by the department's personnel as well as the official title or
record type. In the inventory, you are identifying the medium (paper,
computer disk, CD-ROM), the type of record (form, report, correspondence,
etc.), and also the record's function. The function should give a brief summary
of the purpose the record serves. Also, identify whether the record is created
within or outside that department. If outside, it is probably a copy and may
not have to be kept.

After the inventory and identification of each record, decisions must be
made as to the value of each record title. Value may be assigned as "useful,
essential, vital" or "administrative, regulatory, extended."

It is assumed that records are retained because, and only so long as, they
serve a worthwhile purpose. Probably 90 percent of all corporate paperwork
over a year old is rarely, if ever, referred to again. When it is time to pitch it,
file it in the paper shredder for notepads or packing stuffing, or burn it.
Although certain documents have permanent value, the majority have only a
limited period of usefulness. This period of usefulness depends upon legal
requirements and office use. Rather than being shredded or burned, large
numbers of records are moved from active to inactive files. After a designated
period in the inactive files, they are shredded or sent to permanent storage if
they have been so designated. Storage should not mean the need for more and
more space, because most documents should eventually be destroyed.

Only *vital records* should be kept indefinitely. Vital records are those
necessary to reconstruct the organization in the event of a disaster. These
records include the corporate charter, major contracts and deeds, and legal
documents. They may include finances, research, engineering, manufacturing
data, and information vital to stockholders, employees, and customers. Some
records are saved for historical or archival purposes, such as information
dating back to the company's founding and any current records regarding
acquisitions or mergers. The loss of essential documents can cause serious
financial loss or legal difficulties for a business, and might even cause a
company to go out of business.

A functional method may be used to determine which records are vital.
The functional method is based on:

Determining what operating functions are vital for the continuation of
the company

Determining what information must be available to reconstruct and carry
out each vital function

...ing the records that have the information necessary to perform ...n vital function

Creating or having available any record needed to carry out each vital function.

The Oklahoma ARMA chapter lists the following steps for vital record information:

1. The department manager requests a Records Analyst to review the department's records for the purpose of determining which records should be considered vital.

2. A Vital Records Questionnaire is completed by the analyst on each type of record considered vital.

3. The Vital Records Questionnaire is submitted to the Vital Records Administrator for review.

4. The Records Analyst prepares a Vital Records Master List on those records determined to be vital to the company.

5. A Vital Records Coordinator and an Alternate are selected to represent the department by the department manager.

6. Authorization Cards are signed by the department's Vital Records Coordinator and Alternate.

7. The department's Vital Records Master List and Authorization Cards are forwarded by the Vital Records Administator to the Vital Records Correspondent.

8. The Vital Records Administrator furnishes the department's Vital Records Coordinator and Alternate a copy of the approved Vital Records Master List.

A vital record analysis might look like the one in figure 6.3, page 137.

Vital records need special treatment. Duplicates, and often microfilm copies, are made for central records and various other locations, and the originals are frequently kept in another building in fire-resistant cabinets or vaults. There are even commercially operated vital records centers established in old mines and caves throughout the country. It is essential that a complete and up-to-date index be kept on all materials sent to permanent storage. Such a form might look like figure 6.4, page 137.

Regulatory records are the easiest to determine because they are ones a company is legally bound to keep for a set period of time. These regulations are promulgated by federal and state statute and federal and state regulatory agencies. Actually, few laws, either federal or state, mention specific record-keeping requirements. The statutes of limitations found in the laws refer to

vital records classification: accounts receivable 001
vital records documents: 001A general ledger
                  001B form 627: invoices
retention schedule: 001A general ledger 6/18 months
               001B invoices 3/18 months
distribution of copies: records center
                vice-president accounting
                purchasing manager
reason for protection: 001A to reconstruct status of accounts
                receivable
                001B to provide daily protection for changes to
                accounts receivable
protection method/instruction: 001A records management to microfilm
                accounts receivable ledger at six-
                month intervals—January and July
                and forward one copy to vital records
                center, one to vice-president account-
                ing, one to purchasing manager.
                001B general accounting department
                to produce additional copies of form
                627, as issued and every three months
                forward to records center where addi-
                tional copies will be duplicated and
                sent to vital records center, vice-
                president of accounting and purchas-
                ing manager.
filing method: chronologically
retention: 001A film is replaced every six months and destroyed in 18
       months
       001B film is replaced every three months and destroyed in 18
       months
cost: $65.00 annual maintenance

Fig. 6.3. Vital record analysis.

Division							
Department		Department Number			Location		Date
name of record and description	record number	storage status	retention period	storage method	destruction date		initials

Fig. 6.4. Vital records storage form.

litigation rather than record keeping, but they can be used as a guide for creating a retention time schedule. A sample retention time schedule based on statutes of limitation appears in table 6.1.

Table 6.1.

Retention Time Schedule

State	Simple Contract	Written Contracts	Sealed Instruments	Open Accounts	Promissory Notes	Judgment of Record
Alabama	6 years	6 years	10 years	3 years	6 years	20 years
Alaska	6 years	6 years	10 years	6 years	6 years	10 years
Arizona	3 years	6 years	5 years	3 years	6 years	5 years

Most companies are bound by regulations of very diverse state and federal agencies, such as the Justice Department, National Labor Relations Board, Internal Revenue Service, and the Occupational Safety and Health Administration. There are over 900 federal and state regulations requiring retention periods for documents. Donald S. Skupsky's three-volume *Legal Requirements for Business Records* (Denver, Colo.: Information Requirements Clearinghouse) is a basic primer for beginning a search. The *Code of Federal Regulations* (CFR) is published annually; the *Federal Register* provides daily updates. The *Federal Register Guide for Records Retention Requirements* (Washington, D.C.: Superintendent of Documents), last revised in 1977, is another source of helpful information for making record retention judgments. This guide covers all companies and organizations that might come under the domain of a U.S. government department. It tells what must be kept, who must keep it, and for how long, and provides a citation to the law in the Uniform Commercial Code. For example:

> Wool product manufacturers. The requirement is to keep records of the various fibers used in wool products. The records should show not only the fiber content of wool, reprocessed wool and reused wool, but also any other fibers used. Such records should contain sufficient information whereby each of the wool products manufactured can be identified with its respective record of fiber content including the source of the material used therein.
>
> Retention record: Three years. 16 CFR § 300.31 (*Federal Register* part II, 29257 [June 7, 1977]).

Eastwood Publishing Company (Orem, Utah 84058) publishes *National and International Records Retention Standards*, a compilation of retention practices from states, provinces, private businesses, and national and international associations. Also, several suppliers of consumable filing aids will give customers generalized retention schedules that can be adapted by many companies.

Unfortunately, many times, in doing a statute or regulatory agency search, no retention period will be found—as high as 50 percent of the time. If you write a regulatory commission for guidelines, their response becomes law for your company. Or, you can follow the Paperwork Reduction Act of 1980's guidelines, which state that no records other than health, medical, or taxes must be kept longer than three years. The record then falls back into the category of "administrative" records that should be kept for their technical and operating value.

It is imperative that you list the authority for each record retention decision made. That is, list your source and agencies consulted to document your retention schedule. This shows that your system was systematically developed in the ordinary course of business (and not thrown together to protect yourself in a court case). *Extended records* are those which come into operation whenever your company is involved in a lawsuit. That is, the normal following of the procedures manual for retention and destruction is superseded.

Once the retention requirements have been determined, each record or record series on the inventory list must be matched with the specific retention periods to create a new list. This draft of your retention schedule should include: format, report, or the file number or record series name; retention period; government agency requiring the retention, with specific reference number from the agency's rules or a notation indicating that the retention is dictated by administrative or historical needs.

A *retention schedule* must be created and inserted in the procedures manual. Sometimes a committee must be formed to evaluate what constitutes vital, essential, useful, and nonessential records. Each category of records needs its own section with appropriate definitions, examples, and forms. (See figure 6.5.)

Department			Location			Date		
item number	name of record	record number	retention period	usage restriction	storage location	storage method	remarks

Fig. 6.5. Essential record control card.

For instance:

Essential records are those records with a retention length longer than 10 years. Essential records comprise financial statements, ledgers, stockholders' records, insurance policies, fixed asset records, audits, tax reports, etc.

Creating a records retention program is a labor-intensive decision-making process, and each organization must do it locally, but once established the retention schedule is invaluable (see figure 6.6).

description of record	record number	filing code	period of retention	remarks	transfer to inactive storage date	disposed date	supervisor

Fig. 6.6. Useful records retention schedule.

Many professional associations have produced records guides. The following is an excerpt from one produced by the National Society for Professional Engineers:

Permanent Retention

By statute or administrative decision one copy of the following records should be retained permanently:

tax returns, tax bills and statements, depreciation schedules, dividend register, annuity or deferred payment plans

corporate annual reports, capital stock ledger, charters, incorporation records, authority to issue securities, stock transfers

contracts and claims and litigation concerning contractual and tort liability, trademarks and copyrights

general ledger records, accounts payable ledger, note register, balance sheets, bonds, check register, certified financial statements, P & L statements

executive correspondence, directives from officers, systems and procedures records, file copies of forms used

community affairs records, internal publications, employee activities and presentations, health and safety bulletins, injury frequency charts, training manuals

Period Retention

2 year

payroll checks, periodic financial statements, accounting work papers, job descriptions

3 year

> accounts payable invoices, bank deposits and statements, budgets, voucher checks, expense reports, labor cost records, payroll registers, petty cash records, travel expense records
>
> time cards, purchasing contracts, moving expenses, entertainment gifts and gratuities, audit work papers

4 year

> employee withholding, public relations releases

5 year

> accounts receivable invoices and ledgers, cost accounting records, machinery maintenance and repair records, employee security case files

6 year

> dividend checks, office equipment records, employee contracts

7 year

> personnel attendance records, cash receipts records[1]

After a draft retention schedule has been prepared, it must be sent to each department involved for review and revision. Generally, during this review and revision stage, department managers and records managers are negotiating. Department managers have a tendency to want to keep records longer than the records manager's documentation warrants. Then corporate lawyers may or may not want to review the schedule. If the corporate lawyers make changes, those changes take precedence over departmental wishes. If the corporate attorney has a plaintiff's viewpoint, the retention periods will be longer than if the attorney has a defendant's viewpoint.

After the revisions are made, the record list and retention schedule must be published and distributed to all those involved. To ensure compliance, this document should be issued by the authority of the highest management possible, such as the chief operating officer.

Finally, the schedule must be implemented. Records should be systematically transferred and destroyed as provided in the manual's timetable. Included in this section of the procedures manual should be instructions for the method of transferring and the method of receiving at the other end from active to inactive storage and instructions for disposing of records. (See figure 6.7, page 142.) Also included should be the names of the departmental personnel responsible for each phase of transfer (see figure 6.8, page 143).

CONTAINER #	RANGE	SECTION	SHELF	DESCRIPTION OF MATERIAL	DATE & DISPOSITION

Fig. 6.7. Form to record destruction of files. Courtesy of McDonnell Douglas Aircraft Company.

name of record	record number	record classification	department	dates covered

storage location	date moved from location	initial	date received at disposition center

initial	date destroyed	method of destruction	supervisor

Fig. 6.8. Record transfer form.

Sample instructions based on the ones used at McDonnell Douglas to transfer files from active to inactive are:

1. Call the Records Center for a review of records to be stored and to obtain the necessary form (see figure 6.9, page 144) for type and number of boxes.

2. When the requested boxes arrive, there will be a Records Center transmittal card included and a sticker for the outside of the box. Completely fill out the transmittal card, one per box. Place the card inside the front of the box as your first piece of filing. Place one card in each box.

3. Pack the boxes as if they were file drawers. The quality of how well the files are organized will determine the speed with which items can be retrieved. Records are to be packed in the same order in which they are maintained in active files.

4. When the boxes are packed and ready for transport, place the sticker on the outside of the box and call the Records Center for pickup.

5. Make a photocopy of each Record Center Transmittal card to hold temporarily while your shipment is in transit to and being processed into the Records Center.

6. After processing by the Records Center, you will receive an updated Record Master inventory report from the Records Center listing all of the new boxes received for storage. Check this report against your copies of the cards for accuracy; then destroy your copies of the cards.

7. Some general rules of thumb to help you:
    Limit the contents of any box to a single records series. Generally this is a group of records, filed together in a unified arrangement, which results from or relates to the same function or activity. If this is truly impractical, because of very low volume of the same series, then limit the contents of a single box to series having the same retention period.

REQUEST FOR FILES FROM RECORDS CENTER

PAGE _____ OF _____

THE FOLLOWING RECORDS ARE REQUESTED BY:

NAME _____ DEPT NO _____ MAILCODE _____

PHONE _____ FAX NO. _____ EXPECTED RETURN DATE _____

(PLEASE TYPE OR PRINT LEGIBLY)

RECORD NAME	RECORD TYPE	COMPUTER ID NUMBER	DATE		FOR USE OF RECORDS CENTER * BOX NUMBER *
			FROM	TO	

DISTRIBUTION: Original and 2 copies to Records Center
Requester retain last copy

DATE PROCESSED _____

BY _____

METHOD _____

NO 178469

Fig. 6.9. Form to request file from inactive storage. Courtesy of McDonnell Douglas Aircraft Company.

All file folders must face the same direction to facilitate rapid retrieval.

Leave approximately 1½ inches (two finger widths) in the container to facilitate servicing. Where future interfiling is required, adequate space should be left according to the amount of material to be added. Avoid overpacking.

Use only approved Records Center cartons.

Do not mix record media (i.e., microfiche with paper records).

Do not write on cartons except to number boxes (i.e., 1 of 10, 2 of 10). Keep writing to an absolute minimum.

Do not include hanging file folders or three-ring binders. Remove contents of hanging file folders and three-ring binders and place in clearly identified file folders or file pockets. Binders and hanging files damage both the records and the boxes. Reuse the binders and hanging files.

Whenever possible, send a floor plan, map, or diagram indicating where the boxes to be picked up are located, plus the key contact's name and phone and an alternate contact. The better the information provided, the faster and easier the pickup of the boxes.

Another company's procedures might follow this format:

Procedures for Moving Files
from Active to Inactive Files

Plan the new files four weeks in advance of transfer date.

If you are transferring the entire file, leaving only guides in the file drawers, prepare new folders for the new file beforehand. Prepare only those folders that will definitely be needed. Use a new color for folder labels and indicate the year as well as the title.

If the folders and the guides are to be retained in the file, prepare an inexpensive set of folders to hold the material in the transfer drawers or boxes (see figure 6.10). Put titles on these folders identical to those in the current file, with dates, and have them ready in advance of the transfer date.

For most efficient results, have two people work on a drawer—one pulling out the folders and the other packing them in the transfer files. If folders and labels have not been prepared in advance, have a typist do this work during the transfer operation.

Pack the transfer files tightly. Fiberboard corrugated files are nearly as safe from destruction by fire as metal files when packed tightly.

Fig. 6.10. Transfer file boxes.

Label all transfer files on boxes. Clearly indicate contents of file, dates, etc., on labels and affix them to the containers so that they can be read easily. It is imperative that a destruction date be placed on the storage carton when materials are transferred to the storage center. Papers of longer-lasting value will not be placed in storage in the same carton with documents of shorter life span.

Alert the inactive storage center to make certain that ample storage space is available for the old files and that the transfer files of boxes fit the conditions in the storage location. Storage boxes can be piled to the ceiling to conserve space.

Update the master inventory index file. It is essential that a complete and up-to-date index record be kept of all materials sent to a storage center.

Material is transferred from active to inactive files in many ways. One method is periodically to clean out the files and transfer them in bulk to storage. Some companies have an actual schedule for this transfer. Other groups transfer files whenever they run out of file space. To transfer the bulk of the files effectively at one time, you must allocate a block of time to prepare the transfer and to make the transfer. It means that the files are empty, or nearly so, and it also means that there is no ready reference to material that may be only a few weeks or months old.

Another method is to have active and inactive files in the same filing unit. The top two drawers of a four-drawer cabinet are active files; the bottom two drawers are inactive. From inactive, files are moved to storage when the active files are moved below to the inactive drawers. This works as well with open-shelf filing.

Another method could be considered the *perpetual, periodic,* or *maximum-minimum* principle of retention. Records are in active storage for a maximum stated period of time and never for less than a stated minimum time. When the maximum time is reached, files are purged to the minimum time. For example, the policy might be eighteen months maximum, six months minimum. In practice, this means that on December 31, the files contain 18 months of records, the maximum allowed in the retention schedule. On January 1, the files are purged to June 1, six months earlier. Thus, files from June of two years ago through those of June of last year—a year's worth of records—are moved to inactive storage. That leaves six months of records in active storage.

The end of most records is eventually to be destroyed. Some should be destroyed immediately after reading. Time and money are wasted in filing and keeping large amounts of unnecessary material. If the matter is neither sensitive nor on slick paper, it can be placed in a box for general recycling.

Many documents, though, should be shredded. Shredding protects confidentiality. Many computer passwords and sensitive internal communications have been retrieved from trash bins by corporate pirates for the purpose of industrial sabotage. Throwing something away is not good practice for the environment or for corporate security. Burning can destroy paper and fiche, but nearly all communities have ordinances that prohibit incineration unless strict clean-air requirements are met. Incinerator maintenance is also expensive.

Since 1935 many companies have been shredding sensitive material such as correspondence, interim drafts, extra photocopies, personnel documents, payroll data, computer printouts, blueprints, customer lists, business plans, production schedules, engineering notes, bids and quotations, labor negotiations data, minutes of meetings, obsolete forms, marketing plans, patent applications, vendor files and quotes, old applications for employment, resumes, salary information, periodic and year-end state reports, bills of material, paper documents after microfilming, old purchase orders, memos, sales reports, financial statements, contracts, and administrative and accounting records. In addition, computer disks and tapes, audio and video tapes and cassettes, typewriter ribbons, printer cartridges, staples, paper clips, photographs, film, microfilm, and microfiche can all be shredded.

A shredder uses sharp, rotating metal disks, called *cutters*, to shred paper and other materials into strips or small particles. There are laptop shredders that fit in a briefcase and personal desktop shredders that can shred 1 to 50 sheets of letter-size or computer-printout paper at a time. There are conveyer-fed models that can handle thick stacks of computer printouts, audiocassettes, and multiple sheets of microfiche. They can also handle crumpled papers and other wastebasket contents without manual sorting. High-volume, conveyer-fed shredders can handle from 500 pounds of paper per hour to many tons of paper per hour. They can also destroy three-ring binders, microfilm reels, videocassettes, cardboard boxes, beverage cans, and even metal cabinets.

Three common shreds produced are strip-cut, particle-cut, and cross-cut. Strip-cut shredders cut materials into narrow strips, with widths ranging from ⅛ inch to 1 inch. These are relatively low in cost, operation, and maintenance. Particle-cut shredders cut materials into short strips ranging from about 1 x 1½ inches to ½ x 2½ inches. Particle-cut shredders provide greater security and produce less bulk, which allows the shredder bag to hold more material. Cross-cut shredders provide the greatest security. These materials cut materials into very narrow strips, generally about ⅛ x ½ inch, confetti-size. However, most cross-cut shredders are limited in capacity and in their ability to shred nonpaper items such as staples and paper clips.

Shredders can be placed in individual departments, in central places, or be mobile. They can be small or massive. Placing shredders where they will be used immediately reduces unnecessary documents, but one larger central shredder may be cheaper than multiple smaller units. Naturally, higher capacity units handle large volumes better.

Security cabinets can be part of, or separate from, the shredders. Security cabinets hold the paper until it can be batch-fed or steam-fed to the shredder.

Shredders range in price from $149 for a "personal" model to over $30,000. Before purchasing a shredder, consider anticipated volume, size and type of material to be shredded, level of security needed, and number of machines needed. Try to plan for the future. It is less expensive to buy additional capacity up front than it is to replace an inadequate unit in a year's time. Some service companies will also come on-site for a few days to do shredding.

If you are shredding film, look for the Underwriters Laboratory seal for safety, as enough heat is generated during the process to melt the film, which can be disastrous for the cutters.

Check the warranty. Shredders can take a lot of abuse, but make certain you are protected against breakdown. Read the warranty to discover not only the time covered but also whether individual components and labor are handled and whether repair will be made on-site or off-site.

Once material was shredded primarily for space and security. Now the environment is also a major concern, and shredders are being used to recycle as well as destroy. Some companies even make money recycling their trash. Today, employees are separating their paper, fiche, and cassettes and putting them into special bins to give the record cycle an afterlife as recycled material. A corporation of 500 employees can generate anywhere from one to five tons of paper per week. Each office worker generates about ten pounds of waste paper monthly, a half-pound per day. Shredded material can be recirculated in-house as packing material. Or, if hauled away, shredding reduces bulk and thus trash removal costs.

Paper that need not be shredded for security purposes can be separated and sent to a recycler for deinking and reprocessing for resale as plain paper. Current recycling of nonstrategic paper saves more than 200 million trees a year. Recycled paper uses 64 percent less energy and 58 percent less water to produce. Manufacturing recycled paper produces 74 percent less air pollution and 35 percent less water pollution than virgin paper production processes. Right now many companies are voluntarily recycling, but it may soon become mandated nationwide. A few Northeastern states and California already mandate recycling. The American Paper Institute's goal is to recover and reuse 40 percent of all the nation's waste paper. EPA guidelines currently state that printing and writing grades of paper must contain 50 percent recycled waste paper.

Like any records program, recycling needs planning, corporate support, training, and commitment.

Steps for recycling should begin with the directive from top management, guidelines on what can be recycled, names of recycling vendors selected for paper and nonpaper, responsible departmental personnel whose task it is to train and implement the procedures, equipment used to hold material until recycled, location of equipment, schedule for recycling, and steps for monitoring compliance. It is easiest to begin with separating paper from nonpaper. Because the definition of *paper* differs from recycler to recycler, beginning with white, nonglossy office paper is quickest and simplest. Some vendors accept "mixed" paper, such as colored, glossy, and envelopes; some do not. The records manager is the logical coordinator for the recycling effort. Designated containers must be convenient if they are to be used.

Naturally, any destruction and recycling procedures should be included in your procedures manual, as in the following example.

Procedures for Destroying
Nonessential Records

Records to be destroyed are to be sent to Baker Street Warehouse via company vehicles.

Records to be destroyed must have on the record transfer form the appropriate dated signature of supervisor designating destruction.

The date of disposal, method of disposal, and supervisor of disposal are added to the record transfer form, which now becomes a certificate of record disposal kept by the central records administrator.

Records are disposed of by being shredded into lengths and widths no longer than 5 x ½ inch. The shredded paper is to be used as packing material in boxes.

The destruction of nonessential records is to be supervised by the records control center assistant administrator.

Storage locations for active, inactive, and permanent storage should be specified for vital, essential, useful, and nonessential records (see figure 6.11).

Division		Department		Date		
name of record	file method	retention schedule	location	transferred	disposed

Fig. 6.11. Active storage location of useful records.

The type of equipment, including brand names and specifications required for each piece of equipment, should also be included in the manual. For example:

Equipment and Supplies Used
in Inactive Storage

File boxes are drawer style, with outside dimensions of 9 x 5 x 24 inches, made of corrugated fiberboard with interlocking self-stacking framework (see figure 6.12). File boxes must be able to withstand 275 pounds per square inch without steel supports.

Fig. 6.12. Open storage inactive records. Photo courtesy of Penco Products, Oaks, PA.

Drawer fronts are reinforced with steel and have handles and card holders.

Labels are white, 4 x 6 inches, and marked with box number, inclusive dates, destruction date, contents, and department from which sent.

Acceptable brand names for boxes are ABC Supplies and XYZ Manufacturers.

Label forms are printed in-house.

Boxes are stacked ten high, six rows wide back-to-back, with three feet of aisles between boxes.

Destruction of organizational records (DOOR) liability insurance is available. This insurance protects an organization, individual records management personnel, officers, directors, and partners from liabilities arising from the inability to produce documents required under a legal proceeding because the document(s) were voluntarily destroyed under a systematic records management program, or were inadvertently or accidentally destroyed.

Because record retention regulations change, the records retention schedule section of the procedures manual has to be evaluated and revised periodically.

DISASTER PLANNING

It is not possible to plan for record destruction without also planning for catastrophic disasters and recovery. Forty-three percent of the companies without a disaster plan who lose their information through some catastrophic event go out of business.

A very few companies have to worry about terrorists, but every company has to concern itself with fire, tornados, hurricanes, floods, earthquakes, and even temporary power failures. The Chicago Loop flood shut down some area businesses for weeks. Every six minutes a fire strikes an American business. A fire test conducted by Factory Engineering and Research showed that in less than seven minutes after a fire ignited in a wastebasket containing typical office trash, flashover occurred and near-ceiling gas reached a peak of 1,600 degrees Fahrenheit. About 90 seconds later flames filled the entire room and consumed all the combustible furnishings.

The First National Bank of Minneapolis, which burnt to the ground overnight, was back in business the following morning because it had a program to protect and recover its vital records.

Since 1983, the federal government has said that all financial institutions must have a detailed recovery plan to protect or restore crucial computer data. Meridian Bank in Philadelphia is grateful that it not only had a contingency disaster plan but had also practiced it. Two years before an actual fire, a simulated fire put the program through its paces, pointing out weak points. When the real crisis occurred, everyone knew what to do and business was restored within 48 hours, with minimum disruption to customers.

A videotape should be made yearly of your office layout, furniture, and equipment. A "call-chain" should be kept in each employee's personal possession.

A plan for disaster recovery that includes all your records should appear in your procedures manual. These records are part of your company's assets. The development of a feasible plan can take some time and require the input of many persons. With business ever more dependent upon computers, the risk of disaster escalates as technology, particularly telecommunications, becomes more complex.

On the most rudimentary level, some very small companies make a back-up tape or disks of all the day's work, and one person is responsible for taking it home each evening for safety. A frequent choice of small companies for disaster planning has been to make reciprocal agreements with nearby companies, or with the corporation headquarters or a similar division, to use their computers in the event of a disaster or the need to reconstruct records. These agreements are simple but require continuous compatibility of equipment. Large companies sometimes opt to build internal recovery centers, but that solution requires tremendous capital outlay.

Another option is to use a site vendor service. Such a service provides ready-to-go, off-site back-up facilities for running essential data-processing applications for a limited period of time. Some are referred to as *hot sites* and are fully operational mainframe computer rooms with the latest telecommunication systems. These are valuable alternatives for companies that conduct most of their business on line, such as banks and airlines. *Cold sites* are shells, rooms with raised floors, air and humidity control, and other features necessary for mainframe operations, but lacking the computer itself. Clients are responsible for obtaining and transporting equipment to the site.

A last option is the use of a disaster recovery service. Such a service will provide for the resuscitation of all aspects of a business, not just the data-processing portion.

Primary steps in developing a disaster plan include assessing the risk; determining the time frame essential for recovery of critical functions and records; defining specific roles for staff to follow; establishing company-wide procedures for maintaining and continually updating the outlined system, including detailed step-by-step procedures and checklists; and testing the plan on a full scale. Again, liability insurance should be considered, not only for the directors of the company but also for data-processing and records managers and key employees, for any financial liability incurred for a breach of the *duty of care*, the "prudent person rule."

A good guide for planning this part of your procedures manual is *Planning Manual for Disaster Control in Scottish Libraries and Record Offices.* An illustrative outline is:

A.   Response phase
      Personnel team by title and disaster duties
      Steps to mobilize team
      Location of necessary supplies

B.   Steps to secure/stabilize the area
      Control the emergency, assess damage, and prioritize actions
      Take pictures

C.   Remove damaged materials and prepare for restoration.

Many governmental agencies also put out planning manuals. Peter Waters's *Procedures for Salvage of Water Damaged Library Materials* (2d ed., Washington, D.C.: Library of Congress, 1979) covers print materials. *An Ounce of Prevention: A Handbook on Disaster Contingency Planning for Archives, Libraries and Record Centres* by John P. Barton and Johanna G. Welheiser, eds. (Toronto: Toronto Area Archives, Libraries and Record Centers, 1985) covers nonprint materials and can be used for input for your procedures manual.

Generally, restoration may be limited to materials with the highest priority, as the cost of vacuum freeze-drying is very high and renders paper more fragile than it was before. Items not consumed in a fire are often both singed and water-damaged. Small quantities of paper can be air-dried by hanging them so that air can circulate around the material, or the paper can be laid on absorptive materials to soak up moisture. Items to be sent for vacuum freeze-drying must be wrapped in freezer or waxed paper and packed single-layered in plastic crates, spine side down. Wrap the crate in plastic and ship or haul to freezer storage or freeze-dry plant within 48 to 72 hours of the disaster. Photographs may be air-dried, although they may lose their gloss. Negatives, microforms, and film, should be kept moist, packed in locking plastic bags, and shipped to a professional processor for treatment. Data-processing material should be retrievable through its off-site backup.

The Association of Contingency Planners offers seminars and courses in conjunction with the Disaster Recovery Institute (5647 Telegraph Rd., St. Louis, MO 63129). These courses can lead to certification, and more information can be obtained by contacting the ACP.

FOR FURTHER STUDY

1. From the information you saved for your subject file, devise a retention schedule and procedures for transferring material from active to inactive, to storage, to disposal for your procedures manual.

2. Add the following sections to your procedures manual. Part III, "Processing Materials."

   Section 1. B. Location of inactive files.

   Section 2. B. Instructions for receiving material in permanent storage and for disposal.

   Section 4. B. Regulations and procedures regarding transfer of material from active files to inactive files, to permanent storage, and to disposal.

   Section 5. B. Instructions for creating a master storage index file. Create your own forms for the file if you do not have access to appropriate preprinted forms. These forms will give a history of the documents as they move from active to inactive, to disposal, or to permanent storage. Include persons, by job title, responsible for the necessary steps.

3. Add to your procedures manual, Part IV, "Retention of Records," the following:

    Section 1. Definition with examples of vital, essential, useful, and nonessential records.

    Section 2. Retention schedule for vital, essential, useful, and nonessential records.

4. Add to your procedures manual, Part IV, Section 3, "Disaster Recovery Process," the following:

    Section A. Paper Recovery

    Section B. Electronic Media Recovery

As you prepare this section, assume that a department, not the entire facility, is affected. Think of specific equipment and files that would be destroyed. Prepare for evacuation procedures as well as an after-hours disaster.

NOTES

[1]*Private Practice News* (Winter 1985): 5.

7

PART V: CIRCULATION _____*PROCEDURES* _____

A library becomes a warehouse if it is not used. A records center becomes a graveyard for papers if it is not used. It is in the retrieval of material with speed and accuracy that a records center achieves its function.

Just as a library has to control materials checked in and out, a records center must develop procedures for effective circulation of material.

The most important rule is to establish a written, uniform, strictly-adhered-to circulation or charge-out procedure. Rank cannot have privileges. Exceptions should not be made, no matter who requests the material or for how long. If it leaves the file, it has to follow charge-out procedures. There should be a central control station. An "honor system," in practice, does not work.

Many records centers, and special libraries, never see the requester of materials. Everything is handled by interoffice mail, telephone, or even computer. The requester fills out a form with his or her name, department, date of request, and identification of items. Just as in libraries, where people ask for books by the wrong author, title, or call number, records are requested with wrong or incomplete information. A manual charge-out form might look like this:

title of document
document number
borrower
date requested
date sent
date due
    copied
    routed

Or, a bar code containing this information is used on the folder and on the borrower's company identification badge. A light pen passes over the code on both the folder and the badge to register the charge/discharge.

As automation becomes the norm in records management, so does use of bar codes for tracking material. As with any step of automation, though, the results are only as good as the input. A bar code is a link between the world of things and the world of electronic information. The ability to locate any item depends on the capability of the system as a system. This means that a bar code will not retrieve anything that has not first been put into the system. Every item to be retrieved must be on the database and the relevant fields indexed. Then the transactions must be captured and the database updated. It is the database system that allows you to locate an item, not the magic wand. The bar code is an item's unique identification. This unique identification does not have to mean anything to a person, but it represents a specific individual folder or item to the computer. Bar coding allows the user to find a specific place in the database without knowing where. When the item's label is scanned, the computer recognizes the bar code and links it to the correct record in the database. Putting a bar code on an item without creating the system for it is thus useless. The bar code scanner will "read" it, but will tell you nothing other than a set of numbers.

One of the advantages of using bar codes is eliminating rekeying. It does not eliminate that first keying. If that first keying is accurate, bar-code scanning ensures that every subsequent "read" will also be perfect, eliminating future typing errors. Periodically, you will need to replace the bar code labels, as the contrast between the lines fades when items are frequently scanned.

Most of the commercial bar code systems used for circulation will:

Check out/check in, using a keystroke or light wand

Give item status immediately

Provide for reserves

Provide statistics on use

Print out reports and overdues

Provide an audit track giving a complete history of all transactions

Create new bar codes

Work on a network

Allow password access for security.

If you are purchasing in modules, that is, a section of a system at a time, plan ahead. Look for compatibility. Because a circulation system does not need as much information as a cataloging/indexing system, many places begin with circulation, but adding the indexing later generally means a lot of additional keying. Purchasing the cataloging/indexing system first generally means a simpler set-up if circulation is added later. If computerized information is in an ASCII format, conversion from one vendor system to another can usually be done, but should be done on a bid basis rather than in house. If you stay within a vendor's "family," all components should build onto each other. If not, if you are making long-range plans, it is better to look for a system that can grow with you. Figure 7.1 shows a circulation workstation.

Fig. 7.1. Circulation workstation. Photo courtesy of White Office Systems, Kenilworth, NJ.

When the proper material is found, either of two things typically can happen:

1. An out guide is placed in the file in the place of the removed document. An *out guide* is a pressboard or other stiff material with the word "out" on the top tab. On the guide there are lines for a duplicate of the information on the requisition slip, plus the approximate due

date. Some out guides have a pocket on the front in which one copy of the requisition slip is placed after the file technician adds the approximate due date.

2. An *out folder* similar to an out guide is placed in the file when an entire folder has been removed. This folder provides a place for filing new materials that arrive while the regular folder is out of the files. The front of the folder has a place for recording or holding the charge-out information.

    The charged-out material might be transferred into a carrier folder or special interoffice mail folder. Another copy of the requester slip is kept in a circulation file. This means there are two records of the charge-out: one in the file and another in a charge-out box. The record in the charge-out box is filed either by date due, person to whom the material is charged, date checked out, or, depending on how the files are set up, alphabetically, numerically, geographically, etc.

Overdues occur in record centers too, but special libraries and record centers are not as concerned with the due dates as are public and school libraries. People using the material have a right to keep it as long as necessary. They may be asked to relinquish it temporarily to someone who needs it for a short period of time, but, just as borrowers place library books on their own bookshelves and forget about them, people tend to forget to return record material they no longer need. Thus, follow-up procedures must be carried out. A length of time for which materials may be borrowed should be stated in your procedures manual even though it may be very generous. This establishes a policy that can be enforced with follow-up reminders. When papers have been out beyond the period allowed, the technician should check with the borrower and either extend the loan period or secure the return of the material. This problem has to be handled tactfully, yet firmly, just as in any public relations situation.

When material is returned, the charge-out slip in the file box must be so marked (or destroyed), and the date returned should be noted on the out guide or out folder next to the date charged out (or the charge-out line may be scratched through), or, if using a bar code, scanned again.

If an item is lost, as happens in even the best of filing systems, the same procedures that were followed for nonretrieved items should be followed to retrieve the item. Whatever can be recalled about the item should be listed on a different color paper and filed in place of the lost document. This will prevent repeated searching for something that has already been thoroughly searched for and declared lost.

Some companies no longer permit the removal of any material from the central filing department. Instead, when a request for material is received, a photocopy of it is made and sent to the person needing it. Sometimes, if it is possible, a notation is made in the central file of the date and the person requesting the material. This information might be useful to subsequent requesters and would give a good indication of file activity for storage and weeding purposes.

In the circulation section of the procedures manual the *right to know* policy must also be spelled out, that is, who has and who does not have access to what information. Confidentiality versus freedom of information is becoming more complicated. Within a company some departments are not allowed access to other departmental files; in a wholly owned private company, this might be successful. If a government contract is involved, it might not be. In fact, if the government is part of the contract, then some of the files may be considered public domain and available to anyone requesting information.

The Privacy Act was passed in 1974 to protect individuals and corporations from certain intrusions. The advent of computer data files makes 100 percent privacy suspect.

Another consideration is professional ethics for all file workers. All information learned from working with files, even seemingly inconsequential, should be kept confidential. This requirement should be specified in the procedures manual.

FOR FURTHER STUDY

Add to your procedures manual, Part V, "Circulation Procedures." Prepare steps for both a manual and an automated system. Include a sample charge-out form.

CHAPTER

8

PART VI: EQUIPMENT
AND SUPPLIES

It is essential that record technicians not only understand the principles and systems of filing but also know the types of equipment and supplies available. *Thomas Register of American Manufacturers* (New York: Thomas Publishing Co.) is an excellent source of names of manufacturers to write for current catalogs. The yellow pages of the telephone book is a source for local dealers. Types, sizes, special features, quality, and price vary greatly. In order to choose and use these products wisely, you must know the purposes of the equipment and supplies and understand your own needs. It is important to choose only those items that will be closely related to the functions they will have to serve in your office. A general rule is to use high-quality equipment and supplies for active files and less-expensive materials for inactive files.

In ordering a *file cabinet* you will be able to choose from:

two-drawer, desk-height

three-drawer (forty inches high), which can be used effectively as a working counter

four-drawer, the most widely used

five-drawer, the most efficient for time and space saving

six-drawer

With six-drawer files the drawer height has been reduced, which creates problems with larger-size papers (i.e., larger than standard size). Also, many people have to stand on a stool in order to file into the top drawer.

Drawer files are not very space-efficient. They stick out the furthest from the wall and require the most aisle space. Only one person at a time can access documents and, because you must open and close each drawer separately to reach the files, filing time is slowed. But they are the most inexpensive cabinets.

Lateral file cabinets come in two-, three-, four-, and five-drawer heights. The drawer shelves roll out laterally and can be pulled clear of the file cabinet itself so that 100 percent accessibility and visibility are possible. Lateral filing is more efficient, because drawers do not have to be pulled out or pushed in, and up to 40 percent of floor space can be saved. Lateral files also contain more actual filing space than vertical. One average vertical cabinet drawer has 25 inches of filing space inside. One lateral cabinet drawer can contain from 28 to 40 inches of filing space.

Mobile files. Space saving is the greatest advantage of a mobile file storage system. With stationary or static storage systems, a designated space must be left before the next static unit is installed. The space creates aisles in order to access the shelving. The concept of mobile or high-density storage is to put those shelves on movable carriages and compact them. The system can be accessed by moving one or more of the carriages to open up an aisle when needed. This improves the storage area by more than 50 percent.

Mobile storage units are mounted on tracks. The storage units, or carriages, move laterally on a track by manual or mechanical means. The carriages in a small system, where one moves one carriage at a time, are manually operated. Electrical systems are used for larger units. These systems have motors mounted within the carriage or mounted vertically on the end panel. The user pushes buttons on a control box to move the carriage. Since you are creating high, dense storage in a smaller area with mobile storage units, there can be floor load considerations.

Mechanized files are labor-saving, motorized devices with many racks or drawers for cards or documents. These are considered high-density files, but, of course, are more expensive. (See figure 8.1.)

All of these files are manufactured to accommodate standard-size letters, cards, or legal-size documents. Locks are available, as are thick, fireproof cabinet walls for documents that need protection from fire damage. The cabinets come with or without rods in the bottoms of the drawers to secure guides. Followers in the drawers move back and forth to the desired position to allow the folders to be held upright even when the drawer is not full. Other cabinets

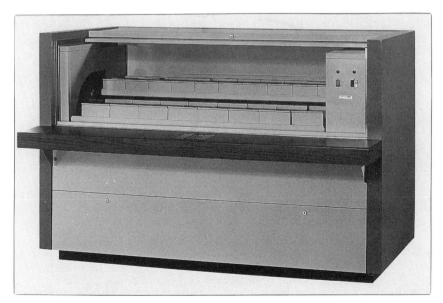

Fig. 8.1. Mechanized file.

have wobble blocks or tilted metal plates that divide the contents of a drawer into small sections and prevent folders from slumping.

Besides cabinets for holding documents, *open-shelf files* are also available (see figure 8.2). Open-shelf files are the same ones used in libraries to hold books. Documents are stored on open, horizontal shelves rather than in closed drawers. Folders are placed vertically on the shelves and are arranged in rows with tabs that face outward for easy reading. Special file supports are used and spaced along the shelves to support the folders and prevent slumping. Open-shelf files are great space savers, saving as much as 50 percent of floor space. Many open-shelf units are available with doors that are easily stored above each row of records when not in use. They can be pulled out and down not only to provide security for confidential materials, but also to protect records from dust or water damage in the event a sprinkler system goes off. The doors can also be locked for security. There are even *motorized open-shelf files* (see figure 8.3). Open-shelf filing is compatible with the numerical system of filing. Alphabetical filing does not work as easily.

Storage files (see figure 8.4) are used for outdated, inactive records. Usually they are placed in a less expensive area such as the basement or a warehouse. They are made of fiberboard or cardboard with steel reinforcement. They are purchased flat and when needed folded along pregrooved lines. They are also constructed so they can be stacked, sometimes from floor to ceiling, in the storage area.

Fig. 8.2. Open-shelf files.

Fig. 8.3. Motorized open-shelf file. Photo courtesy of Kardex Systems, Inc. Marietta, Ohio 45750.

Fig. 8.4. Storage files.

They are labeled as to contents and numbered, and the number is put on the inactive file card (see figure 8.5). For example:

Label

Box no.: 31   Contents: sales correspondence
From: 9-30-85   Sent from: sales department
Through: 9-29-87
Destroy: 9-30-91

Record title: Accounts receivable					Department: Accounting			
year	file range	location	activity	destroy date	initial	other copies	years	format
1979	91	Baker Street	inactive	1989	sg	central records	1960-current	micro-fiche

Fig. 8.5. Inactive file card.

In ordering supplies the technician will have to make many choices from the variety of folders, forms, guides, index cards, and index cabinets available.

File folders are available at a variety of quality levels and in many types of construction. Folders should be carefully chosen to be compatible with filing needs. If documents are not actively handled, a less-expensive, lower-quality folder will handle the work load. Records receiving heavy use would naturally be housed in more durable and consequently more expensive folders.

Folders come in different thicknesses. Thicker folders would be used for extremely busy files. The most common materials for folders are manila, kraft, plastic, and pressboard. Manila is a lightweight, off-white, partially bleached stock. Kraft is an unbleached paper stock that is a dark tan color. It is more durable than manila because it has not been through the bleaching process, which not only lightens the color but also weakens the fibers. The lighter color of manila gives better legibility, but the darker color of kraft is less susceptible to soiling. Plastic is synthetically produced. Plastic file folders rarely show dirt or tear. They are moisture resistant. Pressboard is a hard paper stock built for heavy duty.

Folders have *tabs* or cuts to be used for identification purposes. Staggering the tabs across the tops of the folders make them easier to read (see figure 8.6, page 165). Folders used in shelf filing have the tabs on the sides. The different cuts and their locations help the technician set up the files so the contents of the shelves or lateral file drawers can be easily and readily determined at a glance.

Suspended folders, which hang by hooks from a special metal frame inserted at the top of the file drawer, are available (see figure 8.7). Because the folder hangs from the top and does not rest on the bottom, sagging is reduced. Tabs for suspended folders are plastic frames that can be attached at any one of several positions across the top of the folder.

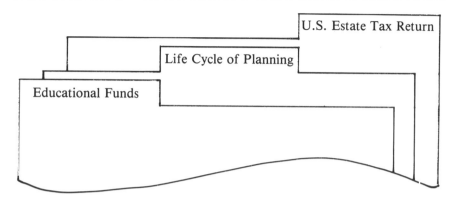

Fig. 8.6. Tabs on folders.

Fig. 8.7. Suspended folders.

Jackets are folders that are closed on both sides as well as the bottom. They look like very large envelopes with out flaps or pockets. The back is higher than the front to allow for easy location. They have side pleats or gussets for expansion. The pleats may be made of the same material as the jacket or be stronger.

Partition or *classification* folders have partitions to divide material and fasteners to keep the material together. They are frequently used by insurance agents and personnel departments, with the newest material filed on top.

Expansion wallets are file holders with protective flaps that close with either an elastic cord, tie string, or Velcro™. Some expansion wallets have inner tabbed dividers to form separate compartments.

Hanging file folders are designed to hang from metal frames. They often hold another folder in their interior.

Labels for folders and guide cards are available in a variety of sizes and colors. They come in rolls, pads, boxes, sheets, or fan-fold arrangement. Some labels must be moistened before they are attached. Others have adhesive backs; their protective backing sheet is pulled off and they are applied directly. Correct any typing errors before these tabs are applied, for once they are applied they cannot be pulled off without ruining the folder. Labels should be printed or typed, not written by hand. One person's legible handwriting is another's scrawl.

Guides are signposts among the folders to guide the technician to the right folder. One of the fundamentals of fast filing is to substitute eye work for hand work. The time saved by spotting the proper guide with the eye before a hand goes into the file can be tremendous. Folder-by-folder fingering is slow, tedious, and time-consuming. Because the guides help support the folders in a drawer and are fingered considerably, they must be strong and rigid. Pressboard or vinyl guides are generally used for very active to average files. Less-active files can be equipped with manila guides. If the file cabinets are equipped with a small rod in the bottom of the drawer, special guides that fit the rod must be purchased.

Along the top of the guide is a raised section called a tab, which, like file folder tabs, can be in various locations. The cuts are available in full-cut, half-cut, third-cut, and fifth-cut. Because the cuts can be staggered across the tops of the guides, it is easier to read the identification on the tabs.

Guides with metal reinforced tabs are available for very active permanent records. Labels can be inserted into these tabs so the guides can be reused. Less-rugged guides with plastic-coated tabs can be used for less-active records. Guides with preprinted or plain tabs and no special reinforcement on the tabs can also be purchased.

Sorters are used to break down the filing before it is interfiled into smaller groups. The sorter is tabbed with the same breakdown as the files and is purchased premarked, but the breakdown can be changed or added to by typing new labels on it. A sorter is an indispensable aid in arranging papers or cards in alphabetical or numerical order.

Out guides are usually a heavy pressboard or cardboard sheet with the word, "out," on the tab. Space is provided on the guide for writing information about the document or folder, such as who has the document or folder, when the material was taken and will be returned, and any other related data.

Once the material has been returned, the recorded information about the charge-out is lined through, and the guide can be used again with the new information below the old. Guides are also available with pockets for charge-out cards on which the information is recorded. Out guides for shelves would have the tab on the side of the guide.

Commercial *cross-reference forms* are available. The document is filed under the most popular name or subject and a cross-reference sheet is prepared and filed under the other name(s) or subject(s). The cross-reference sheets should have spaces available for the second name or subject, the primary name or subject under which the document is filed, and any other pertinent information needed.

Many records are better stored on cards than on sheets of paper. Cards will also be needed for the central index. Card stock comes in many sizes and colors. The most common sizes are 2x4, 3x5, 4x6, and 5x8 inches. Some cards are referred to as *posted records* because information is continually added to them (see figures 8.8, page 168 and 8.9, page 169). Master storage index cards are an example.

Card records are filed vertically in *card cabinets*. Files with one, two, three, or more drawers are available for desktop use. There are also multidrawer card files, as used in a library, for greater numbers of card records. Of course, guide cards are also available in the various card sizes so that card records can be broken down into smaller groups.

Posted records are frequently filed in a *visible file cabinet* with overlapping hinged trays that allow some of the data on the card to show along an edge (see figure 8.10, page 169). The rest of the data are revealed by lifting the cards in front of the desired record. Visible files also come in a horizontal rack or a vertical rack (see figure 8.11, page 170). Addition or deletion of information is handled by simply removing one strip of information and inserting another. Visible files tend to be more expensive and take up more room than drawer files.

Rotary files have cards on wheels. They are compact and efficient to use. Guide cards are available. The cards are not as large usually as those filed in cabinets and thus the space available for information is not as great. They are frequently used for names and addresses.

Readers for microfilm, which double as storage units, are available. A reader is an optical aid that enlarges the microfilm or microfiche material to a legible size.

Bar codes can be purchased commercially or produced in-house either by the software that comes with the scanner or by the circulation/indexing software.

Scanners come in sizes from a light pen to full-page, from plastic wands to metal to laser, from less than $200 to over $1,000.

Storage environment must also be considered. Conservation of material depends not only on the storage equipment but also on atmospheric and other environmental conditions. Temperature should be between 60 degrees and 75 degrees; humidity should be between 50 percent and 60 percent. Air conditioning in the summer not only provides staff comfort; it also keeps out pollution, provides ventilation, filters out dust, and controls temperature and humidity.

(Text continues on page 170.)

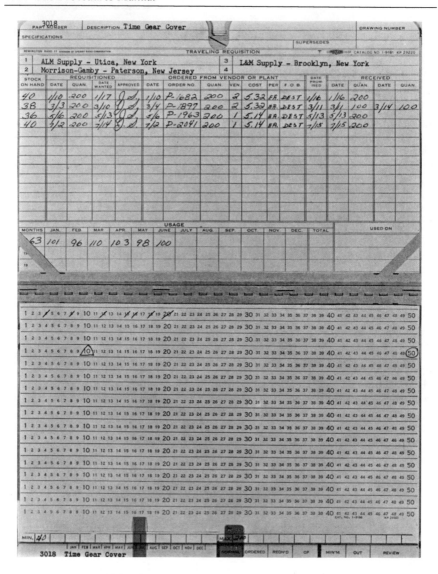

Fig. 8.8. Posted record.

Fig. 8.9. Folder for posted records. Photo courtesy of Kardex Systems, Inc. Marietta, Ohio 45750.

Fig. 8.10. Visible file cabinet.

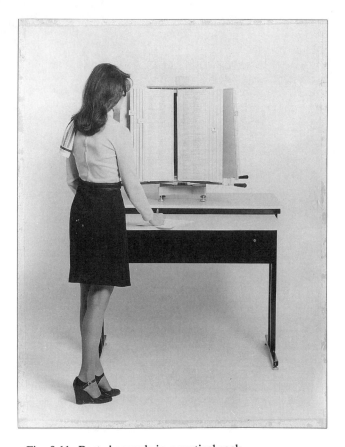

Fig. 8.11. Posted records in a vertical rack.

File cabinets should be dusted regularly. Open shelves need to be vacuumed regularly.

Incandescent lighting is best. It might be necessary to have the lights on all the time to repel insects and rodents. Litter and food should also be kept away if an in-house exterminator is to be avoided.

Film and tape of any kind need to be kept in metal cabinets, in a cool place with air circulating. Too much heat makes them brittle. Commercial cleaners are available for both film and tape. Protection from scratching is, of course, also very important.

Photographs and papers going into permanent storage need to be protected in acid-free folders or reproduced onto acid-free paper and kept from light.

Computer tapes and disks can be filed in special cabinets or racks, or on open shelving. There are specialized diskette hanging files, including some that will hold both disks and copy pages.

Cabinets are also available which will hold mixed media: tape rolls, disk packs, disk cartridges, printouts, manuals, binders, forms, cards, microforms, cassettes, or documents.

Data security has become a top priority. The chief danger is fire. Heat or fire can ruin computer media in seconds. Paper starts to smolder at 350 degrees, but a temperature of just 125 degrees can destroy a computer diskette. Thus, several manufacturers are offering data safes which are fire-resistant, impact-tested, and have special locks.

As environmental issues become not only personal concerns but also mandated, some records managers are assuming the role of facility manager, if not corporate-wide, at least for the department. A facility manager coordinates the physical workplace with the people and work of the organization. This involves office layout, ergonomics, airgonomics, acoustics, environmental liability, and also cost as it affects profitability.

Modular furniture and panels have created an open workstation concept. These replace closed-door offices down the sides of the building. Trying to integrate the need for easy communication with privacy when necessary can lead to layout problems when using open workstations.

Office furniture and accessories are being designed for both aesthetics and ergonomics. The more adjustable an item, the better. People are not uniform in size and should not be expected to spend 40 hours in uncomfortable chairs and desks, using computers that cannot be customized to their bodies. Studies show that the extra cost of adjustable furniture is repaid in more productive work. One study showed a 3 to 12 percent increase in productivity by switching from conventional chairs to fully ergonomics one. Couple that with an adjustable workstation and the additional cost is more than justified—and may save a company a lawsuit from an employee for repetitive strain injury. Laws in New York and California now affect ergonomics and some bills have been placed in front of the U.S. Congress.

Solving sick building syndrome is healthy for the occupants and may also protect the company from liability. Indoor air quality, indoor radon, lead exposure, electromagnetic radiation, solid and hazardous waste production and storage, water quality, asbestos, noise, and task lighting must all be addressed. Many products are on the market for each area to be addressed, and an investigation should be made on the comparable qualities of each.

A study by the International Facilities Management Association revealed that only 11 percent of the members had a written in-house hazardous waste substance production, treatment, or disposal program. Record keeping here may also prevent future litigation. Purchasing or selling a site now involves an environmental assessment. Hazardous waste liability and astronomical cleanup costs have become a major concern in commercial and industrial real estate transactions because, under the Comprehensive Environmental Response, Compensation and Liability Act (CERCLA), the federal government can move in and clean up contaminated property and then seek reimbursement from the property owner. The Resource Conservation and Recovery Act (RCRA) mandates that the owner or operator of a business that accumulates hazardous waste—even as little as a pound for some—at its facility must obtain a storage permit and comply with waste regulations or face a fine. The terms *hazardous substance* and *hazardous waste* are broadly defined and somewhat vague, and may differ from community to community and state to state. Common solvents such as acetone and isopropyl alcohol, corrosive acids or alkalis, benzene and toluene, degreasers, pesticides, and petroleum products are frequently listed.

Safety must also be considered, not only OSHA safety standards but also simple practical matters such as preventing shelves from toppling or closing on someone, having adequate sprinklers and smoke alarms, and restricting access to the department by persons from outside the company.

Finally, because equipment and supplies are an obvious line item on a budget, cost must be considered. Actually, the largest cost in the department is labor. If a consumable such as color-coded file folders can eliminate misfiles and speed filing and retrieval time, their extra cost over non-color-coded file folders can be justified. Do you save by sending your forms-printing work to an outside service rather than duplicating them on a copier? The answer is probably yes. Strangely, supplies made from recycled paper are more costly than ones not, but maybe it is the environmentally conscious thing to do. Bulk buying is not always the wisest decision if storage is at a premium. Equipment is amortorized over its life and can eventually be recycled to other departments as replacements are purchased. Floor space is frequently rented from the parent company and if so, must be put in the budget, including the record center's share of common corridors, restrooms, and parking spaces. A *budget* is a plan formulated for an operation to be carried out at a certain cost level over a certain time span. Budgeting is a matter of forecasting. Some departments budget for one year with quarterly or monthly breakdowns. Overhead or operating costs such as utilities must be considered. Equipment can come under the heading of long- or short-term capital outlay. Quantifying the benefits of equipment and supplies is a consideration. Part of labor's cost are the benefits in addition to salary, such as social security, medical, cafeteria subsidy, and pension.

FOR FURTHER STUDY

1. Obtain office equipment catalogs from dealers and familiarize yourself with the array of supplies and equipment available. Interview three salespeople regarding a select few of their particular product lines and ask them to present the strengths of these products. From the first interview you will gain insights to questions to ask the next salespeople.

2. In your procedures manual, add Part VI, "Equipment and Supplies." Give a brief synopsis of your interviews with each salesperson and draw a concluding paragraph on equipment and supplies.

9

PART VII: CENTRALIZATION
VS. DECENTRALIZATION

This manual has discussed records as if they were housed in a central area. Actually this is the exception rather than the rule. All the procedures that have been presented for organizing files are valid for decentralized as well as centralized files. Centralization of records (see figure 9.1, page 174) is still not standard practice, as many libraries fight the idea of shared cataloging and processing because the individual library has to sacrifice some of its idiosyncracies. Many companies fight the advantages of central records because individual departments do not want to give up unique privileges.

Some common problems found in decentralized files are: incomplete files, disagreement about what file a record belongs to, duplication of files, wrong file numbers typed on letters, poor indexing, slow retrieval, fragmented filing systems, records and files not available when needed, lost files, files not identified as being checked out, and records not returned for filing.

The larger the organization, the more obvious the need for centralized control of records. A company with many branch offices needs uniformity. A central records control can emphasize cost. For instance, by charging back to individual departments or branches the cost of storing inactive records, one can demonstrate the advantage of not keeping a record longer than necessary. One hundred fifty thousand boxes of inactive records at 34 cents per box per month becomes an obvious drain on the department or branch office paying the storage bill.

There are several advantages of centralized files:

1. The standardization of filing procedures produces efficiency, speed in filing and retrieval, and easier personnel supervision.

2. Centralization eliminates, or cuts down on, duplicate files, saving equipment, supplies, and space.

3. Centralization requires fewer people. Responsibility rests with one person, or group of people, minimizing oversights and loss of records.

Fig. 9.1. Centralized files and open workstations. Photo courtesy of Spacesaver Corporation, Fort Atkinson, WI.

4. Charge-out and follow-up procedures are more consistent.

5. Uniform regulations and procedures for transfer of material to inactive and storage files will be instituted or in effect.

Yet, as mentioned, departments and personnel inevitably feel a loss of control over centralized files and are loath to give up their private interests. And, decentralization may be faster if the personnel can really put their hands immediately on the desired material.

An excellent compromise to the problem is the development of (1) a central records control center containing the files used by multiple groups or persons and (2) various personal or departmental files, containing records relating only to individual offices. A forms file should probably be centralized, but sales quotas may be more accessible if filed in departmental files. The departments could move the records from active to inactive files in central records, but storage of records would be the responsibility of central records.

Other advantages of centralization, including standardization of rules and procedures, would carry over to departmental files if the records center were responsible for the development of the system and all filing personnel were trained by central records personnel. Deviations from procedures in the filing manual should be discouraged, or at least noted in the central records procedures manual. An index of records housed in individual departments should be kept in central storage.

FOR FURTHER STUDY

1. Visit an organization with a central records center and one with decentralized records. Ask the technicians in each what they see as a prime advantage and disadvantage to their method. While there, learn the methods of filing classification they use, as well as their methods of coding for filing and for storage and retention. Ask to see their forms for transferring material from active to inactive, to storage, and to disposal. Learn their circulation method.

2. In your procedures manual under Part VII, "Centralization vs. Decentralization Files," write a few paragraphs explaining which method you prefer with explicit reasons why.

THE PAPERLESS
FILES

10

MICROGRAPHICS

Microphotography is almost as old as photography itself. The first micro-image was produced in 1839, the same year the Daguerrotype process was introduced. By the 1850s "circus curiosities" such as the "Lord's Prayer" on a pinhead were being produced. Technically the process of microphotography offered few problems, but practical applications were difficult to foresee. It took a war to make the new technology practical and important. During the 1870 Franco-Prussian war, pigeons were used to fly microfilmed messages in and out of Paris. The fact that each pigeon could carry 50,000 messages proved microfilm's capabilities as a medium for the economical transmission of information, but after the war this experiment was dropped rather than improved and expanded upon.

In 1871 an insurance company's records were filmed, but there was no rush by other companies to follow suit, and it appeared as though the fad for microphotography would eventually disappear. But in 1929 the rotary camera was invented by a banker. This made possible the rapid recording of checks and replaced time-consuming handwritten check descriptions. This camera, combined with the microphotography process, enabled information to be stored on microfilm very quickly. Soon banks, insurance companies, libraries, newspapers, and government agencies were using microfilm for space-saving, economical, archival storage, but retrieval was a problem. Locating a specific frame on a roll of film was a slow, tedious process that no one wanted to go through very often. "Film it, file it, and forget it" was the motto. It took another war to make microfilm an active rather than inactive information transmission tool and, as in 1870, the impetus was the need to transmit large numbers of messages. Letters to the soldiers overseas were microfilmed for transportation then blown up to eye-readable form at the other end of the line. By the end of the war over one billion messages had been sent in this fashion.

Also, Uncle Sam was experimenting with secret information and micro-photography. The Office of Strategic Services (OSS) gathered a huge file of photographs of enemy territory. By 1943 the OSS was filing over 250,000 photographs a month. Microfilm could solve the space problem that such a collection posed, but there was the problem of accessibility. In time of war the speed with which information is accessed is often literally a matter of life and death.

During the war computers were also being used for the first time on a large scale, and the technologies of these areas of microphotography and data processing were fused with the aperture card. Frames of film were mounted onto IBM cards punched with identifying data. Now the computer could search for a particular picture far faster than a human.

After the war two members of the OSS formed a company to explore peacetime applications of the aperture card. One of their first customers was the police, who wanted a more efficient means of handling "mug shots" in files. Soon engineering departments were microfilming engineering drawings. But retrieval was still a problem until high-speed, low-cost viewers came on the scene. The next major advancement occurred in the 1950s when producing a blown-up hard copy of the microfilm image became a dry rather than a wet process.

Computer output microfilm (COM) was developed in the 1950s, experimented with in the 1960s, and was in wide usage by the 1970s. COM is a tool for the recording of computer-generated data onto microfilm. COM is created on a COM recorder, which can be either offline or online with a host computer. The data are transferred directly from the computer to the COM recorder producing the microfilm. With an offline COM recorder, a magnetic tape generated from a host is mounted on the COM recorder to produce the microfilm. Now lasers are being used in the combined technologies of microphotography, computers, and printers.

The technological advancements of microphotography and computers in the last 20 years has led to myriad uses of these technologies. Telecommunications has linked with them and is daily introducing more applications. In 1987 53 percent of all companies were using microforms. The paperless society is not near, but this new technology is here to stay and everyone needs to be aware of its basic operations and applications. Even small companies are investigating microforms as a solution to their storage problems. However, before moving into the area for the first time, a company should carefully study its problems and investigate all possible solutions to those problems. A business owner or manager conducting such a study should: (1) read about microforms and speak with colleagues who have encountered the same storage problems (private consultants are available for consultation); (2) attend professional meetings where representatives of many equipment vendors display their wares; (3) develop a list of requirements and an evaluation checklist; (4) contact individual vendors; (5) actually operate equipment to determine training needs; and (6) calculate upkeep and maintenance costs. Before any purchase or change is initiated the following questions should be answered:

What are the objectives in implementing a micrographics system?

Is it for the security of a backup, for space saving, for faster, more accurate customer service?

What are the characteristics of the file to be microfilmed?

How many items does the file contain; will the documents require conversion before they can be microfilmed; are additions or modifications made to the records frequently; how frequently is the file consulted; how long must the file be retained?

What are the characteristics of the documents to be microfilmed?

Are all the documents of uniform size; are they in good condition; are they paper documents or computerized?

What are the anticipated retrieval needs of the files?

Will the retrievals be one per day or one per week or year?

How many individuals must have access to the files or documents?

Are these people in the same or in different buildings? Must they access the entire file or just single documents within the file?

What will be the cost of equipment, space, and personnel or of hiring a service bureau?

How much space will equipment occupy; will more personnel be needed; what is the turnaround time for a service bureau?

What will be the cost of consumable supplies, including film, developer, filing supplies?

What will be the maintenance cost? (Labor is 60 percent of a filing operation's annual operating cost.)

As a rule, micrographic media and equipment and purchasing decisions should be based on the types of applications involved. Micrographics applications can be classified as either transaction processing documents or document time value. Transaction processing can be uniformly designed documents with sequential serial numbers. Each document stands alone as a record. Examples are invoices and checks. These documents can be readily stacked in an auto-feeder, microfilmed onto roll film, and indexed. Transaction processing can also be case file documents, gathered over a period of time, but usually related in subject matter.

The second application, document time value, includes questions on archiving documents. If they are to be stored for retrieval only, they can be placed on roll film with automated retrieval functionality.

Some forms of microphotography are described below.

Microforms are miniaturized formats for information: microfilm, micro-cards, microfiche, aperture cards, microprint, and COM.

Microfilm designates a size of microform on a continuous roll of either 8, 16, or 35 millimeters. Microfilm rolls are available in a variety of container formats such as reel, cartridge, cassette, and jacket. A *reel* is a cylinder container that turns on its axis and is used for winding a roll of microfilm. Microfilm reels were one of the first microforms; they are still a popular choice because large quantities of information may be stored in very little space at very low cost. A 16-millimeter roll 100 feet long includes up to 2,000 data frames. Thirty-five-millimeter microfilm is used for oversized documents. Because the rolls can be spliced, microfilm reels are very desirable where information is added continuously in sequence and where updating is infrequent. Eight-millimeter film is used for microsheet and filed behind or in front of the first. A 16-millimeter cartridge holding 3,000 to 4,000 8½-x-11-inch images costs $6 to $15 and can be processed and sent back with a duplicate for $16 to $25.

Ultrafiche is a sheet of transparent film that contains images reduced more than 90 times, thus permitting thousands of images to appear on a single fiche.

Microcard is a term referring to a 3-x-5-inch sheet of transparent film, or its positive.

Micro-opaque refers to the positive image of microminiaturization. The image is viewed as any "hard copy" of paper with black lines on a white background.

An *aperture card* is a 3-x-7-inch card with an opening for a single frame of microfilm. The rest of the card can be computer-coded or hand-coded for identifying, filing, and retrieving the frame. Available now are aperture cards that allow for updating and adding single frames to the other single frames.

Readers or *viewers* are optical aides that enlarge the microimages so they can be read by the human eye. Some readers do a better job of enlarging and making the images readable than do other readers. Typically, readers are square boxes that utilize a rear-projection process to enlarge and project the image onto a screen, though front projection is also available. Some readers can handle only certain microformats such as reels or microfiche; others can handle several formats. Some can make paper copies; others cannot. Some are as large as 65 x 107 inches; others can be held in the palm of one hand like a single slide viewer. Some are mechanized; others are hand-operated. Some are simple to use; others are not. Some locate the desired image very quickly; others are time-consuming. Some are quiet; some emit an annoying noise. Some are easy to maintain; others have replaceable parts that are difficult to reach. Low-end systems include simple readers and flat-film readers, costing under $100. These units are manually operated and include portable units. Also falling on the low end are reader/printers that are semiautomated. They are motorized, so the user does not have to crank-roll film. These devices rely on manual indexing and retrieval systems that are not highly sophisticated. They are cost-justifiable for making 15,000 to 20,000 printouts per year. Their cost runs $3,000 to $4,000. The mid-range units, $4,000 to $12,000, consist of reader/printers able to support 25,000 to 60,000 prints per year. They are more automated, usually image-mark retrieval systems. At the high end are computer-assisted retrieval (CAR) reader/printers with automated motorized capabilities that search an index for a micrographic image, get the cartridge and frame number, and then access the image frame in a minute or less. They usually cost $12,000 to $15,000 but can go as high as $25,000.

A number of factors determine the quality of a reader/printer. Of utmost importance are screens and lenses. Screens are usually one foot square, although some are oversized for dual-page projections or projection of over-sized documents. Screens come in several colors and may be fixed or tilting. Most use rear projection and some offer degrees of control over lamp brightness. Buyers must make certain that readers and reader/printers support the same magnification ratio as the reduction ratio used for microfilming. For example, if a document is reduced by 32 times during filming, a reader/printer must support 32X magnification. Buyers should check whether a number of lenses are supplied and that the magnification range is sufficient, along with focus controls.

In recent years, the reader/printer market has shifted sharply to plain-paper machines that use toner-and-drum electrophotographic technology to print on ordinary copier bond paper. The reason for change: lower cost of plain-paper printers, lower cost per copy, and longevity. Coated papers tend to fade in sunlight. Most plain-paper machines are xerographic electrostatic systems, especially on low-end reader/printers. A second type of electrostatic printer prints on coated paper and can create a positive image from a negative microform, or vice versa. Plain-paper electrostatic printers should be used for ordinary applications. On some high-end units, laser printers are used. Dry-silver printers are also available. They produce more detailed and dimensional images than those produced by plain paper. Color printers are also entering the micrographics area.

COM (computer output microfilm) is the eye-readable printout from a computer in microfiche or microfilm format. Developed in 1954, COM is an efficient, economical information tool that reduces characters up to 48 times smaller than those produced by traditional computer printing methods. Similar to laser beam printers, the units use lasers to write images on the screen and to expose the film. The data that are stored on the magnetic or floppy disk can now be transferred to film. Data from source documents can be replaced by digital input through computer-to-computer linkup. There are three ways to control data formatted by a COM system. Least expensive is offline COM where a stand-alone unit does not tie into the main computer terminal. The computer's print data must be matched with camera commands to produce the microfiche. Print tapes are formatted with these commands and the unit converts COM-formatted tapes to microfilm. The second option is a minicom-puter-controlled recorder that reformats standard print tapes to meet specific requirements. As the recorder does all the formatting, this method is especially useful when multiple formats are needed or when a data center uses a variety of different central processing units (CPUs). A third possibility is online COM where the recorder interfaces with the computer and accepts data over the CPU channel. This method guarantees maximum CPU output efficiency as the recorder does its own internal reformatting and eliminates handling and storage costs. But not all CPU units are capable of reformatting.

COM can also be used to produce a bar code system. Some banks are using this to put a strip on the back of checks. The computer then picks up the code and automatically microfilms the check. Chase Manhattan Bank in New York processes over 11 million checks this way each month. McDonnell Douglas in St. Louis has used COM since 1963. Their system runs 24 hours a day, 365 days a year. Many schools use COM for student records.

CAR (computer-assisted or -automated retrieval) is an indexing system that provides the address of the document on film allowing the user to locate it and reproduce it. Sometimes CAR can be created by integrating an inexpensive reader/printer with a software program like LOTUS 1-2-3. A computer in CAR can be used as an indexing device that calls up a menu or acts as an odometer. Then the operator manually pulls up a roll of film and inserts it into the reader/printer, which is driven by the computer console. The film is reviewed on the screen and, if desired, copies can be made. There are predictions that soon robots will be used to automatically select the microfiche from the CAR system, insert it in the reader/printer and make the hard copy.

Before CAR systems, indexes were kept manually, leaving companies to go through each roll of film to count frames or add *image marks*, or blips on the film, with a special device, with one mark for each record or file. One way to combat the indexing problem is with bar codes. Bar-coded labels can be attached to documents which are then scanned and photographed. CAR-based systems then automatically index the document by bar code, which can be put in numerical sequence beforehand or printed on the spot to match invoice numbers. Compatible CAR-based reader/printers can search, find, and display bar-coded images on an automated basis. Taking advantage of bar-code indexing means either purchasing bar-code-based micrographic cameras for in-house microfilm production or making arrangements with service bureaus. Not all documents are CAR indicative. CAR is better for documents with a short active and legal life, when records are highly computerized, immediate response is desired, and there is a predicted growth. If users of the files are decentralized, the files are usually analyzed rather than used to answer specific questions, are relatively inactive, and have a permanent or extended life, then a microfilm jacket might be the better application.

The reader/digitizer scans microfilmed images and digitizes them for further computer and data communications processing. They merge imaging and micrographics, cost $20,000 to $40,000, and are important as labor-saving systems as well as for their speed.

Other trends in microphotography are intelligent recorders that can reformat data. The recorders can also add titles and indexing information to the film. These intelligent recorders are dropping in price, which will increase their usage. Another trend is toward more sophisticated interfacing with personal computers and the interfacing of all formats of micrographics using telecommunications. With these one can bypass the hard copy altogether and simply send the image to a fax machine. Multifunctional micrographics workstations allow for direct fax hookups and plug into local area networks.

What are the advantages of microforms? Obviously their size saves filing space. One hundred sheets of paper occupy four filing inches in a cabinet; one microfiche containing the images of 100 sheets of paper occupies less than one-fourth of an inch of filing space in a cabinet; eight fiche cards equal 2,000 pages of paper. The use of microforms improves space utilization of equipment and reduces labor in filing. Updated microforms also file easier than dozens of sheets of paper. In addition, microform records do not suffer the wear and tear that original documents do, and they can withstand more rugged handling than paper. The noncombustible mylar base reduces the hazard of fire. Vital records can be microfilmed and then stored away from disasters such as fire or flood in underground caves. Microforms will last at least 100 years.

Microforms are easily and inexpensively duplicated and placed in branch locations, and the master is always available, whereas original records will deteriorate from age and constant use. Microforms could be used for reference, saving the original copies. Readers are available that will make a print on paper of the microfilmed record if one is needed.

A hundred paper pages reproduced onto a single microfiche is much cheaper to mail than 100 pages of paper. Retrieval of a particular page from a document is faster with the mechanized indexes of microfilm equipment than it is with hand searching. Uniformity in filing is possible. Paper comes in all sizes and shapes, but a selected microform standardizes those sizes and shapes.

With all these advantages of microforms, why have they not replaced paper? Even though microforms are cost-saving they are still expensive. Even though they save labor and time, they still require specialized people and preparation time.

A serious study should be undertaken before deciding to convert paper records to microforms. Microforms are not always practical when the preparation will necessitate complete revision of indexing and filing operations, and creation of a cross-reference index for retrieval purposes. At one time microforms were not practical when color in the original document was needed to interpret the information, but today color can be reproduced. Microforms are not always practical when records are of various sizes, because refolding, stapling, or pasting records slows down the microfilming process and increases cost. Microforms are not always practical when information is stored on both sides of the document or when there is a need to compare several different records. Nor are microforms practical where records are being entered continuously or where additional information needs to be entered much later. One document or span of accounts is photographed on one reel or fiche. Once a record has been microfilmed no information can be added. Splicing film shortens the life of the reel. Film jackets might solve the problems, but they may not be practical for other reasons.

Generally microfilming should not be considered when the cost exceeds the cost of storing records for the period of time required by the retention schedule. Generally it is cheaper to keep the document for 10 years than it is to microfilm it.

A roll of film or fiche is made as a complete filing unit. The finished product is then filed. Rolls can be stored in boxes labeled with the contents and filed numerically, alphabetically, geographically, phonetically. Or color-coding by subject, or a combination of methods, can be used. The scheme selected must allow for updating material and interfiling. Microfiche and microcards can be stored in an envelope labeled with the contents and filed according to the system in use. Microfiche and microcards can also be stored

in pockets in binders and the pockets and binders labeled, or in special microfiche holders (see figure 10.1).

Fig. 10.1. Microfiche holder. Photo courtesy of Nb Jackets—
Martin Quint Advertising Company, 303 Lexington Ave., New
York, NY 10016.

Aperture cards can be labeled with the contents and filed according to the
system in use, or keypunched and stored randomly. To retrieve a particular
record, the proper fiche or film is first retrieved by hand, machine (see figure
10.2), or computer; then a particular page is retrieved by rapid machine-
scanning of the film or fiche. When the page has been located it can be
reprinted on paper by the optical scanner. Floppy disks can be stored in jackets
or binders according to the system in use. The microphotography itself can be
done in-house in a print production department or it can be contracted out to
microfilming companies.

The demise of micrographics is being predicted as more and more organizations turn to optical disk, but at this time micrographics still dominates.
Since micrographics has evolved to provide image digitization for links to

Fig. 10.2. Motorized microfiche filing. Photo courtesy of Kardex Systems, Inc. Marietta, Ohio 45750.

computers and facsimile and automated document indexing via bar-code technology and automated computer-assisted retrieval (CAR), micrographic systems are matching or outperforming optical technology. Nevertheless, most eventually see a marriage between micrographics and imaging during the 1990s. Currently some scanners can take an image on microfilm or fiche, digitize the image, and then transfer it to optical disk. At this point the microfilm becomes a backup.

In your procedures manual, reference needs to be made to the user's manuals for each piece of equipment. As a precaution against loss, one set of all manufacturer's procedures manuals might be part of the record center's procedures manual. It is important that the record center's procedures manual provide a schematic of the work flow and any particular care needed along the work flow, such as making certain all pages are turned the proper direction for filming.

FOR FURTHER STUDY

It may not be possible to visit a micrographics service center or a company that does in-house microfilming. If there is a chapter of the Association of Records Managers and Administrators or Special Libraries Association in your area, try to attend a meeting in which microfilming is on the program agenda and add your notes to your procedures manual under "Part VIII: Micrographics." If you have a user's guide for a projector, photocopy it to add to Part VIII to illustrate that equipment manuals are often part of a procedures manual.

11

_____*COMPUTERS*_____

If one described a computer as merely a fast, counting machine, the first computer would have been an abacus. But of course today a computer can do much more than an abacus.

The computers of 1950 are very primitive compared to those of the late 1980s. In fact, when one considers the advancements made in the computer field in the last five years compared with the ten years before or the twenty before that, it does not seem possible that experiments were being conducted as early as the 1600s. Blaise Pascal developed one of the first mechanical calculating machines in 1612. The mind of man could already conceive the idea of a computer, but the technology was simply not available to build one. Pascal's machine could only add; by 1642 a multiplying calculating machine had been invented. Punched cards were developed in 1725. The concept of a machine that could make comparisons was formed in 1786, and by 1833 a difference machine had been invented. By 1833 the idea of an analytical machine existed, but again technology had not advanced far enough for a practical working machine to be built. The 1890 census used punched cards and sorting machines to save enormous amounts of human labor. Once information was key-punched onto a card it could be used over and over. The company that was to become known as International Business Machines (IBM) was begun in 1911. An analytical machine was brought to fruition in 1939 with *Mark I*. World War II spurred the development of computers and proved their value. The mass production of computers after the war introduced the technology and competition that has enabled them to do more, and to do it faster, with smaller and less equipment. The first advancement in this area was the ability to store the program, or instructions, in the machine along with the numbers used for computation. A major change in computers and the acceptance of computers occurred in 1981 when IBM introduced the first "PC" (personal computer). At that time company officials predicted 500,000 units would be sold. Forty million units later, sales have not stopped.

Basically, there are two types of computers: digital and analog. A *digital computer* is primarily a mathematical problem-solving machine while an *analog computer* solves problems by comparing one quantity with another. For example, an adding machine is a primitive digital computer, and a speedometer on a car could be classified as an analog computer because it measures speed.

A computer can provide central records management just as a group of filing cabinets or shelves can. The term, "computer," actually refers to many pieces of equipment called *hardware* together with a collection of routines or programs called *software* used with the computer equipment.

The hardware consists of an input unit, a storage unit, a control unit, and an output unit. The *input unit* feeds information in input format into the computer. The basic function of the input unit is to accept information in some format and act upon it so that the data, or information, can be used by the rest of the equipment. This information must be in some regular coded form that can be sensed and converted into electrical impulses. In the early 1950s through the 1970s, this coded form, *input format*, often was punched paper or punched cards. Now input is almost universally done via a typewriter-like keyboard or a scanning device. The type of character inputted is presented to the central processor for conversion into an electrical impulse. A *cathode ray tube* (CRT) or screen/monitor, can be both an input format and an output format. This screen shows what the keyboard is "saying" to the *central processing unit* (CPU) and what is being stored in memory. Thus it acts as an inputer. The CRT unit can also retrieve and display information stored in the computer and being acted upon by the CPU. Input formats can also be *magnetic tape* or *disks*. Stored information on the tape or disk becomes input format to the CPU. The tapes and disks can also become storage media for the output of the CPU. Data stored on magnetic tape or disk is much more efficient and economical than information stored on punched cards or paper, and retrieval is much faster. Magnetic tape and disks are also highly compact and durable and are easily transportable.

The *storage* or *memory unit* of the computer is like an indexed filing cabinet in which stored material is instantaneously accessible. The computer "remembers" by storing in its memory information or data needed to solve a problem, perform a calculation, or update information. Each location, position, or section in the storage unit is numbered so that stored data can be readily located. The amount of information that can be held within the computer at any one time depends on the size or capacity of the storage unit formats. Like the input unit, the storage unit also manipulates various formats. Until hard disk drives arrived, rarely was information stored within the equipment, per se, but rather it was stored on disks, tapes, or microfilm. Even today some companies place only the software program on the hard disk and keep the data files on floppies.

The *central unit* equipment controls the operation of the other units of equipment. It directs the flow of information in and out of the computer and manipulates the information inside the computer. It coordinates and programs the functions of the various parts of the computer and ensures the execution of the sequence or *program* of instructions given to the computer. The central unit thus acts as a processor.

Originally the control unit and the storage unit were separate pieces of equipment. With the advent of minicomputers they now constitute one piece of equipment known as the *central processing unit* (CPU). This single unit stores and processes the data; that is, it computes mathematically or arranges the data logically. Thus, it both stores and controls the program. The term *online* describes equipment, devices, and persons that are in direct communication with the computer's CPU. Conversely, *offline* describes any equipment, devices, and persons not in direct communication with the CPU; but rather connected (usually) via a telecommunications channel.

Output is the information released by the computer that can be interpreted by the operator. The operator cannot use the computer's solution if it is in the form of electrical impulses. The equipment for producing the output format is the *output hardware.* Typically, typewriters, high-speed printers, or cathode ray tubes (screens) are output equipment. Besides print, other output formats are punched cards, paper tape, magnetic tape, and magnetic disks. These need an additional translation from their coding to be read by the operator. A *microcomputer* is also called a *personal computer.* The input unit, central processing unit, and output unit all appear to be one piece of equipment. Today's desktop microcomputers have more computing power and operate faster than the *mainframe computers* of the 1950s. A *minicomputer* is larger in terms of equipment needs and memory size than a micro, but smaller than a mainframe.

A local area network (LAN) is an arrangement where two or more personal computers are connected into a single system that allows all users on the network to have access to a common data and storage area. This storage area can be partitioned so that, by the use of a password, users can be allowed access to only those programs and data which they need to use. More than one person can use a single set of programs and data at the same time. *Record locking* allows one person to update a particular record. While that record is being changed, no one else may search it, although searchers have access to all the other records in the database. Another advantage of a LAN is that all users can share the same printers on the system. In a company with only a few printers, the requested information may stack in the printer's memory until work currently being processed is completed. Because all programs and data are stored in a single location, the network host drive, backups to a tape cartridge are easy. The connection of PC workstations to a LAN is accomplished by installing a device called a *network interface card* in each of the PCs. These cards connect the PCs to the network cable, which is usually a coaxial cable about one-quarter inch in diameter, or a set of telephone-type twisted-pair wires. One of the PCs on the network is equipped with a disk drive (data storage device) that has large enough capacity for all the programs and data the organization will use. This machine is called a *file server.* Finally, a special software program called a *network operating system* is loaded on the file server. This network operating system allows the many PCs on the network to use the same programs and data and manages the access security and printer sharing. In large networks, the file server is not used as a workstation computer, but is dedicated to the task of managing the network activity. In small networks, the file server can also be used as a workstation. Local area networks for mainframes are called WANs (wide area networks).

The differences between computers are the capacity of the memory, the speed of the processing unit, and the number, variety, and speed of the input and output units.

An *automated records system* refers to the integration of equipment, software, methods, and procedures designed to support the day-to-day records management activities of an organization.

Software is the program used with the computer equipment. It is possible to key in one's own program, but most companies use programs developed commercially or in-house. A program tells the computer what to do. Some types of software are described below.

Word processing. Word processing software manipulates or edits typed information. Microcomputers designed to do only word processing are frequently used in secretarial pools. Many commercial and public domain software disks are available which can be inserted into the disk drive of a microcomputer and do word editing or manipulation.

Word processing software can also be used in records management—for example, in correspondence control. A letter a typist prepares using the word processing software is edited, saved, and printed out. A second copy does not have to be printed because the letter has been saved on the disk. If another copy is needed, the word processing software's word-search capability can be used to call up the name of either the sender or the receiver, or to call up all letters sent on a certain date or dealing with a particular project or subject.

Database management system. A database management system is software designed to store and retrieve related pieces of information about entities (documents, customers' accounts, etc.). A database is composed of any number of records. A *record* is all information in the computer concerning a single entity (a document, an employee, an account, etc.). This record contains *fields* which categorize the various kinds of data in the record. Examples of fields in a document management database are: date, originator, addressee, document location, subject. A field may be *required*, that is, it is always necessary to put data in that field in order to complete the record. Or a field may be *optional*, that is, data are entered only if available and at the discretion of the user. The item of data or information entered into a field is called a *value*. If only one item of data is allowed in a field, that field is said to be single-valued. For example, the field "date received" would be single-valued if only one date was accepted. A multivalued field allows more than one item of data to be entered. In multivalued fields the values are separated by delimiters such as commas, slashes, etc. Some fields require that a value be in a specific *format*, that it be expressed in a consistent arrangement that the computer can recognize. For example, a date might be YYMMDD; e.g., June 30, 1994 would be expressed as 940630. Sometimes specific formats are required because the data that are input into the record are checked or *validated* against a table. A *table* is a list in the database of acceptable terms allowed to be input in a given field. There can be any number of validation tables. Fields that use validation tables to control the format in which data may be entered are said to have a *controlled* vocabulary. If data can be entered in any form the field is described as *free-text* or *free-form* vocabulary. Some databases are designed so that when certain data are entered in one field the computer automatically fills in additional data. This is called *autogeneration*. For example, in a correspondence control application, entering an employee's name may autogenerate his or her office location. When all required data have been entered and corrections have been made, it is necessary to *file* or *save* the record. Filing tells the computer to permanently store the record in the database. Once a record has been filed it can be called up again and displayed through the process of *retrieval*. To search for, retrieve, and display one or more records, a user must execute a query. A *query* is the translation of what the user is looking for into terms the computer can understand. Databases that allow the user to look for data in more than one field in a query are said to have *multiparameter* search capability. How queries must be expressed varies tremendously from system to system. In some systems the user is told how many records have been found as a result of the query before the records are displayed. These are called *hits*. Information contained in the records of a database can usually be displayed on the screen or printed out in different ways. This is accomplished using the *report generator* function. Some systems allow *ad hoc reports* to be produced. This is output in which the user specifies what data should be displayed and how those data should be arranged in the printout or on the screen. *Standard reports* are those in which the format and the data displayed have been pre-programmed and cannot be changed by the user.

Application software. An application software is the specific function a system is designed and implemented to do. Examples are correspondence control, engineering drawing tracking, inactive (archival) records management, retention and destruction scheduling, and, of course, document retrieval. A database application management system may be used for multiple applications. Examples of specific application software programs are word processing, spreadsheets, and computer automated drafting (CAD) engineering programs. Some of these CAD programs also have reports management functions built in so that after the drawing is made, it is saved to a "history" file from where it can be retrieved by project number or designated name. Such a process saves having to print and file a paper copy. There are also large numbers of commercial programs for inventory control management. One of the case studies in this book illustrates how PFS:FILE software has been used in records management. Another commercial program, *Eloquent Librarian*, has also been used as a case study. There are also specific industry application programs for real estate, insurance, farmers, retail stores, etc. Before purchasing a specific applications program one should talk with other users of the software, because often those users have learned more about the software's strengths and weaknesses than the salesperson of the software has.

Prices for applications software can run from under $100 to hundreds of thousands of dollars. Here is a checklist of features to look for in commercial records management applications software. Does it:

Log in new files or documents

Index files or documents

Print file folder labels

Print bar codes

Scan or log documents out and in

Find files and documents along the paperwork route

Track active files, inactive files, historical and vital records, and off-premise storage

Produce transfer notices

Track nonpaper documents such as PC disks, hard disks, microforms, optical media, audiovisual media, drawings, etc.

Perform searches, such as key-word or full-text index, multiple field, boolean, etc.

Have the ability to add new index fields or redefine existing ones

Provide for reserves, wait lists, or flags for files or documents

Generate file activity reports by location, department, and user, and report on delinquent or overdue files and documents

Generate inventory reports by user, department, project number, contract number, etc.

Provide an audit trail of activity

Provide for chargeback billing data

Provide records retention and disposal guidelines

Generate destruction procedures, such as authorizations, destruction certifications, etc.

Have frequent and easy-to-use help screens

Have security and password provisions

Work on a network

Interface with COM, CAR, and CD-ROM

Include an operator's manual and adequate documentation

Have a free demonstration or preview policy

Have installation support

Have online or hotline help

Offer training, either on-site or at software headquarters?

You may not desire all these features for your particular application usage, but they are features to look for when evaluating several programs.

Public domain software. Public domain (PD) programs are programs which have been placed in the public domain by the programmer and are available to the general public free or very inexpensively. They range in quality from terrible to outstanding. Many commercial programs began as experimental public domain programs. If one is versed in computer usage PD programs can be an excellent source for finding out what one needs in a commercial program. One limitation is that instructions are often weak and the user really has to understand the operation of a word processing, spreadsheet, or database program before being able to use the PD version. Public domain programs are available from computer bulletin boards, computer clubs, direct mail vendors, and even some commercial vendors.

In-house programming. In-house programs by systems analysts will provide tailor-made programs for specific applications. For companies with their own programmers this may be the ideal solution. In-house programming may be less expensive or more expensive than using a commercial program.

With all software, factors that affect "user friendliness" are the "help aids," messages the user can call up on the screen for information on what to do at a given point. Two types of help aids are menus and commands. A *menu* system presents a series of choices to the user. Upon choosing one option from the menu another set of menu options may appear, and so forth, until the user arrives at the desired destination. Menu-driven systems are easier for novices to use but are slow for experienced users of a particular software program. *Command* systems require that the user know in advance what instructions to input in order to obtain the desired result. Command systems usually require more user training. The newest trend in microcomputer software is the switch from a character-based user interface to a graphical interface using icons and a mouse.

Another addition to computer records control is the use of the *bar code* (see figure 11.1).

Fig. 11.1. Bar code or zebra label.

To file, store, and retrieve information contained in a bar code a computer requires the special equipment described below.

1. A bar code *label printer* makes the bar code labels specifically designed for the program. These labels are then attached to the folders or data items to be filed.

2. A *data entry system* provides for the transfer of the data from the bar code to a temporary storage unit by way of a light pen that reads the information imprinted on the code by passing over the label. This transmits the information on the bar code to a tape inside a cartridge much faster than typing, or keying, the information. This cartridge acts as a temporary storage unit. Some light pen units also have a keyboard for adding information to the information just transmitted onto the tape in the cartridge. Thus the information is updated as well as stored.

3. The *master computer unit* stores and updates information from many light pen data systems.

4. An *output device* can be a printer, microform, or CRT screen.

Hospitals have found the bar code computer method of filing invaluable. One use has been to keep track of the location of a patient file in a hospital system and to keep the billing current to the minute. Before bar coding, a patient's file was to be returned to central files after each department had handled it. In medical records it was checked in and checked out to the next department needing the patient's records. The reality of the system was that the patient would spend a day moving from department to department for treatment but the file would stop somewhere along the way. When the doctor would arrive at the patient's room to read the record for the day, the record would still be sitting in the X-ray department. But no one would know that immediately. With the bar code system an identifying bar code appears on a patient's folder. Each department has a series of identifying labels for each treatment, service, or billing. When the patient and folder arrive in the department, the folder is immediately read by the light pen to log the patient in. When the patient has had the treatment, the appropriate treatment and billing labels are added and again read by the light pen. This procedure is much faster than hand-posting would be. The patient, who is now logged out of the department, leaves with the folder for the next department. The patient and the record stay together. At the end of the day all the information stored on cassettes inside each of these light pen data devices in every department is sent to the master computer to be updated and filed onto the master file of medical records.

It is not surprising that the federal government with its vast records was one of the first to institute automation on a large scale. The National Personnel Records Center has the responsibility of storing and servicing more than 74 million noncurrent personnel records. Each morning some 7,500 requests for information from these records are received. The records themselves are stored in the format in which they are received, either paper or microform; but automation has been used to establish a locator index for this extensive file. A unique registry number is assigned to each record retired to the center. This sequentially assigned number identifies the file location reserved for the record. The registry number and other identifying data are added to the registry index to document record receipt for future retrieval and reference. An automated request system serves as the request, file locator/charge-out card, and transmittal form for returning the record to the requestor. A separate automated system keeps track of the orderly retirement and disposal of records and of the availability of shelf space.

The Mercantile Trust Company (St. Louis) has also automated its storage function. The following information, which used to be on a manual control card, is inputted into a computerized database: accession number, a unique number that identifies the department; date the record was received by the records center and a control number; shelf location number; volume or size of the information constituting the record; inclusive date of the record; disposal date; and a written description of the record. From the master database a number of reports are generated for records control, including a master list of all items in the record center, eligible disposal list, space availability, holdings summary by department, and audit records. Within a year this automated method brought a 20 percent reduction in retrieval time, an on-time destruction schedule, an ability to analyze needs department-by-department, and a reduction in personnel.

In 1990 the U.S. Postal Service offered businesses a discount if they would bar-code their mail. In 1990 165 billion pieces of mail were delivered to 110 million residences and businesses. This is expected to grow to 200 billion pieces to 120 million destinations in 1995. Indianapolis Power and Light, which sends out 400,000 pieces of mail, figures it saves over $100,000 annually as a result of bar coding and other in-house mail-handling efficiencies.

By the year 2000, it is likely that all records managers and library managers will have evaluated, tested, and installed some sort of computer-based records management system. Besides hardware, network, and software, consideration must also be given to adequate wiring, atmosphere, and surge protectors for power outages and peaks and valleys of high or low voltage. Without a surge protector, data can be lost, software programs can be inadvertently reconfigured, and even the semiconductors on the power board can be damaged. If a computer is in use during a brownout, the system will shut down, with all unsaved data lost. This is minor compared to losses that will result if a power outage occurs when the disk heads are updating or just resting over the File Allocation Table (FAT) area. When the FAT area is erased, the computer loses its ability to track data on the hard disk and the information becomes permanently lost. Standby power supplies (SPS), or an online uninterruptible power supply (UPS), are back-up power solutions. When a power failure occurs, the SPS switches on. It provides the electrical equipment with back-up power from a battery supply until the equipment is shut down or power is restored. A UPS provides power to a computer via an inverter which electronically generates its own pure power. Mainframes are generally protected by UPS systems.

Surge protectors provide one form of computer security. Besides power fluctuations, another threat to computer security comes from viruses. A *virus* is a computer program, designed as a prank or sabotage, which replicates itself by attaching itself to other programs, including the system software, and carries out unwanted and sometimes damaging operations. The effects of a computer virus may not be detected for quite a long time, during which every disk inserted into the system comes away with a hidden copy of the virus. Eventually the effects of the virus manifest themselves. The consequences of a virus range from prank messages, to erratic system software performance, to catastrophic erasure of all the information on a hard disk. A study of 2,500 large sites with 400 or more computers revealed that 50 percent had a virus infection. Damage can be minor or run into hundreds of thousands of dollars. If a virus in a stand-alone computer is bad, one running rampant on a LAN is worse. Many inexpensive software virus detector programs are available and certainly worth investigating. The problem with them is that they provide protection only from known past viruses, not ones that have not yet been devised. Most viruses appear through telecommunications, such as e-mail and modems, downloading PC or shareware programs that have not been screened for viruses, and pirated software, although some have also shown up on software from reputable manufacturers.

More serious than viruses is outright data theft or damage. The most widely used computer access security and control technique involves confidential character strings known as *passwords*. A password can be defined as any character or numeric string intended to remain confidential and used to control access by individuals to computer software. Unfortunately, these are frequently stolen and sometimes revealed by carelessness, such as putting a password on scratch paper and then pitching the note in the wastebasket. Sometimes passwords are stolen because they are too "easy" (initials, birth date, phone number, name, spouse's name, etc.). Long, randomly generated passwords are the most difficult to compromise, but are more likely to be written and thus subject to theft. Passwords should be changed frequently. Good password security should provide security by user, application, function within application, and transaction within the application. For example, access to search *Eloquent Librarian* can be by RES (research). A cataloger with rights to add to the database is by ALL. Each cataloger saves data added to the database with his or her own password code. The only person who can actually change the configuration of the database is someone who signs on with SYS and a "silent" password that does not show on the screen. Good password security should also monitor unused or inactive passwords; monitor passwords with excessive usage; produce a terminal activity report which indicates the sign-on and sign-off time, program accessed, and functions performed for each terminal user; produce a security violations report that shows all unauthorized attempts to access the system; randomly generate passwords; encrypt passwords; automatically log off terminals after a predetermined number of invalid access attempts; automatically log off users when their terminals remain inactive for a specified time, to reduce the risk of unattended terminals; inform the user after each log-on of the last successful access by the user and any unsuccessful intervening attempts, which would alert the user to any suspicious events; and provide an audit trail of all current and past passwords.

Another security measure is backup. For hard-disk backup, the most widely used method is quarter-inch cartridge drive and tape. A quarter-inch cartridge system is comprised of a drive unit and one or more removable, portable tape cartridges. The cartridges are loaded with 1,000 feet of 8¼-inch magnetic-coated tape installed either with the computer system hardware, or as a stand-alone, plug-in unit. Data is recorded on 32 tracks along the tape, usually in a serial fashion.

Ergonomics, the science of designing machines, tools, and computers so that people find them easy and healthful to use, cannot be forgotten when planning workstations and purchasing peripherals. In San Francisco there is now a law affecting all businesses with more than 15 employees who spend at least 50 percent of their workday in front of CRT terminals. It requires businesses to:

Provide workers with adjustable chairs, terminals, keyboards, and proper lighting

Provide, upon request, wrist rests, foot rests, and document holders

Provide anti-glare screens

Allow 15-minute paid breaks from continuous CRT work every 2 hours

Provide programs of employee education concerning proper use of the equipment and the health hazards associated with extensive CRT use

Implement these measures (estimated cost of $250 per worker), or face fines of $500 per day.

This legislation is a response to widespread concerns about the health hazards associated with computer-intensive work. These include repetitive stress injuries, stress, eyestrain, musculoskeletal ailments, and conditions related to prolonged radiation exposure. Repetitive strain injuries accounted for 52 percent of all workplace illnesses in 1989. The most common complaints involve the wrist, including carpal tunnel syndrome. A number of factors can influence this, including chair elevation, desk height, and even clothing worn. It is obvious that a good keyboard height for a five foot, six-inch person is too low for a six-footer.

Computers are becoming multifunctional by interfacing with microfilm and optical disks. The computer will rapidly search through the database and display all the entries containing the requested information. If the computer is attached to the CAR or optical disk equipment, the image of the document will automatically appear when it is located by the computer. Both CAR and optical disk systems have online and offline capabilities. In a roll microfilm CAR system, the computer might display the number of the roll of film on which the requested image is located. When that roll is inserted into the CAR equipment, the film fast-forwards to the desired frame.

Many programs have appeared on the scene for records or library data management. A bibliography in this book lists a few. The appearance of so many commercial records management software programs has meant less in-house program design. Commercial data management programs comprise two types: flat file management and relational databases. File managers, the less complex of the two, are also less powerful. They have the ability to manage data without allowing users to establish relationships between fields, the way relational databases can. The simple name list would need only a file manager, but more sophisticated applications require the power of a relational database. An inventory system, for instance, can be linked to a separate order system by related fields, so that the depletion of products triggers the reordering of them. Some of the commercial products available do specific applications (inventory tracking, circulation). Others must be preconfigured for special applications but, once configured, run on menu screens. Someone knowledgeable regarding specific record needs must do the configuring. This person does not have to know how to program but must understand the retrieval needs. Once configured, the programs run on menus, and anyone can add to, search, or delete from the database. Before purchasing any software, define your needs and actually try out several products on the job, that is, put them through their paces according to your needs. Many producers and dealers allow a 30-day trial either free or for a modest fee.

If your records are already machine-readable and you want to change systems or application software, you need to know if the new system can read or translate the old records. If not, you will have to plan a conversion time. This conversion can be done in-house, by the software vendor, or by a service bureau.

If your records are currently not machine-readable, then a retrospective conversion will have to be done. Again, this can be done in-house, by the software vendor, or by a service bureau. The advantages of doing it in-house is that you can ensure that it is being done by your standards. Also, inconsistencies and errors in records can be found and cleaned up as part of the conversion process. Service bureaus can accomplish conversions more quickly and possibly cheaper than in-house.

If something should happen to your computerized records because of power failure, hard-disk drive failure, or even human error, all is not necessarily lost. Good disaster planning calls for backups, and programs are available to help restore erased data. Of course, there will also be a record of your computer software (see figure 11.2).

Software		Release date	date received
Modification no.	date rec'd	updated	comments

Fig. 11.2. Computer software record.

Modern computers can do only what they are programmed to do, but the day of a "thinking computer," like Hal in the movie *2001*, is in the making. Computers with artificial intelligence or neural networks that mimic human brain function are past the design stage. These computers will make decisions on indeterminate inputs and will usher in a new age of computer usage.

FOR FURTHER STUDY

If you have access to a personal computer, write several records management software companies to obtain demonstration disks and literature. In your procedures manual, prepare "Part IX: Computers." Write your observations regarding the software demo disks and make a chart comparing the products. Add this chart to your procedures manual.

12

_____OPTICAL DISKS_____

When most of us think "CD" (compact disk), we think of audio and the recording industry. The technology for creating CDs began to develop back in the 1950s, but it was not until the mid 1980s that the commercial possibilities exploded. CD-ROM (compact disk-read only memory) technology benefited from the acceptance of audio, mass-market CDs, the proliferation of personal computers in businesses, and the need for information providers to find non-paper alternatives to distribute increasingly higher volumes of information. The financial success of audio CDs has acted as a subsidy for funding spin-off technologies.

Some futurists believe that the impact computers have had on our lives will be minimal when compared with the impact of compact disks. They tout optical disks as the replacement of both micrographics and computers in offices.

The creation of optical disks began in the 1950s with a digitizer and a scanner. The first optical character reader was a ball or font and a ribbon with magnetic ink, similar to the device on a typewriter or computer printer that digitizes characters on paper.

Today optical character recognition, or OCR, technology is a data-entry technique whereby letters, numbers, or other symbols are scanned or "read" to produce electronic images on paper. The basic components of an OCR system are a paper mechanism, which feeds the page through a scanning device; a scanning mechanism, which uses a strong light source to scan each character and symbol on the page, converting each image into an electrical signal; and some type of an output logic, which analyzes these electrical signals and converts them into machine-readable form. To perform these functions, the OCR scanner compares black and white patterns on a page to sets of prepro-grammed characters and symbols. Once recognized, these characters or symbols are processed by the computer and recorded on floppy disks or other recording media. Using automatic paper feeders, the scanning operation can be performed almost unattended. A scanner functions as the computer's "eye" to translate images into computer-readable digital code. Simply put, a scanner is a reverse computer printer. It converts printed characters to electrical digital signals.

In the technology's early stage, it was expected that OCR would replace keypunch entry in data processing and word processing. The logic behind using OCRs was, therefore, why retype information into a computer when you can scan it by waving a wand over the paper? What a typist can do in an hour the scanner can do in two-and-a-half minutes. A single sheet of paper can be scanned in 15 to 25 seconds. One minor drawback is that a scanner may make two errors per page—but the average typist will make five.

Magnetic ink character recognition (MICR) is used extensively by banks for inscribing information on checks and deposit slips. Employing specially shaped magnetic ink characters, MICR devices are designed to read, encode, and sort checks into compartments, converting characters into pulses for processing by a computer.

Another common application of OCR technology is the use of different types of bar codes read by bar-code readers. *Bar codes* are the lines (zebra) of variegated length printed on products of every sort to be read by scanning.

Image (or intelligent) character readers (ICR) can recognize and convert handwriting, with limitations. One of the most difficult tasks in ICR is character separation. Until documents are standardized, people are not likely to print clearly and cleanly on documents.

Voice recognition, another offshoot of OCR technology, is a device that accepts human voice input through a microphone, thereby converting analog speech waveforms into digital form. In the process, the computer matches each speech sound against an internal (defined and limited) repertoire of sounds and words. The major inherent technological problem in voice recognition is the infinite variations in the ways people speak and pronounce words, including dialects, accents, and pitch.

After the information has been fed to the computer by the scanner, the computer saves it on a magnetic disk or tape. This disk or tape then becomes the master for reproducing optical disks, called CD-ROMs. Production of the first CD-ROMs through a service bureau cost $50,000 to $100,000. Today, a corporation can install a complete CD-ROM hard drive (see figure 12.1) for

Fig. 12.1. Optical disk hard-disk drive, software, and CD-ROM. Photo courtesy of Pioneer Communications of America, Inc. Optical Memory Systems Division.

$700. This will read a WORM (Write Once Read Many times) commercial disk, such as a 20-volume encyclopedia with over 10,000 pages. The cost for mastering and replicating 100 disks of such an encyclopedia has fallen from $5,000 to $1,500. Also, a hard drive that will let a company produce its own read-only CDs can be purchased for about $8,000 to $12,000. A special authoring software product, for another $300 (up to $50,000!), is needed to work with the drive. A system to make the master will cost from $20,000 to $50,000. Equipment to do the work in-house should pay for itself within two years to be cost-effective. If not, a service bureau should be considered.

What is interesting about WORM disks is that they actually can be erased and reused. In the process, the original information also remains on the disk. The term *write-once* means that once the computer system has written to an individual sector, it cannot then erase and rewrite that sector. Re-edits and file updates are accomplished by writing to additional sectors. To the user, the system appears to function identically to any other DOS mass storage subsystem. When a file is recalled, it can be updated and edited, and when a user deletes a file, it no longer appears in the directory. But the difference between the standard hard-disk storage method and the write-once optical system is that somewhere on the WORM disk, transparent to the user, every version of every file is permanently stored, including files that have been deleted. These files can be accessed only in a read-only mode using unique utilities that provide an audit trail. In other words, each of the previous versions of the file can be read, but not altered. In addition there are EROMs (Erasable Read Only Memory) and rewritable disks that can be wiped clean like a floppy and reused. A single 4¾-inch disk can store approximately 130,000 pages of documents. One 400MB (megabyte) write-once disk costs around $100 and can hold more data than 300 standard floppies. A CD-ROM disk can contain 100 times more information than the typical personal computer database, but the rate at which the drive can get to various locations on the CD-ROM disk is at least 10 times slower than on a magnetic disk. In a large optical disk system, disks are kept in a device called a *jukebox* (see figure 12.2). As a disk is requested by the computer, it is removed from its slot and moved to the location of the disk reader (CD-ROM disk drive). After use, it is returned to its slot. Should the amount of storage exceed the number of slots in the jukebox, the less active disks are stored offline until requested from a workstation by a user. In this type of system, document retrieval would depend on an operator's loading the offline disk while it is being accessed.

Some advantages of CD-ROMs are:

Digital media capable of delivering text, data, graphics, and/or sound

Compatibility with personal computers and local area networks. Information can be exported to other computers and software programs, displayed and printed on a wide range of computer platforms, and shared through drives across local area networks.

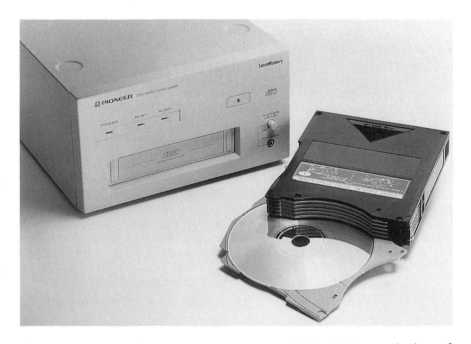

Fig. 12.2. Jukebox minichanger. Photo courtesy of Pioneer Communications of America, Inc. Optical Memory Systems Division.

Very high capacity at a significantly lower cost than other distribution alternatives.

Searching, sorting, and retrieval capability superior to paper, computer output microfiche, microfilm, or online.

Low cost for volume distribution.

Space-saving—rooms of file cabinets can be reduced to feet.

Labor reduction coupled with improved employee morale. The role image of an image processor is higher than that of a file clerk. Productivity will also increase.

If you process at least 5,000 document pages per day, if numerous people per day have to access the same document, if fast retrieval time is important, if departments are separated geographically, and if your competition has moved to image processing, then image technology should be considered.

Some disadvantages of CD-ROMs are:

A mastering step is required to create the master disk and replicas.

The slow speed and large data capacity of optical disks require special software to provide performance competitive with magnetic media.

A special disk drive must be added to the PC.

An indexing system must be devised and applied to the scanner and CD-ROM. Document indexing is a crucial step. Indexes are the key to the retrieval process and an incorrect index can render the scanned document virtually untraceable and unrecoverable. Indexing is the most time-consuming—and therefore expensive—part of document management. Search parameters must be defined. Two-dimensional bar codes that can code both alphabetically and numerically should be considered.

Checking for accuracy is more time-consuming than the actual scan, as is document preparation (removing paper clips, staples). Laser printer paper, because it is whiter, allows the printed image to appear sharper and text more legible, which means it scans better, but relatively few documents are produced on laser printer paper.

Lack of standardization, although this is changing as CD-ROM publishers and hard-disk drive manufacturers adhere to the same specifications.

Legality. Unlike microfilm, electronic images cannot be certified as to authenticity. Information within an erasable optical image, such as text or a signature, can be deleted or modified without a trace. Currently optical disks are not admissible in evidence in most jurisdictions. The National Historic Publications and Records Commission of the U.S. National Archives is studying the use of optical digital imaging for public records.

Unknown lifespan. Micrographics can survive over 100 years. The projected life span of a CD-ROM is 30 years. It is suggested now that they be duplicated every 10 years to avoid deterioration, although an accelerated aging test claims an optical disk will last 700 years.

Cost. Currently, optical disks are 3 to 58 times more expensive than microfilm.

Optical disks have already revolutionized the publishing industry and creation of databases. Full-text documents of materials that were once available only in a bibliographic format with an online search service can now be obtained and updated quarterly at a nominal price.

Three other major users of image processing are the government, the insurance industry, and the financial industry. Optical disks are being used to permanently store city, county, state, and federal records. Since implementing an optical disk system, the Kansas Department of Health and Environment has cut the waiting period of 3 to 5 weeks for a certified copy of a birth certificate to 11 seconds. The new system integrates an IBM mainframe database, NCR microcomputer, and a FileNet image system (consisting of a server, an optical storage unit holding up to 288 12-inch platters of 40,000 certificates each, 2 scanners, 2 laser printers, and 13 imaging workstations). The NCR processes requests for copies and handles the accounting fees.

Insurance companies can store photographs, reports, forms, and documents relating to a claim or client. A single optical disk can store an entire month's bank records for less than half the cost of storing on microfiche. Currently, optical disks and microphotography are seen as dual-storage, stand-alone systems, but more and more they are integrating and becoming multifunctional. (See figure 12.3.) Today, operators at digital workstations are

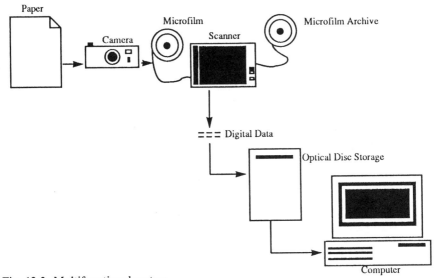

Fig. 12.3. Multifunctional system.

retrieving document images from rolls of microfilm which are then digitized with a built-in film scanner. The digitized micrographic images can be transferred over a network for display on an image-capable workstation. They can be printed on an electronic printer, faxed to a remote location, or transferred to an optical or digital storage medium. It is expected that soon there will be scanners that can capture a film medium and a digital image in a single pass. It is expected, too, that computers will soon be able to output to any medium format. A further integration will occur with broad-band networks, as integrated services digital networks (ISDN) create a digital highway to speed the flow of images. The highest speeds will be reached with fiber optic networks.

The National Association of Government Archives and Records Administrators and the National Archives and Records Administrators recommend:

1. Choose industry standard equipment.

2. Recopy optical disks at least every 10 years, more often if stored in a humid area.

3. High resolution equals high storage. Do not scan at higher resolutions than needed. Reserve high resolutions for highly detailed images like maps and photos.

4. Keep a tight control on who can alter images. Look for systems that allow levels of security and that maintain audit trails.

5. Periodically do a quality control check on your paper documents and scanner. Recalibrate optical drives annually.

6. Maintain original copies of valuable records.

FOR FURTHER STUDY

If you have not used a CD-ROM database, visit your public or local college library. They should have products such as *Info-Trac* for serials searching or *Newsbank*. Add Part X, "Document Imaging," to your procedures manual. If possible, try to watch the product being loaded onto the hard-disk drive. Describe the steps necessary to access the product.

CHAPTER

13

CASE HISTORIES

The following cases present a brief historic overview of indexing, from manual, "first generation" automation to the present. Earlier methods appear laborious and contorted when compared to the ease with which current software programs can perform the tasks. Read these case histories from this viewpoint.

WALKER, MORRIS & WALKER

The following situation encountered by Information Resource Consultants (IRC) is not atypical of small offices. In 10 years Mr. K. L. Walker had become a very successful insurance broker and businessman. He was a salesman par excellence. His secretary was extremely efficient at keeping abreast of daily events, but record keeping had reached a crisis point.

When IRC arrived on request to bring order out of chaos, it was discovered that not only were the filing cabinets overflowing, but boxes of material were stacked in a closet from floor to ceiling—ten years worth of files were everywhere.

The first problem was to identify the kinds of records Mr. Walker had. These grouped into:

- name files
- insurance client folders
- pension client folders
- insurance and pension prospect folders
- product information for each insurance company brokered
- forms for each type of insurance from each of the companies brokered
- professional development material, including expensive subscription series, which had not been updated in years
- correspondence with clients; prospective clients; home offices; legal, church, political, and charitable organizations; and other businesses

- agency files including licenses, expenses, advertising, and professional organizations
- office supply catalogs
- church files (he was an officer in his church)
- political and charitable files (he was an active worker in both fields)
- other businesses he was beginning to invest in, including real estate and automobile leasing
- monthly printouts of sales quotas for each insurance company brokered
- legal contracts for all his various interests
- educational materials for insurance courses he taught at a local college

All this material was literally thrown together, except for his client and prospect files. Still, prospects who became clients were rarely removed from the prospect file.

After the types of material and business interests had been identified, the next step was to find out the frequency of use of material. This was necessary in order to create a floor plan of file location and to estimate the number of additional filing cabinets and inactive storage files that would be needed.

Then came the time to categorize material, and to do this IRC had to learn how the material was asked for. Classification codes and retention schedules for each category of material were developed as was a master procedures manual and index. The final arrangement was not one master filing system but, as is often the case, several filing systems, and typically, a great deal of weeding of material had to be done.

A master index on 3x5-inch cards was created for people, companies, and organizations. An annual chronological file was created for long-term appointments and events. This also included client birthday anniversaries, preceded by a three-month tickler file and a biweekly file of appointments. This was all kept in the secretary's drawer.

Client, pension client, and prospective client files were each made alphabetical and kept separately. Pertinent correspondence was kept in each folder.

The Million Dollar Round Table Information Retrieval (MDRT-IR) System was used for professional development and educational materials, and for Mr. Walker's insurance agency business and the charitable and political organizations in which he was active. One copy of each product line of insurance for each company brokered was kept in the MDRT-IR files. Duplicate copies were used as handouts to prospective clients and were kept in the forms file by number.

A forms file, arranged alphabetically by company brokered and then numerically by form number, was created. Product information, rate books, and company procedures manuals were also kept here.

A personal file was created for Mr. Walker's expenses, monthly sales quotas met, automobile expenses, and real estate ventures.

A separate church file was created temporarily because it was currently a very active file. Later this would be incorporated into his personal file.

Material that was not active but needed to be kept was moved to storage in marked, inactive file boxes.

Material to be disposed was shredded for notepads.

A part-time files technician was hired and trained by the secretary in the systems established. The secretary coded all material and decided retention dates. The file technician filed and retrieved information.

An immediate benefit to Mr. Walker and his secretary was that all of this was accomplished in six weeks' time, because three paraprofessionals came and worked full time on the project, freeing Mr. Walker and his secretary to conduct business as usual except for conferences with IRC and the training required to learn the systems. In reality, Mr. Walker will rarely retrieve from the files himself, but it is important that he understand the concept of the file organization.

Efficient files brought extra productive time to both Mr. Walker and his secretary. More was being accomplished in less time because they knew where to put their hands on required material immediately. The sense of urgency that pervaded the office before was gone.

In a small office it is imperative that only a few people have access to the files; too many fingers spoil the system. As Mr. Walker's firm grows, file access must be limited to Mr. Walker, his secretary, and the files technician. The secretary has remained, but files technicians have come and gone. The secretary believes training time is saved when she requires each new files technician to read the procedures manual through once before doing any filing and to file with the procedures manual for three weeks, or until the systems are mastered.

McDONNELL DOUGLAS AUTOMATION COMPANY (MCAUTO)

The McDonnell Douglas Automation Company (MCAUTO) contacted Information Resource Consultants (IRC) for help in designing a Resource Library Management System involving the control of videocassettes, audiocassettes, manuals, and teaching packets.

MCAUTO Technical Training provides data processing education to personnel in all divisions of the corporation. Some specific courses are also made available to other companies on a course-fee basis.

As a result, every month the company receives sets of videotapes, audiocassettes, and manuals from vendors. Some manuals are theirs to keep, as are some audiocassettes, but others must be returned. The videocassettes are acquired on a rental basis only. In addition, the company owns some videocassette tapes, audiocassettes, and manuals from yet different producers, as well as some books and journals.

Their problems were not knowing

- what tapes and manuals they had;
- who within the company had checked out what, and when;
- when each tape had arrived from the lending companies, and when it was due back;

- which tapes were available by subject and title; or

- how to arrange tapes, manuals, and audiocassettes on the shelves.

As MCAUTO is a computer training center they wanted this information automated with the information printed in book format.

MCAUTO has developed a preprogrammed computer software package called DATA DIALOG®, which is excellent for doing text manipulation. DATA DIALOG can be used with many different terminals and can be connected by telephone lines directly to the central processing unit. Users can also create their own programs with this program product, but for the purposes of establishing the video library this skill was not necessary. All the program and manipulative skills that were required to catalog the collection were already within DATA DIALOG's capabilities. MCAUTO quickly decided to do the indexing/cataloging onto the company's own computers using the DATA DIALOG package. This proved to be very economical as a professional programmer did not have to be called in. Once the worksheet format was established, a technician did the manual input onto paper and then into the computer.

The indexing format devised for the worksheet had to identify specific courses as well as individual videocassettes, audiocassettes, and manuals. Vendors had to be identified, as well as the dates material had been received from the vendors. It also had to be determined whether the material had been returned to the vendors. Subjects had to be assigned to the material and a thesaurus created. It had to be possible to print out all the courses by subject and individual courses by title.

The format devised was very simple. The unique number given to every course by the vendor became the identifying link to the titles, subjects, vendors, and dates.

Below is an explanation from one section of the procedures manual, the worksheet for cataloging/indexing a video set. The information to be placed on the worksheet for videotapes and manuals follows fixed field format. That is, line 1, field 1, always represents the same notation; line 1, field 2, always represents whatever it has been designated to represent. (See figure 13.1.)

In this case line 1, field 1, position 1, is the code area for *title*; the "*" is used for this.

Line 1, field 2, positions 2 through 9, are for the vendor number given to the video course.

Line 1, positions 10 through 15, are for the date acquired from vendor by month, day, year; the Julian date is used for this.

Line 1, position 16, indicates whether the videotape is available. Presence of the "v" means that it is; absence of the "v" means that only the manual is on hand and that the videotape has been returned to the vendor.

Line 1, positions 18 through 126, are for the title. The number of the videotape may be given if only a partial set is in the library.

Line 2 is for vendor information about the material. Positions 2 through 9 are for the vendor number. Positions 18 through 126 are used for the name of the vendor or producer, number of the videocassette or reel, number of the audiocassette, number of the manual, running time if available, and date if applicable.

```
  12345678901234567890123456789012345678901234567890123456789012345678901234567890
1 *vendernodate  v title
2  venderno        vendor/producer no. of video cassettes audio cassettes manuals running time
3  venderno        description
4 $venderno        subject
5 $venderno        subject
6
7

  12345678901234567890123456789012345678901234567890
1 *1401V005061579v programming logic & techniques
2  1401V005        Deltak 5 videocassettes 3 audiocassettes 3 manuals 5 hours
3 $1401V005        FLOWCHARTING
4 $1401V005        ALGEBRA
5
6
7
```

* = title line
$ = subject line

Fig. 13.1. Worksheet for cataloging/indexing a video set.

The number of lines used for each item may vary because each line has the identifying number in positions 2 through 9, which keeps the lines together during sorts.

Line 3 may be used for descriptive notes about the material; if necessary these notes may be continued on other lines. Descriptive information is listed in positions 18 through 126.

The next line is used for subject information. As many lines as desired may be used for this; however, only one subject is printed per line so that subjects may be extracted and sorted alphabetically. Position 1, field 1, is used for the "$" character as this is the character used to extract subject lines for the alphabetical sort. Field 2, positions 2 through 9, are used for the material identification (vendor) number. The subject is entered beginning at position 18. When material is called out and printed by subject, the identifying vendor number, but no additional information, appears. To find a word description of the entire video course one must refer back to the full entry as printed in the book catalog under the vendor name.

DATA DIALOG is preprogrammed to sort alphabetically or numerically. It also allows reformatting of the printout. The typist may not type the information into the storage unit with all capital letters, but if given the command, the computer will print in that fashion. It can also respace all the information.

New material can be added at random. Once a month a new catalog is printed; the commands to extract all titles, videotape listings only, or subject, and to sort numerically or alphabetically, have all been stored on the database. But deletions have to be done line-by-line. Thus, when a videotape has been returned, the complete description of the course must be recalled and the video notation deleted by specific line and field or by a group of lines.

Since the initial printout there has not been an integrated catalog. The latest printout of the currently available material is on top. The older printouts are beneath it, and if one wants to know everything that has ever been ordered, one has to check through all the printouts. However, as there would be little reason to be concerned with materials not on hand, having only available materials in the catalog listing serves the needs of the Technical Training Resource Center for which it was created.

Each printout includes a section by vendor number, title, description, and subjects in numerical order; and one by subjects, with vendor number, in either alphabetical order or numerical order as desired.

The check-out system is still manual at this time. Plans are to have a computerized check-out system sometime in the future. At present, manuals and videotapes are checked out by number and title. The name of the person checking out the material, followed by his or her department, mailing address, phone, and the date borrowed, is recorded. When material is returned, the date returned is added next to the name of the person checking out the material. The check-out sheet looks like the one in figure 13.2.

Videotapes are checked out for one month only. These sheets are kept in a looseleaf binder in numerical order. From looking at the check-out manual one can tell who used what material when, and how often material is being used.

An authority file of 100 words and phrases was created for subjects. This can be increased.

No.			Course title		
Borrower	Dept. Address	Phone	Date Borrowed	Date Due	Date Returned

Fig. 13.2. Check-out sheet.

The cassettes, manuals, and other materials were arranged on the shelves alphabetically by producer. The materials of each producer were then placed in numerical order. Materials are ordered through the librarian who has the resources ready on the date required, or sends them to the borrower when requested.

COMPCARE

Many commercial software programs are available that can be used for document control. Below is a section from the procedures manual for Compcare, a company that uses PFS:FILE software. FILE is an information management program with filing, sorting, and searching capabilities. It was used to create an index of documents and a book catalog of holdings for Compcare. With PFS:FILE software the user designs a form which is then used to record, update, retrieve, and purge information.

A. *Acquisitions*

Each document as it arrives should be marked with the date it is received. This date can be used to search documents by date for weeding.

New documents may be added to the file as they are received. Additions and corrections can be made to the computer file at any time.

Shelf numbers can be assigned to newly received documents from the list of available numbers. Folders bearing these numbers are already prepared. Labels showing the number assigned to each document should be typed and affixed to the document. Available numbers may be found in the back of this manual.

B. *Terms, Including Keys*

1. CTRL = Control Key

CTRL, like "shift," is used in conjunction with other keys. It is used to perform software steps. For example, when you see the following symbol CTRL C it means press CTRL and while holding it down, press C.

2. ESC = Escape

Anytime you press ESC you leave the software operation you are performing and return to the *main menu*. Whenever this menu is displayed, you can perform an operation.

3. RESET

This key should never be pressed while you are using PFS software. If you accidentally press it, the computer will try to reset itself by loading the PFS program from the diskette in drive 1. You will lose the information you are entering.

C. *To Begin*

1. Check that the terminal is turned off.

2. Turn the monitor on first.

3. Insert the PFS program diskette into drive 1.
    a.   To do this, first open the drive door by pulling outward on its bottom edge carefully, keeping your fingers off the disk itself.
    b.   Slip the diskette from its folder into the slot with the label up. The oval cutout in the diskette jacket should enter the drive first. The label itself should enter the drive last. Gently push the diskette until it is entirely inside the drive.
    c.   Close the door by pushing it down.

4.   Turn on the Apple computer. The red in-use light on the disk drive will come on and you will hear the drive as it loads the PFS program from the diskette into the central memory unit of the computer.

When it is finished, the in-use light will go off and the software is now in the memory of the central processing unit (CPU) and ready to use. The PFS menu will appear on the screen.

5.   Gently open the disk drive door and carefully remove the software diskette and put it back into its envelope.

D. *Formatting a Disk — Designing a File*

The CPU, the central memory of the computer, now contains all the information from the PFS software.

The next step is to format a blank disk so it contains that basic memory information in a specific manner useful to the library or document indexing.

All diskettes containing documents classified by state in the library will be called "Library." All diskettes containing unclassified documents will be called "Unclass." These will be their *file names.*

Formatting will be skipped when adding to either file, but every time a new blank disk is used, the following steps must be undertaken:

> When the PFS software has finished loading from the disk drive into the CPU, a *function menu* appears on the CRT screen (monitor).

It looks like this:

PFS FUNCTION MENU

1. Design File	4. Search/Update
2. Add	5. Print
3. Copy	6. Remove

Selection Number:

File Name:

This menu, or index, tells you what operations (functions) the software can perform.

The name of the blank disk you will format will be either "Library" or "Unclass." This will be its file name. (A file name must have eight or fewer characters.)

To keep track of the library as it grows, number the disks needed. The first disk is, of course, "Selection Number" one (1). After keying in the words "Library" and "1" in their appropriate places, press the CTRL C keys to continue. This locks the information onto the software.

The "Design File" function (number 1) provides the tracks upon which information will be stored on the disk in the format desired. When you "design file" you are creating a format (form) that will be used to hold the information from the documents you will be indexing.

The *design file menu* appears after you press the numeral "1." It looks like this:

DESIGN FILE MENU

1. Create File

2. Change Design

Selection Number:

"Create File" allows you to create a blank form for specific needs, in this case, indexing the library materials.

"Change Design" allows you to change the form which was designed in option 1 (Create File).

To create a file, press numeral 1 and the CTRL and C keys.

The screen will look like this:

Put Diskette in Drive 1

WARNING

The Diskette in Drive 1 will
be completely overwritten

(This is to warn you that you will be erasing any disk that you have used for any other purpose. Make certain you have inserted a blank disk, and definitely NOT a disk already formatted for "Library.")

Note: Information in the CPU can only be lost when the power to the terminal is turned off.

Press ESC to abandon this operation

Press CTRL C to continue

Since you want to continue after you key in CTRL C the screen will be blank with a cursor (blinking white square) in the upper left corner.
The bottom of the screen will look like this:

% full

File: Library   Design   Page 1

"% full" = how much available space has been used (not what is left) from the diskette. "Page" = the page number of the form you are on. Documents to which the contents of the article have been added may require more than one page of diskette usage.

A *form* is made up of *items* that are to be filled in. Each item has a name followed by a colon (:). The form for the library file will contain the following items in the following order:

ST: DT: SN:

TITLE:

CONTENTS:

This form is used for both sorting and retrieving information. ST (State) is the first item on the form because it is the item most frequently searched. The computer can go directly to the first item, otherwise it searches the rest of the form sequentially and the search time is longer.
The following keys allow you to move the cursor around the screen:

$$\begin{matrix} & & T \\ \text{CTRL} & & \text{F G} \\ & & V \end{matrix}$$

CTRL F   — moves the cursor left one character

CTRL G   — moves the cursor right one character

CTRL T   — moves the cursor up one line

CTRL V   — moves the cursor down one line

RETURN — moves the cursor to the beginning of the next line

Position the cursor to the left of the screen and type the desired item name, ST: (for "state"); punctuate the end of the item with a colon; type in the next item, DT: (for "date"); and finally, type in SN: (for "shelf number"). Now press RETURN to move to the next item and type TITLE: (skip one line in case the title requires many characters). After each line press RETURN. Type CONTENTS:. This completes the form.

** After the blank form has been created with all the items correctly typed and in their correct order it is important to *store* the form onto the diskette. To do this, press CTRL C. This blank library form is now on the diskette in drive 1.

When you are ready to leave the "Design File" function, press the ESC key. Do not press the ESC key until you have saved the form with CTRL C or you will have lost rather than saved the form.

E. *Storing Information*

Until a disk is full at which point you repeat Step D, you will be inserting the Library disk into drive 1 and moving immediately to Step E, Storing Information. You will store, or index, the information using function number 2 of the main menu (PFS Function Menu) and that is "Add."

When you have the main function menu on the monitor, press number 2 (Add) and CTRL C. The blank form for the library should appear:

ST: DT: SN:

TITLE:

CONTENTS:

Besides the cursor control keys previously mentioned, the arrow keys (◄———) will also move the cursor. The left arrow moves it back one space, and the right arrow (———►) moves it to the next item on the form. You cannot move the cursor into an item name. They are protected from being overwritten.

CTRL N will bring up the next page of a form.

CTRL P will bring back the previous page of the form to the screen.

CTRL E allows you to erase all the information entered on the current form. Information on other pages is unaffected. The item names are not erased, only the added information.

When all the information for the document has been entered on the form, press CTRL C. This form is now stored on the diskette file. A new blank form appears on the screen for the next document. Documents can be entered in any order. The searching function of the software eliminates the need for keeping all states or all subject contents together as they are entered. The program will do all the traditional "hand filing" when it searches. The person inputting information need only be concerned with a proper shelf number for each document and that number should be on the work form. This is not added at the terminal.

After the last document has been indexed into the computer and CTRL C is pressed, press ESC to return to the main menu.

F. *Copy*

Before quitting for the day, or any time you stop entering material into the computer, make a backup disk of that day's work. The third function on the PFS main menu is number 3 "Copy." There are usually three options with the copy function: (1) copy only the blank form (this allows you to continue to add forms on a new diskette when the diskette you are currently using becomes full); (2) select certain forms on a master diskette onto a new data diskette; (3) copy the entire diskette file, including both the blank form and all the filled-in forms (this gives you an exact duplicate of the original diskette). You always want at least one backup disk of the library's holdings. In fact, two backup disks are better. This will ensure that three library disks are always available in the event of a catastrophe (power failure, error in inputting, copying, etc.).

To make a copy when the PFS function menu is on the screen, press function key number 3 (Copy) and CTRL C. The diskette you want to copy *from* should be in drive 1. The diskette you want to copy *to* should be in drive 2.

The copy function menu will appear:

COPY FUNCTION MENU

1.   Copy Design Only

2.   Copy Selected Forms

3.   Copy Whole Diskette

Selection Number: 3

File Name: Library

Options 1 and 3 will destroy all information on the diskette in drive 2. This diskette should either be a blank or one you want to overwrite (erase).

Enter a selection number and new file name. These can be 1-A and LibraryA or an exact duplicate of the disk in drive 1 (1 and Library).

When option 1 or 3 is selected, the following screen appears:

Put File in Drive 1

Put a Diskette in Drive 2

WARNING

The diskette in Drive 2 will
be completely overwritten

Press ESC to abandon this operation

Press CTRL-C to continue

If you decide not to copy the file now, you can press ESC and return to the PFS function menu.

If you pressed CTRL C the copy function begins. When it is complete, the monitor will return to the PFS function menu.

Since there is only one design on the library diskettes, option 2 should not be used.

** Remember to always make two copies of any newly input information before turning off the computer.

Copy function 2 can be used to split and merge files. To do this refer to the PFS Basic Procedures Manual.

H. *Search/Update*

After the indexing of the library documents has been completed, the diskettes will be used primarily to search until it is time to input new documents.

The disk becomes the card catalog, or index, to the library documents. It is also possible to print a catalog from the disk.

With the "Search/Update" function you indicate which forms (documents) you want to see by recalling the blank form from the diskette file and filling it in with information that describes what you want to find. The items you enter onto the blank form are called *retrieve specifications*. These can be:

1. *Full Item Match*

If you are looking for specific information, then type the characters that exactly match the information in the item you want to find. Fastest retrieval is in the first item, ST. If the name of the state is typed, the items will be found within seconds and called to the screen one by one.

Abbreviations are not used because of possible user unfamiliarity with terms.

In searching for items, the spaces before the first character and after the last character are ignored. Multiple spaces within the items are treated as a single space. Thus the machine can find:

...hospital

hospital...

...hospital...

For example, if a document containing information on adolescent alcoholism is desired, press 4 ("Search/Update") from the PFS menu. A blank form from the diskette file will appear. Since the state, date, shelf number and title are unknown, leave those areas blank, move the cursor to the contents area, and type in ...adolescent alcoholism.... The machine will search its file until it finds a document containing the subject "adolescent alcoholism." When the file or files are found, each form will be displayed on the screen.

2. *Partial Item Search*

Usually searching can be done completely by following 1, a full item match, but if a more sophisticated search is desired, use a partial item search strategy.

If a document contains several pieces of information, you can isolate those portions that interest you. The retrieval specifications consist of the character you are interested in preceded and/or followed by a special symbol ... This symbol ("...") means to ignore unwanted characters. The software takes the characters preceding and/or following the symbol (...) and tries to find an occurrence of them anywhere within the item. For example, if you are searching for everything relating to "alcoholism," by typing "...alcohol..." you will retrieve: alcohol, alcoholics, alcoholism.

The PFS software will also do a "Boolean" search using "and/or/not" which means you can enter as many retrieval item specifications as you want and the computer will search for and match only those that meet all retrieval specifications. For example, you can search the title items for "drug abuse *and* alcohol." You could search the contents area for "drug abuse *not* alcohol." You can search both the title area and the contents area. You could limit your search to only certain years, or years not before or not after....

Symbols used for these specialized searches are:

@   means "at sign" and will match any single character except a blank space in the "@" position (it will thus match the following: "@orn" will produce a match for "born" and "corn").

/   is used to produce a "not" search; it reverses the sense of the retrieval specification (/B will find all items not beginning with a "B") /...er will find all items that do not end in "er."

=   means "equal" and can be used for a numeric range search (=6...9 means to find all values between the range of 6 and 9 inclusive).

/ =   means "not equal."

X number = numeric item match—less than

X number = numeric item match—greater than

characters = full item match

...characters = partial item match—ignore beginning

...characters... = ignore both beginning and ending, search for these anywhere they appear in a word.

As each document meeting the specification(s) is found, it is displayed on the screen. You can review it, make changes to it, print it, or remove it from the file. When you have finished viewing this document's index on the monitor, press CTRL C to call up the next one that meets the exact specifications being searched.

To select the "Search" function from the PFS function menu, press option 4 and CTRL C. The blank form for the library indexing should appear on the screen:

ST: DT: SN:

TITLE:

CONTENTS:

To search for a specific document or all documents meeting the required specifications, fill in the item area with the desired retrieval specifications.

For example, to search for all the items relating to the state of Alabama, after ST: type Alabama and all the appropriate documents will be found.

If a document deals with a region rather than a state, but the states in that region appear in the title, next to TITLE type ...Alabama... and the title area will be searched.

In this same way the contents area can be searched for specific words. To search for anything relating to "alcohol," type ...alcohol... to retrieve all possibilities.

If you want to research the topic "death since 1985," search the title area for ... death..., search date area = 1985...1989; and search contents area for ...death.... If the computer throws out everything that does not match "death" in both title area and contents area, then search each item separately.

Refer to the PFS:FILE procedures manual for further Boolean searching.

When all retrieved specifications have been typed in, press CTRL C to begin the search function. While the software is searching for the desired document, the screen is blank except for the message area at the bottom. When a document is found, it is displayed on the screen.

To browse through the document (form) appearing on the screen, use CTRL N (and CTRL P for multiple pages) to move through the document and the terms that you have indexed in the CONTENTS area. When finished, press CTRL C to return to the beginning of the document. When finished, press CTRL C and the software will continue its search for the next document.

If you want to make any changes to the information stored on the form, position the cursor to the item you want to change and enter the new information. When finished, press CTRL C to store this changed or updated information onto the diskette and to continue the search.

You can output the found document to the printer by pressing CTRL O or you can print out only the shelf number for the desired document.

You can also remove this document from the file by pressing CTRL R.

After the last document that meets the search specifications has been reviewed, the following message appears on the monitor:

Forms Found: (#)

CTRL C to continue

Pressing CTRL C returns you to the PFS function menu. If at any time you want to abort the search (you have found the exact, or sufficient number of documents), press ESC to return to the main menu.

I. *Print*

Quarterly, or whenever a large number of documents have been added or removed from the index, a catalog should be printed. As many copies as desired can be produced. And the catalog can be printed in any sorted order (state, title, search words, etc.). It is also possible when doing a machine search to print out only specific documents found, or even only shelf numbers. The print format can also be custom designed or left in a preprogrammed format.

To use the "Print" option, from the PFS function menu, press number 5 ("Print") and CTRL C. The print menu will appear:

PRINT MENU

1. Print Forms
2. Define Print Specifications

Selection Number: 5

"Print Forms" allows you to select documents, indicate the way they are to be printed, and print them.

"Define Print Specifications" allows you to define and name sets of print specifications and use these at future printings.

If "Print Forms" is selected (1), a blank form from the Library file will appear on the screen:

ST: DT: SN:

TITLE:

CONTENTS:

If no print specifications are entered, the entire form is printed.

If you want only certain items printed, use one or more of the following characters by the items you want printed:

X = print this item, then advance the printer to the next line

+ = print this item, but do not advance to the next line—skip two spaces instead (this allows you to print more than one item per line).

S = sort the printout based on this item. An S does not automatically cause that item to be printed, you have to use SX or S+ to sort *and* print.

T = treat this item as text. The item is printed eighty columns wide with word wrap at the end of each line (sixty-six-line page). Again, an X or + must be used with the T to treat text *and* print.

A TX next to the contents area should be used for the printed book catalog.

Items are printed in the order in which they appear on the screen. If the shelf number is the only item desired, put an X next to just that item.

When all the print specifications have been entered, press CTRL C.

NOTE: If nothing happens here, check to make sure the printer has been turned on and the paper is properly loaded.

After the last form has been printed, the following message appears:

Forms printed: (#)

Press CTRL C to continue

Pressing CTRL C returns you to the PFS function menu.

If you want to stop printing at any time, press ESC. The form currently being executed will be completed and the printing option will end.

If you want to predefine the print specifications, see the PFS:FILE procedures manual.

J. *Removing Unwanted Documents—Weeding*

When documents have become obsolete, you can erase them from the diskette using option 6 ("Remove") from the PFS function menu.

Before automatically removing any documents, it is recommended you first do a "Search/Update" to put the appropriate documents onto the screen for double checking before they are eliminated from memory, or to work from a printed book catalog.

Return to the main menu with ESC. Use option 6 ("Remove") to call a blank form to the screen and, using the book catalog for a guide, fill in the items with the necessary information. Press CTRL C. The screen will show:

Selected Forms About to Be Removed

Press ESC to abandon this operation

Press CTRL C to continue

After CTRL C is pressed, the screen shows:

Forms Removed: 1

CTRL C to continue

Pressing CTRL C returns you to the PFS function menu where you can continue using option 6 ("Remove") to weed from memory all outdated material.

This material should also be removed from the shelves. The shelf numbers can now be reused next time you are inputting new documents into the files.

JGA, INC.

JGA, Inc., a small process engineering firm, uses WordStar (Micro-Pro) word processing software for organizing its journal collection.

The company subscribes to, or receives as part of its membership dues, numerous technical journals. Many of these journals are never indexed in professional indexing services.

The titles to the articles in the journal are so descriptive that a very simple file has been created using WordStar word processing software. There are many ways to use word processing software for tracking journals or for other forms of record keeping. The method employed by JGA is a very basic, simple one. The method described here presumes the file "Journal" has already been properly established, or opened, on a formatted disk.

WordStar has been permanently installed on the hard-disk drive to an IBM-PC microcomputer. After the computer has been turned on and DOS has "booted" (started) the system, type "ws" at the C>drive command and insert the data disk "journal" in drive A.

After WordStar loads into the CPU memory, the opening menu appears on the screen:

D	open a document	L	change logged drive/directory
N	open a nondocument	C	protect a file
P	print a file	E	rename a file
M	merge print a file	O	copy a file
I	index a document	Y	delete a file
T	table of contents	F	turn directory off
X	exit WordStar	ESC	shorthand
J	help	R	run a DOS command

Press D to open a document. When the screen prompts "document to open?" meaning type in a document name, type "journal."

For JGA, Inc. each article from the various journals is entered sequentially onto this form, which is typed each time:

Title:

Author:

Journal:

Date/pages:

The form could be saved and recalled, but the typist has found it quicker to reenter the headings with each article. Some examples are:

Title: Flocculation—excerpts from a symposium
Author: S. Lee Shipton
Journal: Mining Engineering
Date/pages: May 1987, 356-357

Title: Polymer Processing: an overview
Author: C. G. Gogos
Journal: Chemical Engineering Process
Date/pages: June 1987, 33-79

Title: Alternate Scrap Metal Technologies
Author: R. J. Freehan
Journal: Iron & Steelmaker
Date/pages: June 1987, 15-20

At the completion of entering the articles, the typist types CTRL KD to save the information onto the data disk.

The typist can print the titles entered for the day to distribute to the engineers by typing "P" after the main menu reappears.

The data disk "journal" becomes the index to the company's periodical holdings. If someone wants to search for a particular topic, the same steps are followed as for entering the journal titles, that is, D is pressed from the opening menu to open a document. The document "journal" is named. The contents of the disk are then loaded automatically into the CPU memory. The search command CTRL QF is used for finding a specific topic. After CTRL QF is pressed, the screen asks for the string of letters to find. The user has the option of searching for whole words only or truncated words, or the word within a word, and to ignore upper and lower case characters, and the choice of searching from the beginning or end of the document or globally throughout. To find all the articles that deal with flocculation, type that word when the screen asks for the string of letters you are searching for. The cursor will then search page by page and stop at the first occurrence of the word. The user then needs to use CTRL W to open the screen for the full entry to find the journal, date, and page numbers. The program is designed to now replace that word with another if so desired, but you do not want to do that; instead, use CTRL L to move the cursor to the next occurrence of the word "flocculation." Continue using CTRL L until the disk has been searched for all articles dealing with that topic.

Using WordStar as the catalog for the journal holdings has been a time-saver over typing and filing 3-x-5-inch cards. Frequently the entire contents of a journal are entered on the disk.

GEOTECHNOLOGY, INC.

Because Geotechnology, Inc., did not have any record when the author was contacted to set up an information center for them, she inquired whether they would consider an automated record. This appealed to them and she left several demo products for them to evaluate. They selected *Eloquent Librarian* (Eloquent Systems, Inc., North Vancouver, British Columbia) as one they would like to examine further. The product itself was obtained for a 30-day preview. The person doing the evaluating was accustomed to working with a dBASE product with fixed fields. The fact that *Eloquent Librarian* could be customized and that no field was limited in length was the selling point for the product. The author was brought in to do a quick catalog of materials, with in-house staff planning on doing the upkeep.

The product is MARC compatible, but because relatively few of the company's items were on a MARC database, that module interface was not purchased. Everything was entered as original cataloging. The classification scheme chosen was one developed in-house, based on Geodex subject headings and expanded in-house into the environmental area. The cataloging module purchased creates both an online catalog and a Boolean searching OPAC (online public-access catalog).

Once the template and method of examining material are explained, one does not have to be a professional librarian or records manager to index the materials to the database.

Because newer trade books have CIP (cataloging in publication) data, this was used to explain parts of the template. For older materials, or material lacking CIP data, information appearing on the template which cannot be found (ISBN, LC card number, etc.) can be defaulted away with "return." Below is an example of the template using CIP material.

01 (field) KEY: 200 [This is the computer's identifying number, similar to an accession number.]
02 TITLE: Worker protection during hazardous waste remediation
03 VARIANT TITLE: [not used, so defaulted away]
04 01) Edition   2nd ed.
    02) Place   New York
    03) Publisher   Van Nostrand Reinhold
    04) Collation   xxi, 391 p. : ill. ; 24 cm.
    05) General note   includes index
    06) Supplementary notes
    07) Responsibility Lori P. Andrews [can also be an association, conference, etc.]
    08) Main entry   (if printing cards)
05 SUMMARY: 01) necessary steps to take to prevent accidents and what to do if one occurs. [This field can be as long as necessary and can provide an in-depth look at the chapters.]
06 01) Call number   705 [Geotechnology's call number based on the classification scheme devised by them]
    02) Publ. date   1990
    03) Series # [defaulted away if there is none]
    04) ISBN 05900747/5X
    05) Dewey call number   363.72
    06) Library of Congress call number QH701.4
    07) Library of Congress card order number 90-45321
    08) Price $39.95
    09) New copies 1
07 USER CODES
    01) GMD (general media designation) — The default is "book," but it is also programmed to automatically accept other media such as audiocassettes, maps, periodicals, slides, videocassettes. Any may be modified to accept whatever designated
    02) LOC (location) — The default is "library," but the program can also catalog books in departments
    03) OWNER [program was modified to accept this, as some of the material is personally, rather than corporately, owned]
08 AUTHORITIES
    01) Author   Andrews, Lori P.
    02) Subject   Hazardous waste sites — Safety measures
    03) Subject   Industrial safety
    04) Subject Soil remediation [The number of added entries is unlimited. Most material was key-word indexed in depth as well as by accepting CIP information.]

An unlimited number of subjects or searchable key words can be inputted, which means the contents of a work can be closely indexed. The program does not care whether LC subjects, Sears subjects, or in-house subjects are inputted. (The program will print catalog cards, bibliographies, or reports. Because one can mix subjects, a purist might complain about the resulting format of the printed card that can be produced. For most special information centers, however, this is a plus, not a minus.)

At the end of the template an opportunity to correct any errors made is given. If no changes are desired, pressing "return" places the entry on the database. Backups can be made on floppy disks or tape. In Geotechnology's case, because the program had been put on a network, a tape backup is automatically made by the network and stored offsite each night.

One of the nice indexing features for a specialized information center is that for material in sets or for very similar material, a record can be recalled, given a new identifying number (key number), appropriate changes made, and the new record saved without having to rekey material or change all the template.

Customized features are easily made in a basic, "canned" program. This is so easy one does not have to know programming. Some of the customization added for Geotechnology were "journals," "maps," and "reports" to the General Media Designation (books, videocassettes, film strips, etc. were already there). "Location" and "owner" were added because some of the material indexed is not company-owned but individually owned; if someone were to leave the company, they could obtain a printout of their personal material. Also, not all of the material is housed in the library. Some of it is in departments or individual offices.

The program creates its own authority file by which indexing terms are established. Some examples based on the Geodex subjects are "Pile design," "Pile vibration damage," "Pile installation," "Pile lateral resistance." "See" and "see also" references can also be created from this authority file. Thus, "vibration" would also cross-reference automatically to "pile vibration damage." Searching "OSHA" also searches "Occupational Safety and Health Association."

Since the program was placed on a network, the information center's holdings can be searched from any office with a PC. "Library" is selected from the network menu and the user then signs on to the program with "RES" (research). A cataloger can add to or change a record by signing on with "ALL." Only someone signing on as "SYS" (system) and a private password can customize or change the basic program.

Search category options include:

1. Word(s) in title

2. Word(s) in a heading (subject, author, series)

3. Restrictors (type of material—GMD)

4. Word(s) found in Contents Note or Summary

5.   Unique record number (key)

6.   Numbers (call #, date, ISBN, etc.)

7.   Modification date

8.   Operator

9.   Key word

10.   Saved results as a parameter

11.   Saved search as a parameter.

Because the program will search any part of the record (notes, content description, and subjects as well as author and title), the employees generally search by key word, not author, title, or subject. Key words can be linked Booleanly. Searching by key word can be seconds slower but not annoyingly. If the hit rate is too high, it can be narrowed further by linking more words.

Keyword: Groundwater

1)   144   titles

Key word: groundwater seepage (the space means "and")

1)   38   titles

Once an appropriate number of holdings emerge, pressing "return" brings a screen showing call number and brief title.

Browse screen   Selection

1)   80   Groundwater and soil dynamics
2)   80   Sand seepage and groundwater control
3)   80   Groundwater conditions, St. Louis County

Moving the cursor and pressing return will then bring up the full cataloging information if anyone wants to see it.

277.   Groundwater conditions, St. Louis County
Call number 80
Author   Kulhawy, Fred H.
Edition   3rd
Publ. date   1989
Place   Rolla
Publisher   Missouri Department of Natural Resources
Collation   x, 473 p. : ill. ; 20 cm.
General Note   includes index
Subject   Groundwater

Subject   Seepage
Subject   St. Louis County
New Copies   1
Last Updated   27 Aug 1990
Last Updated By   System Operator

One can also have a printout arranged by author, call number, subject, title, etc., in any format desired (bibliography, column, etc.).

A detailed procedures manual comes with the software, but brief "crib sheets" were developed for the cataloger and another for the employees. Separate training sessions were held for the staff on using the database and for the person who would be updating the database.

More and more programs similar to *Eloquent Librarian* and its corollary product, *Gencat* (a broader records management program that must be configured before use) are appearing. These third-generation programs are very good and deciding which one to use requires careful evaluation. Many producers will send the actual program for an on-site trial. This is preferable to using demos, which only illustrate the product or provide for creating a minimal database.

GLOSSARY

Other terms not listed in this glossary are printed in italics and defined in the text.

Accession. Listing records as they are received.

Accession book. A manual in which documents are listed as they are received; provides the next available number for a numerical system of filing. Sometimes it is referred to as a register book.

Active records. Records that are referred to more than once per section per month.

Alphabetical filing. Arrangement of records according to initial character from A to Z.

Alphanumeric filing system. Arrangement of records by a method combining alphabetical arrangement and a numerical arrangement or a system of symbols.

Aperture card. Paper card the size of an IBM punch card (Hollerith card) with a rectangular opening that holds a 35mm frame of microfilm. Retrieval information can be punched into the card.

Archives. (1) A place where vital or essential records are kept. (2) Vital or essential records, themselves, deemed important enough to be kept permanently.

Archivist. The person responsible for determining the importance of keeping particular documents.

ASCII. American Standard Code for Information Interchange. Pronounced AS-kee. The most popular coding method used by personal computers for converting letters, numbers, punctuation, and control codes into digital form.

Audit trail. Record of activity that has occurred in a certain file.

Authorization code. An identifying code, a password, that allows a user access to a system. Used mainly for privacy and security.

Autochanger. See Jukebox.

Backup. As a noun, a duplicate copy of data placed in a separate, safe place — electronic storage, on a tape, on a disk, in a vault — to guard against total loss in the event the original data becomes inaccessible. Contrast with *archive*, which is a filed-away record of data meant to be kept for a long time. As a verb, to "back up" means to physically make the copy. Backups should be made frequently. Their usefulness is over when a more recent backup is made.

Bad sector. Defective areas on a floppy disk or hard disk.

Bar coding. A system of portraying data in a series of machine-readable lines of varying widths.

Batch processing. Conducting a group of computer tasks at one time, instead of steadily throughout the day.

Beam recording. Using an electron or laser beam to record directly onto film.

Bill of lading. A document issued by a carrier to a shipper acknowledging receipt of goods and agreeing to transport them under the conditions stipulated.

Black line. A positive image — black on a clear or white background. Opposite of *white line*, also known as a negative image.

Blip. A mark placed on a microfilm for counting or timing purposes.

CAR. See Computer-assisted retrieval.

Card file. A cabinet designed to hold cards of a uniform size. Cabinets exist for 3 x 5-, 4 x 6-, 5 x 8-inch cards.

Central files/records. One copy of all organizational records maintained and supervised in one records center.

Charge-out. Lending records from a file.

Charge-out form. A record describing the material being checked out and identifying the person taking the material and the date by which it is to be returned.

Chronological filing. Material filed by time period usually for follow-up purposes. It is often called a *tickler file*.

Circulation. The act of issuing, or charging out, materials.

Classification scheme. A logical, systematic arrangement of material usually involving a set of symbols, numbers, or letters.

Code. A system of symbols used to represent words or concepts.

COM. Computer Output Microfilm. The transference of the information stored and retrieved in the computer onto microfilm.

Compact disk (CD). A medium for storage of digital data in machine-readable form, accessible with a laser-based reader. CDs are 4¾ inches in diameter. Compact disks are faster and more accurate than magnetic tape for data storage.

Computer-assisted retrieval. Computer systems that locate or identify data stored on microfilm or paper. CAR systems rely on indexing and cross-indexing, preassigned to the documents, to find all documents related to the CAR search attributes. CAR does key-word or Boolean search or both.

Correspondence. Communication by letter.

Cross-reference. An entry in a file which directs the user from one term or name to another.

Cut. The tabs on guides and folders said to be cut according to the width of the tabs. A tab that is one-third the width of a folder is known as one-third cut. Five one-fifth cut tabs in staggered positions would completely fill the space across the top of the folder.

Database. Data that have been organized and structured in a disciplined fashion, so that access to information is as quick as possible.

Decentralized files. Records kept with the departments responsible for them rather than in one central place.

Decimal filing system. A system of classifying records by subject developed in units of ten and coded for arrangement in numerical order.

Descriptor. The key word, code, or phrase that an automated document retrieval system uses to identify and locate a document.

Desktop publishing. Term applied to the creation of printed documents using a personal computer. The documents may be printed directly from the desktop publishing application software with a desktop laser printer.

Discharge procedure. The act of cancelling the record of material on loan to show it has been returned.

Disk. (Also sometimes *disc*.) A digital storage medium. Frequently used to describe magnetic floppies for a computer or optical storage.

Document. Recorded information in any format.

DOS. Disk operating system. The basic command system for personal computers.

Electronic publishing. Refers to electronically preparing documents that are read by electronic means.

Essential record. Important records generally kept for a long period of time, or permanently, in inactive files.

Faceted classification. Subject classification.

Facsimile (Fax). See Telecopier.

Fiberboard. The heaviest paper product, because it contains the most wood pulp.

Fiche. See Microfiche.

Filing. The actual placement of material into a container in a predetermined order.

Filing caption. The file designation as it appears on the tab of the file folder or guide.

Filing rules. A code for arranging entries into a file.

Filing system. Planned method of indexing and arranging records so they can be found quickly when needed.

Floppy disk. A thin sheet of plastic impregnated with ferrite, which when magnetized is a means of storing words and numbers.

Folder. A container in which papers or materials are kept in a filing unit.

Form. Paper with preprinted constant information and space to record variable data.

Geographical filing system. Arrangement of material by location subarranged by alphabet or number.

Guide card. A heavy card with a projecting tab used to subdivide the contents of a file and to speed the filing and retrieval of material.

Guide file. A file folder with a projecting tab used to indicate the arrangement in a filing cabinet and to facilitate filing and retrieving material.

Hanging files. Files suspended from a metal rod.

Hard disk. Also called *fixed disk*. Installed in a computer and not meant to be removed.

Imaging. Recording "human-readable" images—pictures, images, motion, text, etc.—into "machine readable" formats—microfilm, computer data, videotape, OCR output, ASCII code, etc.

Index. An organized list of terms and names which refers to the locations of records.

Indexing. The act of selecting filing method for a record.

Invoice. An itemized list of goods sent by the seller to the buyer stating their prices and the quantities sold.

Japanese tissue. A very fine paper with high fiber content which binds torn sections of paper together. It is not necessarily made in Japan.

Key word. The word conveying the significant meaning of a document or phrase. The word indicates a subject and is frequently used for indexing.

Kraft paper. Brown paper stock containing very long and tough fibers that make it a strong paper.

Label. The identifying tag on a folder or box which identifies the contents.

LAN. Local area network. High-speed transmission over cables that connect terminals, personal computers, mainframe computers, and peripherals together at distances of about one mile or less. A WAN (wide area network) covers a greater distance.

Laser disk. An optical disk with the same technology as a compact disk, except laser disks are 12 inches in diameter.

Lateral filing cabinet. A cabinet equipped with two rails that move the file folders laterally to the front making all the contents immediately accessible. Filing capacity is greater than that of a vertical cabinet. The cabinets can have doors to keep out dust and provide security.

Letter-by-letter filing. Arranging records according to the letters irrespective of their division into words.

Library of Congress classification. The alphanumeric method of arranging subjects used by the Library of Congress and other libraries following that scheme.

Machine readable. Data in a format (such as ASCII) or on a medium (such as disks, tapes, optical disks, or punched cards) that a computer can understand.

Magnetic tape. Storage medium that uses a thin plastic ribbon coated with iron oxide compound to record data with electrical pulses. Magnetic tape is a sequential storage medium—the next bit of data is recorded after the last bit. To locate a specific bit of data, you have to search through the whole tape until you find it.

Manila. Paper stock made from bleached kraft paper frequently used for folders and envelopes.

Mark. Same as a *blip*. Small character printed or notched on microfilm for timing or counting purposes. On an optical disk, it may be a pit, hole, bubble, or light-reflective area.

Mechanized files. Motorized equipment used to house files and to bring them to the operator.

Menu. A displayed set of options on a computer screen for the user of a software program.

Microcard. An opaque or transparent 3x5- or 4x6-inch card containing miniaturized pages requiring an optical aid to read. The film is in the form of a continuous strip.

Microfiche. A 4x6-inch, transparent negative sheet of film containing miniaturized papers requiring an optical aid to read. Each miniaturized page can be reproduced and enlarged as a positive image.

Microfilm. Eight, sixteen, or thirty-five millimeter transparent negative film containing miniaturized pages requiring an optical aid to read. The film is in the form of a continuous strip.

Middle digit filing. A numerical method of filing whereby a string of numbers is broken into three sets and primary filing is by the middle group of numbers.

Modem. Short for modulator-demodulator. Device that allows digital signals to be transmitted and received over telephone lines.

Numerical filing arrangement. A predetermined, systematic method of filing by numbers.

OCR. Optical character recognition or reader. The ability of a scanner with the proper software to capture, recognize, and translate printed alphanumeric characters into machine-readable text.

Open-shelf filing. Files not contained in a box filing cabinet but on shelves with guide captions on the sides rather than on the tops of the folders.

Optical disks. A direct access storage device that is written and read by laser light. Certain optical disks are considered Write Once Read Many (WORM) because data are permanently engraved in the disk's surface either by gouging pits or by causing the nonimage area to bubble, reflecting light away from the reading head. Compact disks (CDs) and laser (or video) disks are optical disks.

Out folder. A form on a folder on which is recorded the loan of file material. It is substituted for the material borrowed and is large enough to project above the folders, indicating material is on loan.

Out guide. A form on a card on which the loan of material from a file is recorded. It is substituted for the material borrowed and is large enough to project above the folders, indicating material is on loan.

Phonetic filing. Filing by the sound of terms or names rather than by how they are spelled.

Policy statement. The purposes for which a procedures manual or a department has been established; a record of a particular filing procedure or decision.

Posted record. A form for material which is continually being added to rather than a form completed and filed permanently.

Procedures manual. An instruction book detailing objectives, processing steps, forms, and schedules for records management.

RAM. Random access memory. The primary memory in a computer, which can be overwritten with new information. "Random access" comes from the fact that all information in RAM can be located, no matter where it is, in an equal amount of time. This means that access to and from RAM memory is extraordinarily fast, as contrasted with magnetic tape which is seqential.

Reader. A device that uses a rearview projector technique to project a readable image of a microcopy onto a screen. Also called a *viewer.*

Record. Information in any format (paper, computer tape/disk, microfilm, CD, realia) which has been generated or received by someone and deemed important enough to be saved for a specified time period.

Record center. See Central files/records.

Record transfer. The process of moving records that are no longer useful from active to inactive files.

Records management. The systematic program for the organization, maintenance, use, retrieval, and disposition of information.

Register book. See Accession book.

Requestor slip. A form, or card, distributed to users to request information.

Retention schedule. A listing of the time period records must be kept before being transferred from one location to another or discarded.

Retrieval. The act of finding material after it has been filed.

Rotary camera. A microform camera system in which documents are recorded "on the fly"; that is, the documents are fed and the film is advanced simultaneously by synchronized transport systems.

Rotary card file. A wheel-like container in which cards are placed on their edges. The container revolves to bring the desired cards to the top; the cards are prevented from falling out by a fixed retaining implement.

Scanner. A device that optically senses a human-readable image and contains software to convert the image to machine-readable code.

Scope of coverage. A statement in a procedures manual giving the range of information covered.

Search. Seeking requested information in storage.

Serial subscription service. A publication issued in parts which is purchased on an annual basis.

Server. A computer that is dedicated to one task.

Sorter. A device that holds material in a partial breakdown according to a systematic plan.

Sorting. The separation of records into filing groups according to a systematic plan.

Storage files. Fiberboard file cartons made to hold rarely used materials. They can be stacked from ceiling to floor and when packed full are fireproof.

Subject filing. A facted classification scheme in which information is grouped by conceptual categories.

Subject numeric filing. Classification of records by subject, employing a numeric arrangement at the same time.

Suspended folders. Hanging folders. The folders hang from support brackets made from a framework of rigid bars.

Tab. The portion of guide or of a folder that extends above the rest of the folder. It may be in any one of a number of positions from left to right across the top. Each of the positions is considered a tab cut.

Telecopier. A machine that transmits a printed copy of words, numbers, and pictures over a telephone wire. Also called a facsimile (fax) machine.

Telex. A machine that transmits a printed copy of words and numbers over a telephone wire.

Terminal digit filing. A numerical method of filing whereby a string of numbers is broken into three sets and primary filing is by the final set of digits.

Text management. All the techniques and technologies involved in creating, storing, and retrieving text files in an organized and logical manner.

Thesaurus. A dictionary with words grouped as descriptors for subjects in a file, indicating synonyms or near synonyms.

Tickler file. See Chronological filing.

Transfer. Systematic removal of materials from one file to another file.

Unit. A number or word, or a set of words or numbers, by which filing order is determined.

Updating service. A publication issued in parts which is kept current by new or replacement pages.

Useful records. Records that would help prevent confusion after a disaster but that are not essential for reconstruction of business. They are eventually moved from inactive storage to disposal.

Vertical filing cabinet. A cabinet of two, three, or four drawers that move on rollers to the front; each drawer is large enough to take file folders resting on their edges or spines.

Viewer. See Reader.

Visible file. Arrangement of information so that the index to the information is available without thumbing through a file. Frequently used for posted record cards.

Vital record. A record essential for the reconstruction of an organization after a catastrophe. It is kept permanently in a safeguarded location.

Wand. A hand-held scanner used for OCR or for reading bar codes.

Weeding. The process of discarding, destroying, or removing to another location unnecessary material from a file.

Word-by-word filing. A system of arranging items in order first by the first word, then by the subsequent word.

BIBLIOGRAPHY

These works were in print at the time of publication. They are not meant to be exhaustive but rather illustrative of materials available. _Books in Print_ can be used to find other works. Many of the works available, though, are from professional associations, rather than trade publishers, and thus will not always be found in _Books in Print_.

Andover, James. _How to Set Up an Effective Filing System_. Columbia, Md.: National Association of Credit Managers, 1981.

Association for Records Managers and Administrators. _Active Filing for Paper Records_. Prairie Village, Kan.: ARMA, 1989. Includes slides.

_____. _Alphabetic Filing Rules_. Prairie Village, Kan.: ARMA, 1986.

_____. _Disaster Prevention and Recovery: A Planned Approach_. Prairie Village, Kan.: ARMA, 1988.

_____. _Filing and Records Management Fundamentals for Small Businesses_. Prairie Village, Kan.: ARMA, 1987.

_____. _Filing Procedures Guidelines_. Prairie Village, Kan.: ARMA, 1989.

_____. _Guide to the Management of Legal Records_. Prairie Village, Kan.: ARMA, 1987.

_____. _Guideline for Subject Filing_. Prairie Village, Kan.: ARMA, 1988.

_____. _Guidelines to Developing and Operating a Records Retention Program_. Prairie Village, Kan.: ARMA, 1986.

_____. _Handbook for Recovery of Water Damaged Business Records_. Prairie Village, Kan.: ARMA, 1986.

_____. _Numeric Filing Guide_. Prairie Village, Kan.: ARMA, 1989.

_____. *Optical Disk Systems for Records Management*. Prairie Village, Kan.: ARMA, 1988. Includes slides.

_____. *Overview of Records and Information Management*. Prairie Village, Kan.: ARMA, 1985. Includes slides.

Barber, Donald T., and Mark Langemo. *Filing Dynamics: Development in Color Coding for Filing Systems*. Emeryville, Cal.: Marsdale, 1987.

Barton, John P., and Johanna G. Wellheiser, eds. *An Ounce of Prevention: A Handbook on Disaster Contingency Planning for Archives, Libraries and Record Centres*. Toronto: Toronto Area Archivists Group Education Foundation, 1985.

Burwasser, Suzanne M. *File Management Handbook for Managers and Librarians*. Felton, Cal.: Pacific Information, 1986.

Clark, Jesse L. *The Encyclopedia of Records Retention*. Northfield, Ill.: Records Management Group.

Claybrook, Billy D. *File Management Techniques*. Melbourne, Fla.: Krieger, 1983 reprint.

Cunningham, Margaret. *File Structure and Design*. Melbourne, Fla.: Krieger, 1986.

Diaman, Susan. *Records Management*. Watertown, Mass.: AMACON, 1983.

DiLauro, Anne. *Manual for Preparing Records in Microcomputer Based Bibliographic Information*. Lanham, Md.: UNIPUB, 1990.

Donnelly, Don, and Nora Donnelly. *FileSolutions: The Complete Guide to Personal Filing*. Dallas, Tex.: FileSolutions, 1988.

Frosch, Andrew, and Shirley Dembo. *Filing Workbook*. New York: Dictation Press, 1985.

Gorelick, Jamie S., Stephen Marzen, and Lawrence Solum. *Destruction of Evidence*. New York: John Wiley & Sons.

Guyman, Fred E. *National and International Records Retention Standards*. 2d ed. Orem, Utah: Eastwood, 1990.

Henne, Andrea. *Intensive File Management*. 2d ed. Cincinnati, Ohio: Southwestern, 1985.

Huffman, Harry. *General Recordkeeping*. 9th ed. New York: McGraw-Hill, 1988.

Jackson, Van. *Corporate Information Management.* Englewood Cliffs, N.J.: Prentice Hall, 1986.

Johnson, Nina, and Norman Kallaus. *Records Management.* 4th ed. Cincinnati, Ohio: Southwestern Publishing Co., 1986.

Lundgren, Carol, and Terry Lundgren. *Records Management in the Computer Age.* Boston: PWS-Kent, 1989.

National and International Records Retention Standards. Orem, Utah: Eastwood, 1990.

Piper, Joanne. *Filing: Syllabus.* 2d ed. Portland, Oreg.: National Book, 1979.

Roth, Judith Paris, ed. *Essential Guide to Multifunction Optical Storage.* Westport, Conn.: Meckler, 1991.

Safady, William. *Optical Disks vs. Magnetic Storage.* Westport, Conn.: Meckler, 1990.

_____. *Optical Storage Technology, 1992; A State of the Art Review.* Westport, Conn.: Meckler, 1991.

Skupsky, Donald S. *Legal Requirements for Business Records.* (3 vols.) Denver, Colo.: Information Requirements Clearinghouse, 1990.

_____. *Legal Requirements for Microfilm, Computer and Optical Disk Records.* Denver, Colo.: Information Requirements Clearinghouse, 1990.

_____. *Recordkeeping Requirements.* Denver, Colo.: Information Requirements Clearinghouse, 1991.

_____. *Records Retention Procedures.* Denver, Colo.: Information Requirements Clearinghouse, 1991.

Stewart, Jeffrey R. *Records and Database Management.* 14th ed. New York: McGraw-Hill, 1989.

Stewart, R. O. *Workbook Exercises in Alphabetic Filing.* New York: McGraw-Hill, 1980.

Tapper, Garry, and Kenneth Tombs. *The Legal Admissibility of Document Imaging Systems.* Westport, Conn.: Meckler, 1992.

Taylor, Mary. *Clear and Simple Filing and Records Management.* New York: Arco, 1987.

U.S. General Services Administration, Information Resources Management Service. *Electronic Recordkeeping.* Washington, D.C.: Superintendent of Documents, 1991.

Waegmann, C. Peter. *Handbook of Record Storage and Space Management.* Westport, Conn.: Greenwood, 1983.

Waters, Peter. *Procedures for Salvage of Water-Damaged Library Materials.* 2d ed. Washington, D.C.: Library of Congress, 1979.

PERIODICALS THAT FREQUENTLY HAVE ARTICLES ON RECORDS MANAGEMENT

Administrative Management. New York: Geyer-McAllister Publications.

American Archivist. Baltimore, Md.: Monumental Printing.

Computer Law Strategist. New York: Leader Publications.

Computerworld. Framingham, Mass.: Computerworld.

Corporate Systems. Garden City, N.Y.: United Technical Publications.

Datamation. Greenwich, Conn.: F. D. Thompson Publications.

Disaster Recovery Journal. St. Louis, Mo.: Systems Support.

Document Image Automation. Westport, Conn.: Meckler.

FORM. Alexandria, Va.: National Business Association.

FORMAT. Gaithersburg, Md.: Association of Business Forms Manufacturers.

Information and Records Management. Hempstead, N.Y.: Information and Records Management.

Infosystems. Wheaton, Ill.: Hitchcock Publishing.

Journal of Data Management. Cleveland, Ohio: Association of Systems Management.

Journal of Systems Management. Cleveland, Ohio: Association of Systems Management.

Management World. Willow Grove, Pa.: Administrative Management Society.

Microfilm Techniques. Hempstead, N.Y.: Microfilm Techniques.

Modern Office Technology. Cleveland, Ohio: Penton/I.P.C.

The Office. Stamford, Conn.: Office Publications.

PC Magazine. New York: Ziff-Davis.

Prologue: The Journal of the National Archives. Washington, D.C.: National Archives.

Record and Retrieval Report. Westport, Conn.: Greenwood Press.

Records Management Quarterly. Prairie Village, Kan.: Association of Records Managers and Administrators (ARMA).

Special Libraries. New York: Special Library Association.

Systems. New York: United Business Publications.

Word Processing World. New York: Geyer-McAllister Publications.

Words. Willow Grove, Pa.: International Word Processing Association.

For additional information, see *Business Index*, an index of magazines on microfilm published by Information Access Company, 11 Davis Dr., Belmont, CA 94002.

SOFTWARE

This software product listing is not meant to be exhaustive; rather, it is an illustrative list of some products on the market for records retention.

Active Records Management. Laguna Hills, Cal.: Automated Records Management Systems (ARMS).

AI2MS. Hayward, Cal.: Anamet Laboratories.

AIMS+ PLUS. Austin, Tex.: AIMS+ Plus.

AIS-Departmental File Systems. Chadds Ford, Pa.: Assured Information Systems.

AIS-Uniform Central File. Chadds Ford, Pa.: Assured Information Systems.

Archival RM System. Tulsa, Okla.: EWI Systems, Ltd.

Automatic Record Inventory System. Bedford Heights, Ohio: Data Security.

Canonfile 250. Itasca, Ill.: Canon USA.

Check Out. Kenilworth, N.J.: White Office Systems.

Corporate Records Management. Laguna Hills, Cal.: Automated Records Management Systems (ARMS).

D-CAR-E. Minneapolis, Minn.: Microforms.

Docubase. Geneva-Acacias, Switzerland: Docubase Systems.

EZ-Forms. Houston, Tex.: EZX

FastTrack. Norberth, Pa.: Chase Technologies.

FileMaker Pro. Santa Clara, Cal.: Claris.

FileMark. Natick, Mass.: FileMark.

FileNet. Costa Mesa, Cal.: FileNet.

Focus. New York: Information Builders.

Formfiller. Deerfield Beach, Fla.: BLOC Development.

Formscan. Novato, Cal.: Graphics Development International.

Forms-Xpress. Norcross, Ga.: Xpoint.

FROLIC. Worcester, Mass.: Wright Line.

Gencat. North Vancouver, B.C. Eloquent Systems.

ImageTrax. Fullerton, Cal.: Advanced Office Concepts.

IMagic. Westport, Conn.: Westbrook Technologies.

InfoTRAX. Boulder, Colo.: InfoTrax.

InMAGIC. Cambridge, Mass.: InMagic.

IZE. Madison, Wis.: Perfsoft.

Kardex Record Control System. Marietta, Ga.: Kardex.

Kodak Imagelink. Rochester, N.Y.: Eastman Kodak.

Personnel Policy Expert. Petaluma, Cal.: Knowledge Point.

Professional File. Mountain View, Cal.: SPC Software.

ProFound. Phoenix, Ariz.: WANG/Informatics Legal and Professional Systems.

Ready, Aim, File! Beverly Hills, Cal.: VSoft Systems.

RecFind. Vista, Cal.: GMB Support.

Record-Master. Costa Mesa, Cal.: CISD International.

Record Trakker. Houston, Tex.: ATM Technologies.

Retention. Denver, Colo.: Information Requirements.

Retention Management. Laguna Hills, Cal.: Automated Records Management Systems (ARMS).

Scan Type. Novato, Cal.: Graphics Development International.

SECUREcard Network Security System. Nashua, N.H.: Datamedia.

TextWare. Park City, Utah. TextWare.

TIM. Broomfield, Colo.: Engineered Data Products.

T-R-I-M-S (Total Records & Information Management Software). Sarasota, Fla.: Alan Negus Associates.

Versatile. Denver, Colo.: Information Requirements Clearinghouse.

VIDEO

Buried Alive: Document Retention. Boston: Commonwealth Films.

Data Security: Be Aware or Beware. Boston: Commonwealth Films.

Protecting Your Information Assets: The Executive's Guide to Information Security. New York: Ernst & Young.

Under Wraps: Information Security. Boston: Commonwealth Films.

MANUFACTURERS OF COLOR-CODED FILING SUPPLIES

Clear Index. Waltham, Mass.: Wes Manufacturing.

Dataware Labeling System. Houston, Tex.: Dataware.

Direct Name System. Rochester, N.Y.: Yawman & Erbe Manufacturing.

F. E. Bee Line Filing System. Boston: Filing Equipment Bureau.

Filex Expanding System. Waltham, Mass.: Dunleavy.

Findit System. Waltham, Mass.: C. L. Barkley.

L. B. Automatic. New York: Remington Rand.

Nual Alphabet Index or Amfile Index. Kankakee, Ill.: Amberg File and Index.

Pendaflex. Garden City, N.Y.: Oxford Filing Supply.

Safeguard Alphabetic System. Cincinnati, Ohio: Globe-Wernicke.

Shannolink. Muscatine, Iowa: Home-O-Nize.

Speed Index. Garden City, N.Y.: Oxford Filing Supply.

Standard Alphabetic Expanding System. Chicago: Automatic File and Index.

Super-Ideal System. Muskegon, Mich.: Shaw-Walker.

Tailor Made Index. Muskegon, Mich.: Shaw-Walker.

Tell-I-Vision System Alphabetic Filing. Hastings, Minn.: Smead Manufacturing.

Triple-Check Automatic Index. New York: Remington Rand.

Variadex System. New York: Remington Rand.

Visible Name Filing System. New York: Remington Rand.

VRE Compufile Service. Malvern, Ohio: VRE Compufile Service.

ANSWERS TO
"FOR FURTHER STUDY"

Alphabetical Filing, 1. a) "A" is a word. Hyphenated words are filed as two separate words. Ignore "'s" but count "s'." Ignore conjunctions, punctuation, the article "the." File "nothing" before "something." File initials and acronyms as "nothing." File surnames, first names. Interfile names and phrases. Interfile U.S. and foreign. File numerals as spoken.

A-A Award Studio
A-AAA Amusement Co.
A-AAA Amusement (&) Vending Co.
A-Abasco Fire Extinguishers Co. Inc.
A-Able Information Service
A-Admiral Rentals (&) Sales Co.
A Bee C Television Co. Inc.
A Better System Dog Training
A Builders
A-O-K Home for the Elderly
A-Okay Apartments
A-1-AA Book Shop
A-1 Auto Drive School
A-1 Auto Parts Locating Service
A-1 Auto Parts (and) Supply Co.
A-Te-Anna Coiffures
A to Z Insurance Programs Inc.
A-Z Auto Parts Inc.
AA see Alcoholics Anonymous
AA Addressing (and) Office Machines
A (&) A Graphics Inc.
AA Importing Co. Inc.
A (&) A Meat Sales
AAA see Automobile Club of America
AAA Ace Photographers of Canada
AAA Auto Air Conditioning
AAA Auto Parts Co.
AAA Auto Parts Inc.
AAA Auto Salvage
AAA Automobile Club
AAA Insurance Agency
AABC National Insurance Agency
AABCO National Insurance Agency
AAFP Group Disability Plans Inc.
A (&) B Linen Service
ABACO Auto Transport
ABC Battery (&) Auto Parts Warehouse Inc.

ABC Insurers
ABCO Insurers
A (&) E Brake Engineers
A (&) E Company Printers
A (&) E Electronics Corp.
A (&) E Guttering Co.
A (&) E Square Deal Auto Salvage
AFIA Worldwide Insurance
A (&) H Auto Parts
APA (&) Associates
A (&) S Auto Service
A (&) S Automotive Inc.
Aabar Express Co.
Aabco Welding Co. Inc.
Aach, Roy L., 14120 Forestvale
Aach, Roy L., 14122 Forestvale
Aach, Roy L., 112 North Hanley
Aach, Roy L., 112 South Hanley
Aach, Roy L. (&) Associates
Aach see also Asche, Ash, Ashe, Oesch
Aaron-Abbott Commercial Service
Aaron, Alex G.
Aaron, Carl L.
Aaron('s) Catering Service
Aaron, Ferer (&) Sons Inc.
Aaron, James H. Capt.
Aaron, James H. Lt.
Aaron, John H.
Aaron, Jon
Aaron-Jones Service Station
Aarons, Albert
Aarons' Plumbing (and) Sewer Cleaning Co.
Abatis Insurance Agency
Abbey Life Assurance Co. Ltd.
Abeille
Abel, Emmett
Aboussie, Alex (&) Son Insurance

Aboussie Insurance Service
Abramson, Mettzer Insurance Agency
Ackrit Automotive Inc.
Ad-Mac (&) Associates Inc.
Adams (&) Associates Agency
Addams, Jane Vocational High School
Adkinson, C. Stanley, Dr.
Aetna Life (&) Casualty
Affiliated Factors Limited
Afro-American Museum
Agricultural (&) General Insurance Ltd.
Agrippina Ruckeversicherung
Airbanc of Canada
Ajax Engineering Products
Al('s) Auto Parts
Al('s) Auto Salvage
Albingia Versicherungs
Alcan Aluminum Corporation
Alexander (&) Aris Ltd.
Alfa Romeo
All American Life Insurance
All Parts Auto Supply Co.
All Risk Agency Inc.
Alleanza Assicuragioni
Allen, A. Guns Inc.
Allendale Insurance
Allianz Lebensversicherungs
Allianz Versicherungs Aktiengesellschaft
Allparts Ltd.
Allsparts Insurance
Allstar National Agency
Allstate Insurance Co.
Am Versucherungen
Amev, N. B.
Ansvar Insurance Co. Ltd.
Apple, Rosalind, DDS
Asche, Edward

Asche, Edward G.
Ash, Edward
Ash, Edward H.
Ash, Roy L.
Ashe, Roy L.
Associated Engineering Limited
Assurances Generales Compagnie Financiere
 et de Reassurance du Groupe
Assurances Generales de France
Audi NSU
Automotive Agency of America
Automotive Products Limited
Avions Marcel Dassault-Breguet
Avon Insurance Co. Ltd.
Avon Rubber Company Limited
BMW see Bayerische Motoren Werke
 Aktiengesellschaft
Bomar-Thomas Insurance Agency
Booker, Alva
Caen, Leach (&) McLean Insurance Agency
Cage, George H.
Campbell (&) Konering
Chapman-Sander Inc.
Dick, A. B. Products Co. of St. Louis
E (&) E Insurance Company
Eighty-Eight Insurance Consultants Inc.
Elias, Elizabeth
Ellis-Rodes-Meers (&) Co.
Emcasco
Emes, Walter J.
Graves, Joe (&) Associates
Lester, A. B. Booksellers Limited
Miller, A. E. Lock (&) Key Co.
Oesch, Roy L., (Jr.)
Oesch, Roy L. Construction Co. Inc.
Schmidt, A. E. Co.
Service, C. P. Company

Alphabetical Filing, 1. c) Word by word filing. "A" is a word. Hyphenated words are filed as one word. Acronyms and initials are filed as words. Disregard apostrophe-s ('s) in filing. File conjunctions and ampersands as words. File individuals' names before phrases.

A and A Graphics Inc.
A and A Meat Sales
A and B Linen Service
A and E Brake Engineers
A and E Company Printers
A and E Electronics Corp.
A and E Guttering Co.
A and E Square Deal Auto Salvage
A and H Auto Parts
A and S Auto Service
A and S Automotive Inc.
A Bee C Television Service Co. Inc.
A Better System Dog Training
A Builders
A to Z Insurance Programs Inc.
AA see Alcoholics Anonymous
AA Addressing and Office Machines

A-A Award Studio
AA Importing Co. Inc.
AAA see also Automobile Club of America
AAA Ace Photographers of Canada
AAA Auto Air Conditioning
AAA Auto Parts Co.
AAA Auto Parts Inc.
AAA Auto Salvage
AAA Automobile Club
AAA Insurance Agency
A-AAA Amusement Co.
A-AAA Amusement and Vending Co.
Aabar Express Co.
A-Abasco Fire Extinguishers Co. Inc.
AABC National Insurance Agency
AABCO National Insurance Agency
Aabco Welding Co. Inc.

A-Able Information Service
Aach, Roy L. 14120 Forestvale
Aach, Roy L. 14122 Forestvale
Aach, Roy L. 112 North Hanley Rd.
Aach, Roy L. 112 South Hanley Rd.
Aach, Roy L. and Associates
Aach, see also Asche, Ash, Ashe, Oesch
A-Admiral Rentals and Sales Co.
AAFP Group Disability Plans Inc.
Aaron, Alex G.
Aaron, Carl L.
Aaron, James H. Capt.
Aaron, James H. Lt.
Aaron, John H.
Aaron, Jon
Aaron('s) Catering Service
Aaron, Ferer and Sons Inc.
Aaron-Abbott Commercial Service
Aaron-Jones Service Station
Aarons, Albert
Aarons' Plumbing and Sewer Cleaning Co.
ABACO Auto Transport
Abatis Insurance Agency
Abbey Life Assurance Co. Ltd.
ABC Battery and Auto Parts Warehouse, Inc.
ABC Insurers
ABCO Insurers
Abeille
Abel, Emmett
Aboussie, Alex and Son Insurance
Aboussie Insurance Service
Abramson, Mettzer Insurance Agency
Ackrit Automotive Inc.
Adams and Associates Agency
Addams, Jane Vocational High School
Adkinson, C. Stanley, Dr.
Ad-Mac and Associates, Inc.
Aetna Life and Casualty
Affiliated Factors Limited
AFIA Worldwide Insurance
AfroAmerican Museum
Agricultural and General Insurance Ltd.
Agrippina Ruckerversicherung
Airbanc of Canada
Ajax Engineering Products
Al('s) Auto Parts
Al('s) Auto Salvage
Albingia Versicherungs
Alcan Aluminum Corporation
Alexander and Aris Ltd.
Alfa Romeo
All American Life Insurance
All Parts Auto Supply Co.
All Risk Agency Inc.
Alleanza Assicuragioni
Allen, A. Guns Inc.
Allendale Insurance

Allianz Lebensversicherungs
Allianz Versicherungs Atkiengesellschaft
Allparts Ltd.
Allsparts Insurance
Allstar National Agency
Allstate Insurance Co.
Am Versicherungs
Amev, N. B.
Ansvar Insurance Co. Ltd.
A-O-K Home for the Elderly
A-Okay Apartments
AOne Auto Drive School
AOne Auto Parts and Supply Co.
AOne Auto Parts Locating Service
AOneAA Book Shop
APA and Associates
Apple, Rosalind, DDS
Ashe, Edward
Ashe, Edward G.
Ash, Edward
Ash, Edward H.
Ash, Roy L.
Ashe, Roy L.
Associated Engineering Limited
Assurances Generales Compagnie Financiere
  et de Reassurance du Groupe
Assurances Generales (de) France
A-Te-Anna Coiffures
Audi NSU
Automotive Agency of America
Automotive Products Limited
Avions Marcel Dassault-Breguet
Avon Insurance Co. Ltd.
Avon Rubber Company Limited
AZ Auto Parts Inc.
BMW see Bayerische Motoren Werke
  Aktiengesellschaft
Bomar-Thomas Insurance Agency
Booker, Alva
Caen, Leach (&) McLean Insurance Agency
Cage, George H.
Campbell (&) Konering
Chapman-Sander Inc.
Dick, A. B. Products Co. of St. Louis
E (&) E Insurance Company
Eighty-Eight Insurance Consultants Inc.
Elias, Elizabeth
Ellis-Rodes-Meers (&) Co.
Emcasco
Emes, Walter J.
Graves, Joe (&) Associates
Lester, A. B. Booksellers Limited
Miller, A. E. Lock (&) Key Co.
Oesch, Roy L. (Jr.)
Oesch, Roy L. Construction Co. Inc.
Schmidt, A. E. Co.
Service, C. P. Company

Geographical Filing, 1. a) Continent. Country. City. Firm or individual name. Alphabetizing word by word, disregarding punctuation.

British Isles. England. East Sussex. Ansvar Insurance Co. Ltd.
British Isles. England. Kent. Affiliated Factors Limited.
British Isles. England. Kent. Agricultural & General Insurance Ltd.
British Isles. England. Kent. Ajax Engineering Products.
British Isles. England. London. Abbey Life Assurance Co. Ltd.
British Isles. England. London. Alexander & Aris Ltd.
British Isles. England. London. Allparts Ltd.
British Isles. England. Stratford-on-Avon. Avon Insurance Co. Ltd.
British Isles. England. Warwickshire. Associated Engineering Limited.
British Isles. England. Wiltshire. Avon Rubber Company Limited.
Europe. Belgium. Brussels. A. G. Compagnie Financiere et de Reassurance du Groupe.
Europe. France. Vaucresson. Assurances Generales de France.
Europe. France. Vaucresson. Avions Marcel Dassault-Breguet.
Europe. Italy. Milan. Abeille (L').
Europe. Italy. Milan. Alfa Romeo.
Europe. Italy. Milan. Alleanza Assicuragioni.
Europe. Netherlands. Utrecht. Amev, N. B.
Europe. West Germany. Aürich. Albingia Versicherungs.
Europe. West Germany. Aürich. Am Versucherungen.
Europe. West Germany. München. Agrippina Ruckeversicherung.
Europe. West Germany. München. Allianz Lebensversicherungs.
Europe. West Germany. München. Allianz Versicherungs-Aktiengesellschaft.
Europe. West Germany. München. Audi NSU.
Europe. West Germany. München. Bayerische Motoren Werke Aktiengesellschaft.
North America. Canada. Montreal. AAA Ace Photographers of Canada.
North America. Canada. Montreal. Alcan Aluminum Corporation.
North America. Canada. Montreal. Automotive Products Limited.
North America. Canada. Toronto. Airbanc of Canada.
North America. Canada. Toronto. All Parts Auto Supply Co.
North America. Canada. Toronto. Apple, Rosalind.

Geographical Filing, 1. b) The only difference is that individual's names come before phrase names:

North America. Canada. Toronto. Apple, Rosalind.
North America. Canada. Toronto. Airbanc of Canada.
North America. Canada. Toronto. All Parts Auto Supply Co.

Geographical Filing, 1. c) The only difference is Belgium and the Canada entries come before England.

Geographical Filing, 1. d) State. Town. Firm or individual name. Alphabetizing word by word. Disregard conjunctions. File hyphenated words as two words. "A" is a word.

California. Oakdale. AA Addressing.
California. Oakdale. AABC National Insurance Agency.
California. Oakdale. ABC Battery & Auto Parts Warehouse Inc.
California. Oakdale. A & S Automotive Inc.
California. Oakdale. Aaron, James H.
California. Oakdale. Aetna Life & Casualty.
California. Oakdale. Service, C. P. Company.
Iowa. Oakdale. A-A Award Studio.
Iowa. Oakdale. A-AAA Amusement & Vending Co.

Iowa. Oakdale. A Bee C Television Service Co. Inc.
Iowa. Oakdale. ABCO Insurers.
Iowa. Oakdale. Adkinson, C. Stanley, Dr.
Iowa. Oakdale. Automotive Agency of America.
Iowa. Oakdale. Elias, Elizabeth.
Louisiana. Oakdale. A & E Guttering Co.
Louisiana. Oakdale. A-O-K Home for the Elderly.
Louisiana. Oakdale. A-1 Auto Drive School.
Louisiana. Oakdale. AAA Auto Salvage.
Louisiana. Oakdale. Aarons' Plumbing and Sewer Cleaning Co.
Louisiana. Oakdale. All American Life Insurance.
Louisiana. Oakdale. Cage, George.
Nebraska. Oakdale. A-AAA Amusement Company.
Nebraska. Oakdale. A-Z Auto Parts Inc.
Nebraska. Oakdale. AFIA Worldwide Insurance.
Nebraska. Oakdale. Aaron, Ferer & Sons Inc.
Nebraska. Oakdale. Ackrit Automotive Inc.
Nebraska. Oakdale. Allparts Insurance.
Nebraska. Oakdale. Ellis-Rodes-Meers & Co.
Pennsylvania. Oakdale. A-Abasco Fire Extinguishers Co. Inc.
Pennsylvania. Oakdale. AAA Auto Air Conditioning.
Pennsylvania. Oakdale. A & E Square Deal Auto Salvage.
Pennsylvania. Oakdale. Aaron-Abbott Commercial Service.
Pennsylvania. Oakdale. Abel, Emmett.
Pennsylvania. Oakdale. Al's Auto Salvage.
Pennsylvania. Oakdale. Campbell & Konering.
Wisconsin. Oakdale. A-1 Auto Parts Locating Service.
Wisconsin. Oakdale. A & A Meat Sales.
Wisconsin. Oakdale. Aabar Express Co.
Wisconsin. Oakdale. ABACO Auto Transport.
Wisconsin. Oakdale. Al's Auto Parts.
Wisconsin. Oakdale. Caen, Leach & McLean Insurance Agency.
Wisconsin. Oakdale. Schmidt, A. E. Co.

Geographical Filing, 1. e) Alphabetize individual names before phrase names. Consider hyphenated words as one word. Consider conjunctions as words. Consider "A" as a word.

California. Oakdale. Aaron, James H.
California. Oakdale. A & S Automotive Inc.
California. Oakdale. AA Addressing.
California. Oakdale. AABC National Insurance Agency.
California. Oakdale. ABC Battery and Auto Parts Warehouse Inc.
California. Oakdale. Aetna Life & Casualty.
California. Oakdale. Service, C. P. Company.
Iowa. Oakdale. Adkinson, C. Stanley, Dr.
Iowa. Oakdale. A-A Award Studio.
Iowa. Oakdale. A-AAA Amusement & Vending Co.
Iowa. Oakdale. A Bee C Television Service Co. Inc.
Iowa. Oakdale. ABCO Insurers.
Iowa. Oakdale. Automotive Agency of America.
Iowa. Oakdale. Elias, Elizabeth.
Louisiana. Oakdale. A & E Guttering Co.
Louisiana. Oakdale. AAA Auto Salvage.
Louisiana. Oakdale. A-O-K Home for the Elderly.
Louisiana. Oakdale. A-1 Auto Drive School.
Louisiana. Oakdale. Aarons' Plumbing and Sewer Cleaning Co.
Louisiana. Oakdale. All American Life Insurance.
Louisiana. Oakdale. Cage, George.

Nebraska. Oakdale. A-AAA Amusement Company.
Nebraska. Oakdale. AFIA Worldwide Insurance.
Nebraska. Oakdale. A-Z Auto Parts Inc.
Nebraska. Oakdale. Aaron, Ferer & Sons Inc.
Nebraska. Oakdale. Ackrit Automotive Inc.
Nebraska. Oakdale. Allparts Insurance.
Nebraska. Oakdale. Ellis-Rodes-Meers & Co.
Pennsylvania. Oakdale. Abel, Emmett.
Pennsylvania. Oakdale. A & E Square Deal Auto Salvage.
Pennsylvania. Oakdale. AAA Auto Air Conditioning.
Pennsylvania. Oakdale. A-Abasco Fire Extinguishers Co. Inc.
Pennsylvania. Oakdale. Aaron-Abbott Commercial Service.
Pennsylvania. Oakdale. Al's Auto Salvage.
Pennsylvania. Oakdale. Campbell & Konering.
Wisconsin. Oakdale. A & A Meat Sales.
Wisconsin. Oakdale. Aabar Express Co.
Wisconsin. Oakdale. ABACO Auto Transport.
Wisconsin. Oakdale. Al's Auto Parts.
Wisconsin. Oakdale. A-1 Auto Parts Locating Service.
Wisconsin. Oakdale. Caen, Leach & McLean Insurance Agency.
Wisconsin. Oakdale. Schmidt, A. E. Co.

Geographical Filing, 1. f) Town, State, Firm or individual name. Disregard punctuation.

Oakdale. California. AAA Addressing.
Etc. Same as "d" or "e" depending upon other rules followed.
Oakdale. Iowa. A-A Award Studio.
Etc. Same as "d" or "e" depending upon other rules followed.
Oakdale. Louisiana. A-1 Auto Drive School.
Etc. Same as "d" or "e" depending upon other rules followed.
Oakdale. Nebraska. A-AAA Amusement Co.
Etc. Same as "d" or "e" depending upon other rules followed.
Oakdale. Pennsylvania. A-Abasco Fire Extinguishers Co. Inc.
Etc. Same as "d" or "e" depending upon other rules followed.
Oakdale. Wisconsin. A-1 Auto Parts Locating Service.
Etc. Same as "d" or "e" depending upon other rules followed.

Geographical Filing, 1. g) Addresses.

119 E. First Ave.
119 E. First St.
14 S. 31st Ave.
21 E. 31st St.
24 Brown Rd.
11923 Claymount
14120 Forestvale
14122 Forestvale
112 N. Hanley Rd.
112 S. Hanley Rd.
2929 Robert Dr.
2910 Santiago

Phonetic Filing, 1.

A120 Aabco; Aboussie
A132 Abatis
A140 Abeille; Abel; Apple
A141 AbbeyLife
A143 Affiliated
A152 Avions
A155 AvonInsurance
A156 AvonRubber
A162 Aabar
A165 Abramson; Afro-American
A200 Aach; Asche; Ash; Ashe
A223 Associated
A225 Ajax
A261 Agrippina
A262 Agricultural
A263 Ackrit
A265 Assurances
A300 Audi
A325 Adkinson
A352 Adams; Addams; Ad-Mac
A353 Automotive
A354 Aetna
A415 Albingia
A416 AlfaRomeo; AllParts
A421 Allsparts
A431 Al('s) Auto; Allstar
A423 Allstate
A425 Alcan
A425 Alexander

A450 Allen
A452 Alleanza; Allianz
A453 Allendale
A462 AllRisk
A510 Amev
A516 Am Versucherungen
A521 Ansvar
A615 Airbanc
A650 Aaron
A652 Aarons
B260 Booker
B563 BomarThomas
B625 BayerischeMotoren
C155 Chapman
C200 Cage
C500 Caen
C514 Campbell
D200 Dick
E232 Eighty-Eight
E420 Elias
E426 EllisRodes
E520 Emes
E522 Emasco
G612 Graves
L236 Lester
M460 Miller
O200 Oesch
S253 Schmidt

Numerical Filing, 1. Terminal Digit Filing.

348-675-016
358-433-034
418-432-035
338-392-043
338-327-048
318-320-050
328-316-055
498-436-066
178-423-072
248-413-073
168-433-073
138-423-074
348-317-086
198-438-087
378-438-088
298-438-089
458-433-090
358-655-091
348-697-098
198-384-099
488-676-109
308-655-113
338-654-117
348-954-125

468-431-141
368-322-149
418-677-160
418-375-168
248-717-180
238-727-180
478-727-180
268-737-180
448-928-185
498-431-191
428-729-197
208-671-198
478-681-198
248-691-198
138-692-198
308-318-222
328-214-235
158-200-243
478-210-243
158-220-243
128-210-244
128-210-245
458-675-254
318-327-255
258-913-255
388-923-255

268-933-255
208-490-285
478-490-286
288-490-287
278-782-319
368-727-332
148-922-355
278-382-363
438-437-363
468-376-364
378-382-364
298-382-365
418-375-376
308-327-416
438-684-419
148-223-420
228-321-431
228-691-431
338-659-442
278-926-448
488-926-449
438-677-454
138-467-484
248-467-488
188-926-490
288-926-490
328-392-523
458-433-528
428-431-534
298-425-540
378-425-541
208-425-542
298-425-542
228-327-543
158-317-544
498-327-544
158-337-544
408-462-552
388-374-569
408-374-569
228-432-593
448-921-608
428-220-616
368-316-617
398-435-638
208-435-639

238-430-645
168-420-646
398-430-646
268-440-646
218-430-647
198-787-648
488-787-649
188-787-650
308-490-680
238-682-682
398-921-682
288-921-683
288-921-684
258-432-691
168-422-692
168-442-692
258-432-693
448-432-721
468-314-722
448-688-756
178-785-770
468-928-771
198-691-773
488-691-774
188-691-775
138-721-780
238-682-781
268-672-782
388-682-782
258-692-782
328-374-788
458-437-794
318-314-841
148-420-867
368-921-884
318-377-894
358-317-897
358-462-932
428-223-958
148-422-962
178-380-969
498-390-969
178-400-969
128-410-969
278-221-993
378-221-994
188-221-995

Numerical Filing, 2. Middle Digit Filing.

158-200-243
128-210-244
128-210-245
478-210-243
328-214-235
158-220-243
428-220-616
188-221-995

278-221-993
378-221-994
148-223-420
428-223-958
318-314-841
468-314-722
328-316-055
368-316-617
158-317-544
348-317-086

358-317-897	298-438-089
308-318-222	378-438-088
318-320-050	268-440-646
228-321-431	168-442-692
368-322-149	358-462-932
228-327-543	408-462-552
308-327-416	138-467-484
318-327-255	248-467-488
338-327-048	208-490-285
498-327-544	288-490-287
158-337-544	308-490-680
328-374-788	478-490-286
388-374-569	338-654-117
408-374-569	308-655-113
418-375-168	358-655-091
418-375-376	338-659-442
468-376-364	208-671-198
318-377-894	268-672-782
178-380-969	348-675-016
278-382-363	458-675-254
298-382-365	488-676-109
378-382-364	418-677-160
198-384-099	438-677-454
498-390-969	478-681-198
328-392-523	238-682-682
338-392-043	238-682-781
178-400-969	388-682-782
128-410-969	438-684-419
248-413-073	448-688-756
148-420-867	188-691-775
168-420-646	198-691-773
148-422-962	228-691-431
168-422-692	248-691-198
138-423-074	488-691-774
178-423-072	138-692-198
208-425-542	258-692-782
298-425-540	348-697-098
298-425-542	248-717-180
378-425-541	138-721-780
218-430-647	238-727-180
238-430-645	368-727-332
398-430-646	478-727-180
428-431-534	428-729-197
468-431-141	268-737-180
498-431-191	278-782-319
228-432-593	178-785-770
258-432-691	188-787-650
258-432-693	198-787-648
418-432-035	488-787-649
448-432-721	258-913-255
168-433-073	288-921-683
358-433-034	288-921-684
458-433-090	368-921-884
458-433-528	398-921-682
208-435-639	448-921-608
398-435-638	148-922-355
498-436-066	388-923-255
438-437-363	188-926-490
458-437-794	278-926-448
198-438-087	288-926-490

488-926-449
448-928-185

468-928-771
268-933-255
348-954-125

Color-Coded Filing, 1.

Red
AAA Ace Photographers of Canada
Abbey Life Assurance Co. Ltd.
Abeille
Affiliated Factors Limited
Agricultural & General Insurance Ltd.
Agrippina Ruckeversicherung
Airbanc of Canada
Ajax Engineering Products
Albingia Versicherungs
Alcan Aluminum Corporation
Alexander & Aris Ltd.
Alfa Romeo
All Parts Auto Supply
Alleanza Assicuragioni
Allianz Lebensversicherungs
Allianz Versicherungs . . .
Allparts Ltd.
Am Versucherungen
Amev, N. B.
Ansvar Insurance Co. Ltd.
Apple, Rosalind, DDS
Associated Engineering Ltd.
Assurances Générales Compagnie . . .

Assurances Générales de France
Audi NSU
Automotive Products Limited
Avions Marcel Dassault-Breguet
Avon Insurance Co. Ltd.
Avon Rubber Co. Ltd.
Bayerische Motoren Werke Aktiengesell-
schaft

Red/Yellow
Alfa Romeo
All Parts Auto Supply
Audi NSU
Automotive Products Limited
Bayerische . . .

Red/Blue
Abbey Life Assurance Co. Ltd.
Agricultural & General Insurance Ltd.
Ansvar Insurance Co. Ltd.
Assurances Générales Compagnie . . .
Assurances Générales de France
Avon Insurance Co. Ltd.

Yellow
A-1 Auto Drive School
A-1 Auto Parts Locating Service
A-1 Auto Parts (and) Supply Co.
AAA Auto Air Conditioning
AAA Auto Parts Inc.
AAA Auto Salvage
AAA Automobile Club
ABACO Auto Transport
ABC Battery (&) Auto Parts Warehouse Inc.
A (&) E Brake Engineers
A (&) E Square Deal Auto Salvage
A (&) H Auto Parts
Aaron-Jones Service Station
Ackrit Automotive Inc.
Al's Auto Parts
Al's Auto Salvage
Automobile Agency of America

Blue
A to Z Insurance Programs Inc.
AAA Insurance Agency
AABC National Insurance Agency
AAFP Group Disability Plans Inc.
ABC Insurers
ABCO Insurers
AFIA Worldwide Insurance
Abramson, Mettzer Insurance Agency
Abatis Insurance Agency
Aboussie, Alex (&) Son Insurance
Aboussie Insurance Service
Aetna Life (&) Casualty
All American Life Insurance
All Risk Agency Inc.
Allendale Insurance
Allsparts Insurance
Allstate Insurance Co.
E (&) E Insurance Co.
Eighty-Eight Insurance Consultants

Color-Coded Filing. 2.

yellow red yellow 348-675-016
purple red purple 358-433-034
purple red gold 418-432-035
orange red orange 338-392-043
orange red pink 338-327-048
orange red red 318-320-050
orange red gold 328-316-055
purple red yellow 498-436-066
purple red blue 178-423-072
purple red orange 248-413-073
purple red orange 168-433-073
purple red purple 138-423-074
orange red yellow 348-317-086
purple red brown 198-438-087
purple red pink 378-438-088
purple red green 298-438-089
purple red red 458-433-090
yellow red gray 358-655-091
yellow red pink 348-697-098
orange red green 198-384-099
yellow gray green 488-676-109
yellow gray orange 308-655-113
yellow gray brown 338-654-117
green gray gold 348-954-125
purple gray gray 468-431-141
orange gray green 368-322-149
yellow gray red 418-677-160
orange gray pink 418-375-168
brown gray red 248-717-180
brown gray red 238-727-180
brown gray red 478-727-180
brown gray red 268-737-180
green gray gold 448-928-185
purple gray gray 498-431-191
brown gray brown 428-729-197
yellow gray pink 208-671-198
yellow gray pink 478-681-198
yellow gray pink 248-691-198
yellow gray pink 138-692-198
orange blue blue 308-318-222
blue blue gold 328-214-235
blue blue orange 158-200-243
blue blue orange 478-210-243
blue blue orange 158-220-243
blue blue purple 128-210-244
blue blue gold 128-210-245
yellow blue purple 458-675-254
orange blue gold 318-327-255
green blue gold 258-913-255
green blue gold 388-923-255
green blue gold 268-933-255
purple blue gold 208-490-285
purple blue yellow 478-490-286
purple blue brown 288-490-287
brown orange green 278-782-319
brown orange blue 368-727-332
green orange gold 148-922-355

orange orange orange 278-382-363
purple orange orange 438-437-363
orange orange purple 468-376-364
orange orange purple 378-382-364
orange orange gold 298-382-365
orange orange yellow 418-375-376
orange purple yellow 308-327-416
yellow purple green 438-684-419
blue purple red 148-223-420
orange purple gray 228-321-431
yellow purple gray 228-691-431
yellow purple blue 338-659-442
green purple pink 278-926-448
green purple green 488-926-449
yellow purple purple 438-677-454
purple purple purple 138-467-484
purple purple pink 248-467-488
green purple red 188-926-490
green purple red 288-926-490
orange gold orange 328-392-523
purple gold pink 458-433-528
purple gold purple 428-431-534
purple gold red 298-425-540
purple gold gray 378-425-541
purple gold blue 208-425-542
purple gold blue 298-425-542
orange gold orange 228-327-543
orange gold purple 158-317-544
orange gold purple 498-327-544
orange gold purple 158-337-544
purple gold blue 408-462-552
orange gold green 388-374-569
orange gold green 408-374-569
purple gold orange 228-432-593
green yellow pink 448-921-608
blue yellow yellow 428-220-616
orange yellow brown 368-316-617
purple yellow pink 398-435-638
purple yellow green 208-435-639
purple yellow gold 238-430-645
purple yellow yellow 168-420-646
purple yellow yellow 398-430-646
purple yellow yellow 268-440-646
purple yellow brown 218-430-647
brown yellow pink 198-787-648
brown yellow green 488-787-649
brown yellow red 188-787-650
purple yellow red 308-490-680
green yellow gray 288-921-681
yellow yellow blue 238-682-682
green yellow blue 398-921-682
green yellow orange 288-921-683
green yellow purple 288-921-684
purple yellow gray 258-432-691
purple yellow blue 168-422-692
purple yellow blue 168-442-692
purple yellow orange 258-432-693
purple brown gray 448-432-721
orange brown blue 468-314-722

yellow brown yellow 448-668-756
brown brown red 178-785-770
green brown gray 468-928-771
yellow brown orange 198-691-773
yellow brown purple 488-691-774
yellow brown gold 188-691-775
brown brown red 138-721-780
yellow brown gray 238-682-781
yellow brown blue 268-672-782
yellow brown blue 388-682-782
yellow brown blue 258-692-782
orange brown pink 328-374-788
purple brown purple 458-437-794
orange pink gray 318-314-841

purple pink brown 148-420-867
green pink purple 368-921-884
orange pink purple 318-377-894
orange pink brown 358-317-897
purple green blue 358-462-932
blue green pink 428-223-958
purple green blue 148-422-962
orange green green 178-380-969
orange green green 498-390-969
purple green green 178-400-969
purple green green 128-410-969
blue green orange 278-221-993
blue green purple 378-221-994
blue green gold 188-221-995

Subject Filing. 1. Your answer may differ considerably, but the following is a section of the subject classification system devised by the American Automobile Association (Sue Williams, Falls Church, VA, and Linda Rothbart, St. Louis, MO) for its files:

Automobiles

Specific makes, alphabetically
Accessories
Advertising
Automatic transmissions
Batteries and electrical systems
Brakes
Car pools
Care
Cost of driving
Customizing
Design and construction
Design and construction — Safety factors
  see also Motor vehicles — Standards
Diesel
Electric
Engines
Exhaust
Foreign
Gas mileage see Gasoline

Headlights
History
Identification
Mechanical failures
Recalls
Rentals and leasing
Repairing
Rust problems
Safety factors see Automobiles — Design &
  Construction — Safety factors
Shipment
Small — Karts and Karting
Specifications
Statistics
Steam
Theft
Towing
Warranties

INDEX

Ultrafiche, 182
Updating subscription services, 130, 240
Useful records, 135, 140, 149, 240

Vertical files, 15
Viewers. *See* Readers
Visible file cabinet, 167-69
Vital records, 135-38
  disaster planning, 151-53
  retention, 135-38, 140

Walker, Morris & Walker, 209-11
WAN. *See* Wide area network
Warren Filing Association, 15-16. *See also*
  Records Management Association
  of Chicago
Warren School of Filing, 15
Weeding systems, 132, 225, 241
Wide area network (WAN), 191

Word key. *See* Cross-references
Word processing, 171, 192
Word-by-word filing, 34-71, 241
  abbreviations, 48-50, 53
  addresses, 67-69, 80
  apostrophes, 54-55
  articles, 34
  common names, 56-59
  consecutive sequences, 93
  corporate names, 42-46, 52-53
  cross-references, 27-28, 71-72, 120-24,
    235
  foreign words, 61-64
  government departments, 58-61
  guardians, 55-56
  names, 35-41
  nonessential words, 34-35
  numbers, 64-65
  symbols, 65
WordStar, 225-27
Work flow, 8